Arizona Gathering II
1950-1969

Arizona Gathering II 1950-1969

AN ANNOTATED BIBLIOGRAPHY

Donald M. Powell

THE UNIVERSITY OF ARIZONA PRESS
Tucson, Arizona

About the Compiler . . .

DONALD M. POWELL, whose bibliographical skills have assisted thousands of students, faculty, and researchers, has been on the staff of the University of Arizona Library since 1946 when he became head of the reference department. In 1968 he became Associate Librarian and Professor of Library Science. The holder of a bachelor's degree in library science from the University of Michigan, he also has an A.B. with high honors from Swarthmore College, and an M.A. degree from Duke University. He is the author of *The Peralta Grant,* the compiler of several bibliographies including *An Arizona Gathering, 1950–1959, New Mexico and Arizona in the Serial Set, 1846–1861,* and *Arizona Fifty,* and the editor of John Marion's *Notes of Travel Through the Territory of Arizona.* From 1966 to 1972 he also edited the monthly *Books of the Southwest,* an annotated bibliography of nonfiction works.

THE UNIVERSITY OF ARIZONA PRESS

I. S. B. N.-0-8165-0382-6
L. C. No. 72-82946

Foreword

ARIZONA GATHERING II is an outgrowth of a periodic bibliography
which has been appearing twice yearly in the *Arizona Quarterly*
since 1952. It, like the present compilation, has attempted to record
all separately published items of nonfiction about Arizona. However, such state and federal publications as annual reports of departments, statistical series, and similar compilations which appear reg-
ularly, and government publications relating to Arizona which
appear to contain no essential information, have been omitted from
the present work.

In 1960 the Arizona Historical Society (then the Arizona
Pioneers' Historical Society) published *An Arizona Gathering,* a
record of the publications for the decade 1950–1959. *Arizona Gathering II* includes most of the entries for the earlier bibliography
although a number of newly discovered works have been added and
a few omitted in the light of greater wisdom.

In general the criteria for the first *Gathering* are those used for
the second. Only nonfiction is included. Then, the book must be
entirely or in large part about an Arizona topic. Juvenile literature
is not included although a number of books which are equally appeal-
ing to the young and adults will be found here. I have not listed a

considerable number of books dealing with various political careers so only those which are biographical in nature are included; the others belong to the national rather than the local record. In the same vein the masses of printed legal reports and other materials on the Colorado River litigation have been omitted. Also omitted are certain reports, mainly by governmental agencies, which were intended for internal use. Though a few copies have found their ways into libraries, they can not be considered to have been "published."

In spite of high resolve, it is in the nature of the thing that no bibliography can be complete. Inevitably some items escape the attention of even the most painstaking workers, and I do not count myself among those. Although I have searched many sources I am bound to have missed some titles, even, perhaps, something of significance, published locally in a small edition and which drew little attention outside its own community.

I have not been rigid about state borders. Whenever a publication appears to illuminate the Arizona scene, I have included it. Thus almost everything about the Navajo has been listed whether the area was Arizona, New Mexico, or Utah.

Arrangement is alphabetical by author or by title when no author is given. However, anonymous works about places are grouped under the name of the place. A few additional entries are made under a bracketed subject (e.g. [Employment]) when the first significant word of the title would be no clue to the matter. I have tried to describe each item accurately, and in acceptable form, so that it may be located easily in a library; however, I have taken no particular pains to give exact descriptions of official documents, especially those of the state which are issued in a wild confusion of formats, title pages (or lack of them), and imprint data. Square brackets indicate information which I have supplied.

In listing doctoral dissertations I have necessarily used the pagination as given in *Dissertation Abstracts*. It should be noted that in many cases it will differ from the original, since the figure found in that trying publication is actually the number of frames on the microfilm.

A greater use of annotations has been made than was true of the first *Gathering*. Annotations are chiefly descriptive and are used to amplify the titles. Many titles, especially those of doctoral dissertations and scientific works, are completely descriptive of the content and need no comment from me; this also is true of many official publications.

I wish to thank Robert Poland, University of Arizona acquisitions librarian, who over the years has been zealous in calling items of Arizoniana to my notice, and Robert K. Johnson, former University Librarian, who kindly allowed me time from my other duties to pursue my bibliographical vagaries. Thanks go to The University of Arizona Press and Kit S. Applegate, who is everything an editor should be.

DONALD M. POWELL

ABBREVIATIONS

comp.	compiler
diags.	diagrams
ed.	editor
illus.	illustrations
port(s).	portrait(s)
trans.	translator

Bibliography

1. ABBOTT, J. L. AND OTHERS. *Nutrient Requirements of Arizona Cotton.* Tucson: University of Arizona Agricultural Experiment Station, 1955. (Report no. 117) 31 pp., diags.

2. ABERLE, DAVID F. *The Peyote Religion Among the Navaho.* Chicago: Aldine Publishing Co., 1966. 454 pp.
    Also issued in stiff paper wrappers as no. 42 in the Viking Fund Publications in Anthropology.

3. ————. *The Psychosocial Analysis of a Hopi Life-History.* Berkeley: University of California Press, 1951. (Comparative Psychology Monographs vol. 21, no. 1) 133 pp.
    An analysis of the autobiography of Don Talayesva published in 1942 with the title *Sun Chief.*

4. ————. *The Reconciliation of Divergent Views of Hopi Culture Through the Analysis of Life-History Material.* Ann Arbor: University Microfilms, 1950. 440 pp.
    A Columbia University doctoral dissertation.

5. ———— AND OMER S. STEWART. *Navajo and Ute Peyotism: a Chronological and Distributional Study.* Boulder: University of Colorado Press, 1957. (University of Colorado Studies, Series in Anthropology no. 6) 129 pp.

6. ACKERMAN, BERNICE. *Characteristics of Summer Radar Echoes in Arizona, 1956.* Tucson: University of Arizona Institute of Atmospheric Physics, 1959. (Scientific Report 2) 66 pp., illus., tables.

7. *An Action Program for Tucson.* [Washington?]: National Association of Real Estate Boards, Build America Better Committee, 1963. 60 pp., illus.
   Need and proposal for urban renewal.

8. ACUÑA GÁLVEZ, CRUZ. *El Romance del Padre Kino.* Hermosillo, Sonora: Editorial Urias, 1969. 112 pp., illus., map.

9. ADAMS, WILLIAM Y. *Ninety Years of Glen Canyon Archaeology, 1869–1959.* Flagstaff: Northern Arizona Society of Science and Art Inc., 1960. (Museum of Northern Arizona Bulletin 33, Glen Canyon Series no. 2) 29 pp., tables, maps.
   Subtitle: "A brief historical sketch and bibliography of archaelogical investigations from J. W. Powell to the Glen Canyon Project."

10. ———. *Shonto: A Study of the Role of the Trader in a Modern Navajo Community.* Ann Arbor: University Microfilms, 1958. 638 pp.
    A University of Arizona doctoral dissertation.

11. ———. *Shonto: A Study of the Role of the Trader in a Modern Navaho Community.* Washington: Bureau of American Ethnology, 1963. (Bulletin no. 188) 329 pp., illus., tables, diags., folding map.
    The author's dissertation with minor changes.

12. *The Adventures of Don Quixow . . . or the Discovery of the Arizona Market.* Phoenix: Phoenix Republic and Gazette, 1954. 48 pp., illus., tables, diags.
    Arizona as a market.

13. AGENBROAD, LARRY D. *Cenozoic Stratigraphy and Paleo-Hydrology of the Redington-San Manuel Area, San Pedro Valley, Arizona.* Ann Arbor: University Microfilms, 1967. 182 pp.
    A University of Arizona doctoral dissertation.

14. AGEY, W. W. AND V. E. EDLUND. *Flotation and Sintering Studies of Manganese Ores Stockpiled at Deming, N. Mex., and Wenden, Ariz.* [Washington]: U. S. Bureau of Mines, 1962. (Report of Investigations no. 6103) 13 pp., tables.

15. [Agriculture] *An Analysis of Arizona's Agricultural Productive Capacity.* Tucson, 1951. 36 pp.
    Part of a cooperative study by the U.S. Department of Agriculture and the land-grant colleges.

16. AINSA, J. Y. *History of the Crabb Expedition into N. Sonora.* Phoenix, 1951. 51 pp.
    Subtitle: "Decapitation of the state Senator of California, Henry A. Crabb, and massacre of ninety-eight of his friends at Caborca and Sonoyta, Sonora, Mexico, 1857."

17. *Air Pollution in Tucson, Arizona*. Phoenix: Arizona State Department of Health, 1959. 12 pp., illus., tables, diags.

18. *Ajo Area Plan*. [Tucson]: Pima County Planning Department, 1966. 29 pp., illus., tables, maps.

19. [Ajo] *New Cornelia Branch, Ajo, Arizona*. [Phoenix? 1969?]. 16 pp., illus.
    Most attractively produced of several pamphlets on the mine and the town.

20. AKERS, JAY P. *Geology and Ground Water in the Central Part of Apache County, Arizona*. Washington: U. S. Geological Survey, 1964. (Water-Supply Paper no. 1771) 107 pp., illus., maps, diags., tables.

21. ———— AND OTHERS. *Geology and Ground Water of the Red Lake Area, Navajo Indian Reservation, Arizona and New Mexico*. Washington: U.S. Geological Survey, 1962. (Water-Supply Paper no. 1576-B) 12 pp., maps.

22. ALENIUS, E. M. J. *A Brief History of the United Verde Open Pit, Jerome, Arizona*. Tucson: The University of Arizona, 1968. (Arizona Bureau of Mines Bulletin 178) 34 pp., illus., diags.

23. ALEXANDER, CHARLES I. *An Introduction to Navaho Sandpaintings*. [Santa Fe]: Museum of Navaho Ceremonial Art, 1967. 24 pp., illus.

24. ALLEN, ALVIN AND HARVEY F. TATE. *Bulbs for Northern Arizona*. Tucson: Arizona Agricultural Extension Service, 1958. (Circular 264) 16 pp., illus.

25. ALLEN, JOHN E. AND ROBERT BALK. *Mineral Resources of the Fort Defiance and Tohatchi Quadrangles, Arizona and New Mexico*. Socorro: New Mexico State Bureau of Mines and Mineral Resources, 1954. (Bulletin 36) 192 pp., illus., maps, diags.

26. ALLEN, TERRY AND DON ALLEN. *Navahos Have Five Fingers*. Norman: University of Oklahoma Press, 1963. 249 pp., illus.
    Reminiscences of a sympathetic couple who were caretakers for an outstation of Ganado Mission.

27. ALONSO, RAMON *see* CLAVERAN ALONSO, RAMON.

28. AMBLER, J. RICHARD AND OTHERS. *Survey and Excavations on Cummings Mesa, Arizona and Utah, 1960–1961*. Flagstaff: Northern Arizona Society of Science and Art, 1964. (Museum of Northern Arizona Bulletin no. 39, Glen Canyon Series no. 5) 105 pp., illus., tables, diags.

29. *The Amerind Foundation*. Dragoon, Arizona: The Foundation, 1967. unpaged.
    Handsome, illustrated booklet explaining the foundation and its work.

30. AMIN, OMAR M. *Helminth Fauna of Suckers* (Catostomidae) *of the Gila River System, Arizona*. Ann Arbor: University Microfilms, 1968. 202 pp.
    An Arizona State University doctoral dissertation.

31. AMSDEN, CHARLES AVERY. *Navaho Weaving, Its Technic and History*. Chicago: Rio Grande Press, 1964. 261 pp., illus.
    Facsimile reprint of the original edition of 1934. The position of the color plates varies from the original.

32. *An Analysis of Arizona-Generated Scrap Iron and Steel Markets*. Prepared by Universal Operations Research. Phoenix: Arizona Development Board, [1958?]. 34 pp., tables, diags.

33. *An Analysis of Forest Products Potential in Arizona*. Prepared for the Arizona Development Board by Division of Forestry, Arizona State College. Phoenix: Arizona Development Board, [1960?]. 19 pp., illus., maps, tables.

34. ANDERSON, CHARLES A. AND S. C. CREASEY. *Geology and Ore Deposits of the Jerome Area, Yavapai County, Arizona*. Washington: U. S. Geological Survey, 1958. (Professional Paper no. 308) 185 pp., illus., tables, maps.

35. ——— AND OTHERS. *Geology and Ore Deposits of the Bagdad Area, Yavapai County, Arizona*. Washington: U. S. Geological Survey, 1955. (Professional Paper no. 278) 103 pp., illus., tables, maps.

36. ANDERSON, DARWIN AND OTHERS. *Reseeding Desert Grassland Ranges in Southern Arizona*. Tucson: University of Arizona Agricultural Experiment Station, 1953. (Bulletin no. 249) 32 pp., illus.

37. ANDERSON, KEITH M. *Archeology on the Shonto Plateau, Northeast Arizona*. Globe, Arizona: Southwestern Monuments Association, 1969. (Technical Series vol. 7) 68 pp., illus., tables, diags.

38. ———. *Tsegi Phase Technology*. Ann Arbor: University Microfilms, 1969. 446 pp.
    A University of Washington doctoral dissertation.

39. ANDERSON, ROGER Y. AND JOHN W. HARSHBARGER. *Guidebook of the Black Mesa Basin, Northeastern Arizona*. Prepared in cooperation with the Arizona Geological Society. [Socorro, New Mexico? 1958?]. 205 pp., illus., maps.

40. ANDERSON, THOMAS W. *Electrical Analog Analysis of Ground-Water Depletion in Central Arizona.* Washington: U. S. Geological Survey, 1968. (Water-Supply Paper no. 1860) 21 pp., illus., maps.

41. ANGLE, JERRY. *Federal, State and Tribal Jurisdiction on Indian Reservations in Arizona.* Tucson: University of Arizona Bureau of Ethnic Research, 1959. (American Indian Series no. 2) 46 pp.

42. ANGUS, ROBERT C. *Arizona Hay Price-Quality Relationships.* Tucson: University of Arizona Agricultural Experiment Station, 1963. (Technical Bulletin no. 157) 15 pp., tables, diags.

43. ———— AND HAROLD M. STULTS. *Grain Storage in Arizona.* Tucson: University of Arizona Agricultural Experiment Station, 1963. (Technical Bulletin no. 159) 23 pp., diags.

44. ANTHONY, JOHN W. AND OTHERS. *Bibliography of the Geology and Mineral Resources of Arizona, 1939–1952.* Tucson: University of Arizona, 1953. (Arizona Bureau of Mines Bulletin no. 161) 62 pp.
    Supplements Bulletin 146 which indexed the literature to 1939.

45. *Agua Fria Union High School: Report of Survey, March 1964.* [Tempe]: Arizona State University, Bureau of Educational Research and Services, 1964. 68 pp.

46. *Arid Lands Colloquia, 1959–1960, 1960–1961.* [Tucson]: The University of Arizona, [1961]. 73 pp., maps, diags.
    Issued in a very limited number of copies primarily for the use of members of cooperating units of the arid-lands project.

47. *Arizona Agricultural Statistics, 1867–1965.* Phoenix: Arizona Crop and Livestock Reporting Service, 1966. 129 pp., tables, diags.
    Supplemented by annual issues of statistics.

48. *Arizona! America at Its Best.* Phoenix: John R. Manning and Associates, 1961. 48 pp., illus., maps.
    An *olla podrida* of Arizona information in cheap, unpleasant, newsprint format.

49. *Arizona Basic Economic and Manpower Data.* [Phoenix]: Employment Security Commission of Arizona, Arizona State Employment Service, 1949–
    Annual. Title varies. In recent years particularly, contains much useful economic information.

50. *Arizona Business Births and Deaths, 1948–1949.* Phoenix: Employment Security Commission of Arizona, 1950. 77 pp., tables.
    Other editions, 1948–1951, 1951–1962, 1963–1965. Title varies. Subtitle: "An analysis of business births, deaths & growth as trend indicators of Arizona's economy."

51. *Arizona — County Base Book*. Tucson: University of Arizona Bureau of Business Research, 1953. 150 pp., tables.
    "Makes readily available . . . selected statistics covering a wide span of the state's economy."
    — second edition, 1953. 150 pp.
    — third edition, 1958. 151 pp.
    — fourth edition, 1962. 59 pp.

52. *Arizona Directory of Manufacturers, 1954*. Phoenix: Employment Security Commission of Arizona, 1954. 53 pp.
    Products, locations, plants. Other editions issued in 1956, 1960, 1962, 1965, 1968.

53. *Arizona Edition, American Biographical Encyclopedia: Profiles of Prominent Personalities*. Phoenix: Paul W. Pollock, 1967. 343 pp., ports.

54. *Arizona Growth Trends, 1957–1966, Economic, Employment, Population*. [Phoenix: Employment Security Commission of Arizona, 1967?]. 30 pp., diags.

55. *Arizona Hunter's Handbook, 1969–1970*. Phoenix: Phoenix Publishing Inc., 1969. 64 pp., illus., tables.

56. *Arizona Indians*. Hearings. 84th Congress, 1st Session. Senate Interior and Insular Affairs Committee. Washington, 1955. 112 pp.
    Papago rehabilitation, legal control, and other matters.

57. *Arizona Industrial Development Workshop*. Tucson: University of Arizona, [1956–1959]. 5 vols.
    Proceedings of five workshops on industrial and community development sponsored by the university's Bureau of Business and Public Research and Tucson organizations. The third has the title "Progress, Problems and Prospects in Arizona Communities," and the fourth "Planning for Progress." For the fifth see "Arizona-Sonora International Conference. . . ."

58. *Arizona: Its People and Resources*. Edited by Jack L. Cross, Elizabeth H. Shaw and Kathleen Scheifele. Tucson: University of Arizona Press, 1960. 385 pp., illus., maps.
    A compendium of information about the state. Useful and surprisingly readable.

59. *Arizona . . . Its Place in Time*. [Phoenix]: The Arizona Republic, [1960]. unpaged, illus.
    Articles, mostly on Arizona's prehistory, reprinted from the Sunday magazine section of the *Republic*.

60. *Arizona, Land of Promise and Fulfillment*. Tucson: University of Arizona Press, 1955. (General Bulletin no. 18) 30 pp.
    Subtitle: "Addresses delivered by four former presidents on November 16, 1951 . . . at the inauguration of Richard Anderson Harvill as president of the University of Arizona." Participants were Homer L. Shantz, Rufus B. von KleinSmid, James B. McCormick, and Alfred Atkinson.

61. *The Arizona Legislative Process and Bill Drafting Manual.* Phoenix: Arizona Legislative Council, 1961. 66 pp., diags.

62. *Arizona Mining — an Epic.* Phoenix: Arizona Mining Association, 1965. 15 pp.
     Advertisements published in Arizona newspapers.

63. *Arizona Mining: Fabled Past, Solid Future.* Phoenix: Arizona Mining Association, [1969]. 22 pp., illus.
     Advertisements from Arizona newspapers in 1969.

64. *An Arizona Plan for Emergency Health and Welfare Services, Transportation, and Supply.* Phoenix: Arizona Civil Defense Agency, 1953. 40 pp., maps, tables.

65. *Arizona-Sonora International Conference on Regional and Community Development, March 6–7, 1959.* Tucson: University of Arizona [Bureau of Business and Public Research, 1959]. 139 pp., illus.
     Fifth and last in a series. For earlier volumes see *Arizona Industrial Development Workshop.* Covers commerce and industry. At head of title "Proceedings." In English and Spanish.

66. *Arizona Statistical Review.* Phoenix: Valley National Bank, 1946–
     Should be excluded because of its beginning date, but noted because of its great usefulness. Annual.

67. *The Arizona Story.* Phoenix: Arizona Development Board, [1963?]. unpaged, illus.
     Facts and figures about the state for potential investors.
     — revised edition, 1964, 59 pp.

68. *The Arizona Student Exchange Program of the Western Interstate Commission for Higher Education.* Tucson, 1957–
     Annual report to the governor and board of regents.

69. *Arizona, the Grand Canyon State: A State Guide.* Revised by Joseph Miller. New York: Hastings House, 1956. 532 pp., illus., maps.
     The Works Progress Administration guide originally published in 1940. Revision is spotty.

70. *Arizona, the Grand Canyon State: A State Guide.* Revised by Joseph Miller. Edited by Henry G. Alsberg and Harry Hansen. New York: Hastings House, 1966. 532 pp., illus., maps.
     The publisher's jacket claim that this is a new and completely revised edition is misleading. Revision is neither extensive nor thorough. For details see the *Arizona Quarterly,* vol. 22, no. 3 (Autumn 1966), pp. 287–88.

71. *Arizona Transportation.* Edited by Martin T. Farris and William S. Peters. Tempe: Arizona State University, 1961. 52 pp., tables, diags.
     Covers highway, rail, and air transportation, and their place in the economy.

72. *Arizona Watershed Program.* Phoenix: State Land Department, 1957–
    Annual symposium. Title varies.

73. *Arizona Yesterday, Today and Tomorrow.* [Phoenix]: First National Bank of Arizona, 1956. unpaged, illus.
    Story of the bank and its then new building in Phoenix.

74. *Arizona Zinc and Lead Deposits.* Parts I and II. Tucson: University of Arizona, 1950. (Arizona Bureau of Mines Bulletin 156) 144 and 115 pp., illus., maps.

75. [Arizona] *An Era of Arizona Expansion, 1946–1957.* Phoenix: Arizona State Employment Service, 1958. 30 pp., diags.
    Brief text and charts for population, income, agriculture, etc.

76. [Arizona] *Historical Album of Arizona.* Edited by Richard J. Bowe. [Los Angeles?]: Richard J. and Charles G. Bowe, [1957?]. unpaged, illus.
    A pictorial miscellany.

77. [Arizona] *Impact of Industrialization upon Finances of the State of Arizona.* Prepared by Stanford Research Institute for Municipal Industrial Development Corporation, Phoenix. [Stanford, California?], 1955. 41 pp., tables, diags.

78. [Arizona] *State Departments, Elective and Appointive Officers, Boards and Commissions of Arizona.* Phoenix: Arizona Tax Research Association, 1966. 53 pp., tables.
    No more issued?

79. [Arizona] *The State of Arizona.* Tucson: League of Women Voters of Arizona, 1959. (Publication no. 7) 80 pp., tables.
    Useful handbook on state government.

80. [Arizona Daily Star] *Index to Arizona News in the Arizona Daily Star.* Tucson: Arizona Daily Star, 1954–
    Covers the years 1953–1965. Issued annually. Others in preparation. Compiled by the reference staff at the University of Arizona Library.

81. [Arizona Republic] *The Researchers' Guide to Arizona News in The Arizona Republic.* [Tempe: Arizona State University Library?], 1966–
    Compiled by the staff of the Arizona State University Library. Covers January 1966 through June 1967. No more issued?

82. *Arizona's Crazy Quilt of Assessment.* [Phoenix]: Maricopa County Taxpayers Association, 1959. 32 pp., tables.

83. *Arizona's Dynamic Future: An Economic Portrait.* Prepared by the Bureau of Business Services, Arizona State College, Tempe. Phoenix: Arizona Development Board, [1957]. unpaged, tables, diags.

84. *Arizona's Golden Years.* Phoenix: Operation Reach Inc., [1961?]. 160 pp., illus.
    All about Arizona (more or less). An anniversary publication.

85. *Arizona's Manpower Challenge of the 60's.* Phoenix: Arizona State Employment Service, 1960. 37 pp., tables, diags.
    A revision of item 89 below.

86. *Arizona's Men of Achievement.* Phoenix: Paul W. Pollock, 1958. 298 pp., illus.
    Biographies. Would once have been called a "mug book."

87. *Arizona's Tax Structure and Its Administration.* Research report prepared by Arizona State University, Tempe. Phoenix: Arizona Academy, [1967]. 145 pp., tables.
    Eleventh Arizona Town Hall, October 1967.

88. *Arizona's Tax Structure — Revenue Needs and Revenue Sources.* Research report prepared by the Bureau of Business Services, Arizona State University, Tempe. Phoenix: Arizona Academy, [1962]. 172 pp., tables, diags.
    First Arizona Town Hall, October 1962.

89. *Arizona's Trained Manpower Future.* [Phoenix]: Arizona State Employment Service, 1959. 80 pp., illus.
    Subtitle: "The utilization and implementation of Arizona manpower requirements and training needs studies through local action programs."

90. *Arizona's Water Supply.* Research report prepared by the University of Arizona. Phoenix: Arizona Academy, [1964]. 167 pp., tables, diags., maps.
    Fourth Arizona Town Hall, April 1964.

91. ARMER, LAURA A. *In Navajo Land.* New York: David McKay, 1962. 107 pp., illus.
    Reminiscences of a sojourn in the Navajo country in the 1920s.

92. ARMSTRONG, AUGUSTUS K. *The Paleontology and Stratigraphy of the Mississippian System of Southwestern New Mexico and Southeastern Arizona.* Ann Arbor: University Microfilms, 1960. 337 pp.
    A University of Cincinnati doctoral dissertation.

93. ARMSTRONG, C. A. AND C. B. YOST, JR. *Geology and Ground-Water Resources of the Palomas Plain — Dendora Valley Area, Maricopa and Yuma Counties, Arizona.* Phoenix: Arizona State Land Department, 1958. (Water Resources Report no. 4) 49 pp., illus., tables.

94. ARMSTRONG, WILLIAM W. *The Economic Value of Hunting and Fishing in Arizona in 1956.* Phoenix: Arizona Game and Fish Department, 1958. (Wildlife Bulletin no. 4) 36 pp., illus., tables, diags.

95. *Army Electronic Proving Ground, Fort Huachuca, Arizona.* [Fort Huachuca, 1956?]. unpaged, illus.
A pamphlet of some 60 pages describing army operations at the fort.

96. ARNBURGER, LESLIE P. *Flowers of the Southwest Mountains.* Santa Fe: Southwestern Monuments Association, 1953. (Popular Series no. 7) 112 pp., illus.

97. ARNOLD, JOSEPH F. AND W. L. SCHROEDER. *Juniper Control Increases Forage Production on the Fort Apache Indian Reservation.* Fort Collins, Colorado: U. S. Forest Service, Rocky Mountain Forest and Range Experiment Station, 1955. (Station Paper no. 18) 35 pp., illus., tables, diags.

98. ———— AND OTHERS. *The Pinyon-Juniper Type of Arizona: Effects of Grazing, Fire, and Tree Control.* Washington: U. S. Forest Service, 1964. (Production Research Report no. 84) 28 pp., illus., tables, diags., maps.

99. ARNOLD, OREN. *Arizona Brags: All the Wittiest, Wisest, Best-and-Worst Ever Said about Arizona.* New edition. Phoenix: Bob Petley Studios, 1952. 48 pp., illus.

100. ————. *Arizona Under the Sun.* Foreword by Barry Goldwater. Freeport, Maine: Bond Wheelwright, 1968. 220 pp.
Essays on how to live in the sun, what to buy, where to go, and some incidents out of the past.

101. ————. *Ghost Gold.* San Antonio: The Naylor Co., 1954. 71 pp., illus.
The Lost Dutchman again.

102. ————. *Savage Son.* Albuquerque: University of New Mexico Press, 1951. 273 pp., illus.
The story of Dr. Carlos Montezuma.

103. ————. *Thunder in the Southwest: Echoes from the Wild Frontier.* Norman: University of Oklahoma Press, 1952. 237 pp., illus.
"... a re-enactment of certain episodes which took place in the Southwest that our pioneers knew."

104. ARROWSMITH, REX, ed. *Mines of the Old Southwest.* Santa Fe: Stagecoach Press, 1963. 90 pp., illus.
Excerpts from reports by Abert, J. Ross Browne, Mowry, and others. Mostly New Mexico.

105. ARTEAGA, F. E. *Ground Water in Paradise Valley, Maricopa County, Arizona.* Phoenix: Arizona State Land Department, 1968. (Water-Resources Report no. 35) 76 pp., maps, diags.

106. *Artists in the Valley of the Sun.* [Phoenix]: Arizona Arts Publications, 1955. 34 pp., illus.
Issued by the Arizona Artists Guild.

107. ASHE, ROBERT W. AND JOHN B. BARNES. *A Survey of Public School Facilities, Peoria, Arizona, 1962.* Tempe: Arizona State University College of Education, [1962]. 71 pp., illus., maps.

108. ———— AND OTHERS. *A Handbook for Arizona School Board Members.* [second edition]. Tempe: Arizona State University Bureau of Educational Research and Services, 1964. (Research and Services Bulletin no. 16) 85 pp.
    For earlier edition see item 1177.

109. ———— AND ————. *Report of the Survey of Eastern Arizona Junior College.* Tempe: Arizona State College, 1958. 250 pp., illus., tables.

110. ———— AND ————. *Survey Report of Gila Indian Reservation Schools, August, 1959.* [Tempe: Arizona State University?], 1959. 39 pp., tables, maps.

111. ASHURST, HENRY FOUNTAIN. *A Many-Colored Toga: The Diary of Henry Fountain Ashurst.* Edited by George F. Sparks. Tucson: University of Arizona Press, 1962. 416 pp., illus.

112. ————. *Speeches of Henry Fountain Ashurst of Arizona.* Phoenix: Arizona-Messenger Printing, [1953]. 110 pp.
    Collected and published by Barry Goldwater.

113. *Authorizing Long-Term Leases on the San Xavier and Salt River Pima-Maricopa Indian Reservations, Arizona.* 89th Congress, 2nd Session. House Report no. 1855. [Washington, 1966?]. 18 pp.

114. [Avondale] *The Comprehensive Planning Program, Avondale, Arizona.* [Scottsdale, Arizona] Van Cleve Associates, 1967. 2 vols. Tables, maps.
    Vol. 1, Data for Planning; Vol. 2, Planning Studies.

115. AXFORD, JOSEPH M. *Around Western Campfires.* New York: Pageant Press, 1964, 261 pp.
    Reminiscences of life in Cochise County, ranching, mining, etc.; some material on the W. C. Greene family.

116. ————. *Around Western Campfires.* Tucson: University of Arizona Press, 1969. 266 pp.
    Originally published by Pageant; see above. This edition omits some material in the original.

117. *BLM at work in Arizona, 1961.* Phoenix: U. S. Department of the Interior, Bureau of Land Management, [1961]. 22 pp., illus.

118. BABBITT, JOHN G. *The Babbitt Brothers Trading Company: An Address before the Newcomen Society, April 15, 1967.* Flagstaff, Arizona: Privately Printed, 1967. 22 pp., illus.
    Story of a northern Arizona mercantile firm; 500 copies printed by the Northland Press.

119. BABINGTON, SUREN H. *Navajos, Gods and Tom-Toms*. New York: Greenburg, 1950. 246 pp., illus.
    A doctor's experiences on an expedition to the reservation. Observations on medicine and medicine men as well as Navajo life in general.

120. BAHTI, TOM. *An Introduction to Southwestern Indian Arts and Crafts*. Flagstaff, Arizona: KC Publications, [1964]. 32 pp., illus.
    Good, simple text and handsome photographs.

121. ————. *Southwestern Indian Tribes*. Flagstaff, Arizona: KC Publications, 1968. 72 pp., illus.
    Brief description for each pueblo or tribe with excellent illustrations, some in color.

122. BAILEY, FLORA L. *Some Sex Beliefs and Practices in a Navaho Community; with Comparative Material from Other Navaho Areas*. Cambridge, Massachusetts: Peabody Museum, 1950. (Peabody Papers Vol. 40, no. 2) 108 pp.

123. BAILEY, JAMES S. *A Stratigraphic Analysis of Rico Strata in the Four Corners Region*. Ann Arbor: University Microfilms, 1955. 116 pp.
    A University of Arizona doctoral dissertation.

124. BAILEY, LYNN R. *The Long Walk, a History of the Navajo Wars, 1846–68*. Los Angeles: Westernlore Press, 1964. 252 pp., illus., maps.

125. BAKER, ARTHUR, III. *Pyrometasomatic Ore Deposits at Johnson Camp, Arizona*. Ann Arbor: University Microfilms, 1953. 125 pp.
    A Stanford University doctoral dissertation.

126. BAKER, EDWARD W. AND DONALD M. TUTTLE. *The False Spider Mites of Arizona* (Acarina Tenuipalpidae). Tucson: University of Arizona Agricultural Experiment Station, 1964. (Technical Bulletin no. 163) 80 pp., illus.

127. BAKER, RICHARD C. *The Geology and Ore Deposits of the Southeast Portion of the Patagonia Mountains, Santa Cruz County, Arizona*. Ann Arbor: University Microfilms, 1962. 325 pp.
    A University of Michigan doctoral dissertation.

128. BAKER, SIMON AND THOMAS J. McCLENEGHAN, eds. *An Arizona Economic and Historic Atlas*. Tucson: University of Arizona in cooperation with the Valley National Bank, 1966. 40 pp., maps.

129. BALDWIN, GORDON C. *The Warrior Apaches: A Story of the Chiricahua and Western Apache*. Tucson: Dale Stuart King, 1965. 144 pp., illus., maps.
    Simply written account of the Apache past and his life ways with a chapter on the Apache today.

130. BALTHASAR, JUAN A. *Juan Antonio Balthasar, Padre Visitador to the Sonora Frontier, 1744–1745: Two Original Reports.* Edited by Peter Masten Dunne. Tucson: Arizona Pioneers' Historical Society, 1957. 122 pp., maps.
Limited to 600 copies, designed and printed by Lawton Kennedy.

131. BANCROFT, HUBERT H. *History of Arizona and New Mexico, 1530–1888.* Albuquerque: Horn & Wallace, 1962. 19, xxxviii, 829 pp.
A facsimile of the 1889 edition with forewords by Senators Clinton P. Anderson and Barry Goldwater.

132. BANERJEE, ANIL K. *Structure and Petrology of the Oracle Granite, Pinal County, Arizona.* Ann Arbor: University Microfilms, 1957. 112 pp.
A University of Arizona doctoral dissertation.

133. BANFIELD, EDWARD C. *Government Project.* Glencoe, Illinois: Free Press, 1951. 271 pp.
Story of the cooperative Casa Grande Valley Farms established in Pinal County by the Resettlement Administration, 1936–43, and an attempt to explain the project's failure.

134. BANNER, WARREN M. AND THEODORA M. DYER. *Economic and Cultural Progress of the Negro.* [Report] conducted for the Phoenix Urban League. New York: National Urban League, 1965. 193 pp., tables.

135. BANNISTER, BRYANT AND OTHERS. *Tree-Ring Dates from Arizona C–D, Eastern Grand Canyon-Tsegi Canyon-Kayenta Area.* Tucson: University of Arizona Laboratory of Tree-Ring Research, 1968. 78 pp.

136. ———— AND ————. *Tree-Ring Dates from Arizona E, Chinle-De Chelly-Red Rock Area.* Tucson: University of Arizona Laboratory of Tree-Ring Research, 1966. 54 pp., maps.

137. ———— AND ————. *Tree Ring Dates from Arizona J, Hopi Mesas Area.* Tucson: University of Arizona Laboratory of Tree-Ring Research, 1967. 44 pp.

138. ———— AND ————. *Tree-Ring Dates from Arizona K: Puerco-Wide Ruin-Ganado Area.* Tucson: University of Arizona Laboratory of Tree-Ring Research, 1966. 48 pp.

139. ———— AND ————. *Tree-Ring Dates from Arizona N-Q: Verde-Show Low-St. John's Area.* Tucson: University of Arizona Laboratory of Tree-Ring Research, 1966. 63 pp.

140. BANTA, ALBERT F. *Albert Franklin Banta, Arizona Pioneer.* Edited by Frank D. Reeve. Albuquerque: Historical Society of New Mexico, 1953. (Publications in History, vol. 14) 143 pp.
Memoirs of a pioneer newspaperman, guide, prospector, and man of all trades who came to Arizona in 1863 and died at Prescott in 1924.

141. BARBOUR, THOMAS L. *Arthur Frommer's Dollar-Wise Guide to Arizona.* New York: Published for American Airlines by the Frommer/Pasmantier Publishing Corp., 1965. 319 pp., illus.
    Features hotels, restaurants, shopping, and tours; includes discount coupons.

142. BARKER, GEORGE C. *Pachuco: an American-Spanish Argot and Its Social Functions in Tucson, Arizona.* Tucson: University of Arizona Press, 1958. (Social Science Bulletin no. 18) 46 pp.
    Reissue, with additions, of a bulletin published in 1950.

143. BARNARD, BARNEY *see* BARNARD, WAYNE E.

144. BARNARD, WAYNE E. *The Story of Jacob Walzer* .... [Apache Junction, Arizona: The Author, 1954]. 68 pp., illus.
    Apparently an expansion of a pamphlet by C. F. Higham published in El Paso in the 1940s, using some of the same text and illustrations. Frequently reprinted with minor variations.

145. BARNES, JOHN B. AND MERWIN DEEVER. *A Study of Buckeye Elementary District Number 33, Buildings and Site Utilization.* Tempe: Arizona State University Bureau of Educational Research and Services, 1962. 61 pp., maps, tables, diags.

146. BARNETT, FRANKLIN. *Viola Jimulla: The Indian Chieftess.* Prescott, Arizona: Prescott Yavapai Indians, 1968. 43 pp., illus.

147. BARNEY, JAMES M. *A Historical Sketch of the Volunteer Fire Department of Phoenix, Arizona.* Phoenix, 1954. 52 pp., illus.

148. ———. *Yuma.* [Phoenix]: Charter Oak Insurance Company, 1953. 43 pp., illus.
    Yuma history through the territorial period.

149. BARRINGTON, JONATHAN. *Piercement Features near Cameron, Arizona.* Ann Arbor: University Microfilms, 1961. 193 pp.
    A Columbia University doctoral dissertation.

150. BARSALOU, FRANK AND OTHERS. *Yuma: Its Economic Growth and Land Use Potentials.* Prepared by the Stanford Research Institute. [Menlo Park, California], 1956. 178 pp., maps, diags.

151. BARTHOLOMEW, ED. *Wyatt Earp, 1879 to 1882: the Man and the Myth.* Toyahvale, Texas: Frontier Book Co., 1964. 335 pp., illus.
    The Tombstone years; the author's earlier *Wyatt Earp: The Untold Story* covers Earp's career before the Tombstone period.

152. BARTLETT, JOHN RUSSELL. *Personal Narrative of Explorations and Incidents in Texas, New Mexico, California, Sonora and Chihuahua, Connected with the United States and Mexican Boundary Commission, During the Years 1850, '51, '52, and '53.* Chicago: Rio Grande Press, 1965. 2 vols.
    A facsimile of the original of 1854 with an unpaged introduction on Bartlett by Odie Faulk and an additional map.

153. BASSO, KEITH H. *The Gift of Changing Woman.* Washington: U. S. Bureau of American Ethnology, 1966. (Bulletin no. 196, Anthropological Papers no. 76) pp. 113–73, illus.
A Western Apache girl's puberty rite as performed on the Fort Apache reservation.

154. ———. *Western Apache Witchcraft.* Tucson: University of Arizona Press, 1969. (Anthropological Papers of the University of Arizona no. 15) 75 pp., tables, diags., maps.

155. BATEMAN, GARY C. *Home Range Studies of a Desert Nocturnal Rodent Fauna.* Ann Arbor: University Microfilms, 1967. 115 pp.
A University of Arizona doctoral dissertation.

156. BAYLOR, GEORGE W. *John Robert Baylor, Confederate Governor of Arizona.* Edited by Odie B. Faulk. Tucson: Arizona Pioneers' Historical Society, 1966. (Arizona History Series no. II) 38 pp., port.

157. BEAL, MERRILL D. *Grand Canyon, the Story Behind the Scenery.* Flagstaff, Arizona: KC Publications, 1967. 38 pp., illus., maps.
Brief clear text, handsome design, illustrated in full color.

158. BEAN, LOWELL J. AND WILLIAM M. MASON, eds. *Diaries & Accounts of the Romero Expeditions in Arizona and California, 1823–1826.* Los Angeles: For the Palm Springs Desert Museum by the Ward Ritchie Press, 1962. 117 pp., illus.
Not much on Arizona but included because this was an important attempt to open land communication between southern Arizona and southern California.

159. BEAUDOIN, KENNETH L. *The Wuwuchim.* Saint Louis: Salter House, 1951. 8 pp.
Subtitle: "On the saga of the hegira of the Hopi from the underworld to the land of the mesas, rendered into traditional English from the account of a Hopi grandsire." 150 copies printed.

160. BEAUMONT, E. C. *Geology of the Kayenta and Chilchinbito Quadrangles, Navajo County, Arizona.* Washington: U. S. Geological Survey, 1965. (Bulletin no. 1202-A) 28 pp., maps, diags.

161. *Beautyway; a Navaho Ceremonial.* Edited by Leland C. Wyman. New York: Pantheon Books, 1957. (Bollingen Series no. 53) 218 pp., illus.
Includes 83-page Navajo Language supplement in pocket. Myth told by Singer Man, recorded and translated by Berard Haile; variant recorded by Maud Oaks; sandpaintings recorded by Laura Armer, F. J. Newcomb, and M. Oaks.

162. BEE, ROBERT L. *Sociocultural Change and Persistence in the Yuma Indian Reservation Community.* Ann Arbor: University Microfilms, 1968. 478 pp.
A University of Kansas doctoral dissertation.

163. BEESON, WILLIAM J. *Archaeological Survey near St. Johns, Arizona: a Methodological Study.* Ann Arbor: University Microfilms, 1966. 318 pp.
    A University of Arizona doctoral dissertation.

164. BELKNAP, BILL AND FRANCES SPENCER BELKNAP. *Gunnar Widforss, Painter of the Grand Canyon.* Flagstaff: Published for the Museum of Northern Arizona by the Northland Press, 1969. 86 pp., illus.
    Text and color reproductions of paintings.

165. BELKNAP, BUZZ. *Grand Canyon River Guide.* New York: Canyonlands Press, 1969. unpaged, illus.
    Strip maps based on the U.S.G.S. river profile with many photographs.

166. BELL, JACK. *Mr. Conservative: Barry Goldwater.* Garden City, New York: Doubleday, 1962. 312 pp.

167. BELL, WILLIAM A. *New Tracks in North America.* Albuquerque: Horn and Wallace, 1965. 564 pp., illus., maps.
    Reprint of the original of 1870. Subtitle: "A journal of travel and adventure whilst engaged in a survey for a southern railroad to the Pacific Ocean in 1867–1868." Much on Arizona including an account of James White's raft voyage down the Colorado.

168. BELL, YOUNG. *Forty Years in the Cow Business in Texas, New Mexico and Arizona.* Cisco, Texas: Longhorn Press, 1959. 91 pp., illus.
    Cover has label reading "Sixty-Four Years in the Cow Business" pasted over title.

169. BELLAH, ROBERT N. *Apache Kinship Systems.* Cambridge: Harvard University Press, 1952. 151 pp., diags.

170. BEMIS, WILLIAM P. *Temperature Tables and Their Uses in Crop Production for Ten Stations in Southern Arizona.* Tucson: University of Arizona Agricultural Experiment Station, 1962. (Technical Bulletin no. 151) 39 pp., tables.

171. BENNETT, KAY. *Kaibah: Recollection of a Navajo Girlhood.* Los Angeles: Westernlore Press, 1964. 253 pp., illus.

172. BENNETT, KENNETH A. *The Indians of Point of Pines: A Comparative Study of Their Physical Characteristics.* Ann Arbor: University Microfilms, 1967. 192 pp.
    A University of Arizona doctoral dissertation.

173. BENSON, LYMAN D. *The Cacti of Arizona.* Second edition. Tucson: University of Arizona Press, 1950. 134 pp., illus., maps.
    Technical but not too difficult for the amateur to use. Originally published as *University of Arizona Bulletin,* vol. xi, no. 1, 1940. This edition published at the University of New Mexico Press.

174. ———. *The Cacti of Arizona.* Third edition. Tucson: University of Arizona Press, 1969. 218 pp., illus., tables, maps.
Extensively revised; almost a wholly new work.

175. ——— AND ROBERT A. DARROW. *The Trees and Shrubs of the Southwestern Deserts.* Second edition. Tucson and Albuquerque: University of Arizona Press and University of New Mexico Press, 1954. 437 pp., illus., maps.
Originally issued as *University of Arizona Bulletin,* vol. xv, no. 2, 1944, with title *A Manual of Southwestern Desert Trees and Shrubs.*

176. BERGE, DALE L. *Historical Archaeology in the American Southwest.* Ann Arbor: University Microfilms, 1968. 463 pp.
A University of Arizona doctoral dissertation.

177. BERNEY, ROBERT E. AND ARLYN J. LARSON. *Mobile Home Taxation in Arizona.* Tempe: Arizona State University Bureau of Business Research and Services, 1966. 64 pp., tables.

178. BERRY, LEONARD L. *The Components of Department Store Image: A Study of Three Selected Department Stores in Phoenix, Arizona.* Ann Arbor: University Microfilms, 1968. 312 pp.
An Arizona State University doctoral dissertation.

179. BERTON, FRANCIS. *A Voyage on the Colorado, 1878.* Translated and edited by Charles N. Rudkin. Los Angeles: Glen Dawson, 1953. (Early California Travel Series no. 17) 103 pp., illus.
Limited to 300 copies. Originally issued in French in San Francisco, 1878, with title *Un Voyage sur le Colorado.*

180. BETZINEZ, JASON AND WILBUR S. NYE. *I Fought with Geronimo.* Harrisburg, Pennsylvania: Stackpole Co., 1959. 214 pp., illus.
Apache version of the Apache wars and the aftermath.

181. *Bibliography for Industrial Arizona.* Phoenix: Arizona Development Board, [1960]. 25 pp.
Sources of information on industrial development.

182. *Bibliography of U. S. Geological Survey Water-Resources Reports, Arizona. 1891 to 1965.* Phoenix: Arizona State Land Department, 1965. (Water-Resources Report no. 22) 59 pp.
Prepared by the U.S. Geological Survey.

183. BIGELOW, JOHN, JR. *On the Bloody Trail of Geronimo.* Edited by Arthur Woodward. Los Angeles: Westernlore Press, 1958. 237 pp., illus.
Limited to 750 copies. Illustrated by Remington and other early artists of the West. Describes army life in the 1880s, not Geronimo. Reissued in facsimile, 1968.

184. BIKERMAN, MICHAEL. *Geological and Geochemical Studies of the Roskruge Range, Pima County, Arizona.* Ann Arbor: University Microfilms, 1965. 135 pp.
A University of Arizona doctoral dissertation.

185. BIMSON, CARL A. *Transformation in the Desert: The Story of Arizona's Valley National Bank.* New York: The Newcomen Society, 1962. 28 pp.
      An address to the Newcomen Society, Phoenix.

186. BINGHAM, DAVID A. *Constitutional Municipal Home Rule in Arizona.* Tucson: University of Arizona Bureau of Business and Public Research, 1960. (Special Studies no. 16) 66 pp.

187. ————. *Handbook for Arizona Mayors and Councilmen.* Tempe: Arizona State University, 1959. (Bureau of Government Research, Monograph no. I) 48 pp.

188. ———— AND LEONARD E. GOODALL. *Handbook for Arizona Mayors and Councilmen.* Revised edition. Tempe: Arizona State University Bureau of Government Research, 1963. (Research Study no. 8) 46 pp., diags.
      Originally issued in 1950.
      — another edition [1968]. 43 pp.

189. *Bisbee, Arizona: A Community Profile.* [Phoenix?]: Arizona Department of Economic Planning and Development, 1969. 41 pp., illus., maps.

190. BLACET, PHILIP M. *Precambrian Geology of the SE ¼ Mount Union Quadrangle, Bradshaw Mountains, Central Arizona.* Ann Arbor: University Microfilms, 1968. 244 pp.
      A Stanford University doctoral dissertation.

191. BLACHLY, LOU. *Mammals, Snakes and Lizards of the Southwest.* [Tucson], 1964. 46 pp., illus.
      Drawings by Sheridan Oman. Similar to the item below.

192. ————. *Picture Guide to Southern Arizona Wildflowers.* [Tucson], 1963. 40 pp., illus.
      "This guide is written expressly for children and adults living in the plains and foothills area of Southern Arizona." Eighty most common wild flowers. A drawing of the plant and the flower accompanies each brief description.

193. BLACK, ROBERT A. *A Content Analysis of 81 Hopi Indian Chants.* Ann Arbor: University Microfilms, 1965. 524 pp.
      An Indiana University doctoral dissertation.

194. BLAGBROUGH, JOHN W. *Quaternary Geology of the Northern Chuska Mountains and Red Rock Valley, Northeastern Arizona and Northwestern New Mexico.* Ann Arbor: University Microfilms, 1965. 178 pp.
      A University of New Mexico doctoral dissertation.

195. BLANEY, HARRY F. AND KARL HARRIS. *Consumptive Use and Irrigation Requirements of Crops in Arizona.* (Provisional) [Beltsville, Maryland]: U. S. Soil Conservation Service, [1952]. 49 pp., tables.

196. BLOMSTROM, ROBERT L. *Fur Trading: Forerunner of Industry in Arizona.* Tempe: Arizona State University Bureau of Business Services, 1963. 26 pp.

197. BOCK, CHARLES M. *The Distribution of Some Selected Alkali Metals and Alkaline Earths in the Stronghold Granite, Cochise County, Arizona.* Ann Arbor: University Microfilms, 1962. 143 pp.
     A University of Arizona doctoral dissertation.

198. BOELTER, HOMER H. *Portfolio of Hopi Kachinas.* Hollywood, California: Homer H. Boelter Lithography, 1969. 61 pp.
     Sixteen color plates bound in and the same sixteen plates in accompanying portfolio. An edition of 1,000 numbered and signed copies.

199. BOGERT, CHARLES M. AND RAFAEL M. DEL CAMPO. *The Gila Monster and Its Allies.* New York: American Museum of Natural History, 1956. (Bulletin vol. 109, article I) 238 pp., illus., maps.
     The monster in general but much on the Arizona species.

200. BOHRER, VORSILA L. *Paleoecology of an Archaeological Site near Snowflake, Arizona.* Ann Arbor: University Microfilms, 1968. 109 pp.
     A University of Arizona doctoral dissertation.

201. ———— AND MARGARET BERGSENG. *An Annotated Catalogue of Plants from Window Rock, Arizona.* Window Rock: Navajo Tribal Museum, 1963. 29 pp.
     First of a series called Navajoland Publications, unnumbered.

202. BOLD, JACOB AND CHRISTINA BOLD. *With Jesus on the Navajo Road.* Grand Rapids: W. B. Berdmans, 1956. 120 pp.
     A new low in titles. Piety on the reservation.

203. BOLOGNANI, BONIFACIO. *Dalle Dolomiti all' Arizona: Biografia di P. Eusebio Francesco Chini, Gesuita Trentino, Pioniere Scopritore Missionario in Arizona.* Sherbrooke, Canada: Edizione Paoline, 1960. 255 pp., illus.
     Popular biography of Eusebio Francisco Kino.

204. ————. *Un Grande Pioniere Trentino: P. Eusebio F. Chini, S. J., Nei Suoi Scritti.* Trento: Arti Grafiche Saturnia, 1964. 139 pp., illus., 3 maps in pocket.
     A selection of Father Kino's writings.

205. BOLTON, HERBERT E. *Coronado, Knight of Pueblos and Plains.* Albuquerque: University of New Mexico Press, 1964. 491 pp., maps.
     First published 1949 as volume 1 of the Coronado Cuarto Centennial Publications with title *Coronado on the Turquoise Trail;* reprinted jointly by the University of New Mexico Press and Whittlesey House in 1949 under present title. The 1964 edition issued clothbound and paperbound.

206. BOLTON, HERBERT E. *The Padre on Horseback: A Sketch of Eusebio Francisco Kino, S. J., Apostle to the Pimas.* Chicago: Loyola University Press, 1963. 90 pp.
Facsimile reprint of the original edition of 1932, preceding Bolton's full-dress biography, *The Rim of Christendom,* by four years. A sketch of Bolton by John Francis Bannon, S.J., has been added to this edition.

207. ————. *Pageant in the Wilderness: The Story of the Escalante Expedition to the Interior Basin, 1776.* Salt Lake: Utah State Historical Society, 1950. 265 pp., illus., maps.
Includes Escalante's diary and itinerary. Also issued as vol. 18 of the *Utah Historical Quarterly.*

208. ————. *Rim of Christendom: a Biography of Eusebio Francisco Kino, Pacific Coast Pioneer.* New York: Russell & Russell, 1960. 644 pp., illus., maps.
A reissue of the original edition of 1936. An outstanding biography of an outstanding missionary written with affection.

209. BOOK, KENNETH M. *The Investment of Idle Public School District Funds in the State of Arizona.* Ann Arbor: University Microfilms, 1966. 160 pp.
A University of Arizona doctoral dissertation.

210. BOTSFORD, HELEN V. *An Evaluation of Sick Leave Policies in the Public Schools of Arizona.* Ann Arbor: University Microfilms, 1961. 310 pp.
A University of Arizona doctoral dissertation.

211. [Boundary] *Joint Summary Report on Arizona-California Boundary.* Submitted by the Colorado River Boundary Commission of California. [Phoenix? 1954?]. 46 pp., maps.

212. BOURKE, JOHN G. *An Apache Campaign in the Sierra Madre.* Introduction by J. Frank Dobie. New York: Scribner's, 1958. 128 pp.
Pursuit of the Chiricahuas in 1883. Originally published in *Outing* in 1885 and by Scribner's in 1886.

213. ————. *On the Border with Crook.* Columbus, Ohio: Long's College Book Company, 1950. 491 pp., illus.
A facsimile of the original 1891 edition of this classic account of the Apache campaigns.

214. ————. *On the Border with Crook.* Chicago: Rio Grande Press, 1962. 491 pp., illus.
A facsimile reprint. Reissued again 1969, with an index.

215. ————. *The Snake-Dance of the Moquis of Arizona.* Chicago: Rio Grande Press, 1962. 371 pp., 31 plates.
A facsimile of the original edition of 1884.

216. ————. *With General Crook in the Indian Wars.* Palo Alto, California: Lewis Osborne, 1968. 59 pp.
Reprinted from the March, 1891, issue of *The Century Magazine.*
About half deals with Crook's early campaigns against the Apaches.

217. BOURNE, EULALIA. *Nine Months Is a Year at Baboquívari School.* Tucson: University of Arizona Press, 1968. 270 pp.
Teaching young Mexican-Americans at a small rural school in the Altar Valley, delightfully told.

218. ————. *Woman in Levi's.* Tucson: University of Arizona Press, 1967. 208 pp., illus.
Ranching in the San Pedro Valley and the Galiuro Mountains.

219. BOWIE, JAMES E. AND OTHERS. *Use of Water by Riparian Vegetation, Cottonwood Wash, Arizona.* Washington: U. S. Geological Survey, 1968. (Water-Supply Paper no. 1858) 62 pp., illus.

220. BOYD, GERTRUDE A. *The Status of Kindergartens in Arizona.* [Tempe: Arizona State University Bureau of Educational Research and Services, 1962?]. (Research and Service Bulletin no. 11) 32 pp., tables.

221. BOYER, GLENN G. *An Illustrated Life of Doc Holliday.* Glenwood Springs, Colorado: Reminder Publishing Co., 1966. 64 pp., illus.

222. ————. *Suppressed Murder of Wyatt Earp.* San Antonio: The Naylor Company, 1967. 135 pp., illus.

223. BOYKIN, CALVIN C. AND OTHERS. *Economic and Operational Characteristics of Arizona and New Mexico Range Cattle Ranches.* Washington: U. S. Department of Agriculture, 1966. 25 pp., tables, diags.

224. *Brand Book and Supplement, State of Arizona.* [Phoenix]: Arizona Livestock Sanitary Board, 1953. various paging, illus.
All brands recorded to and including May 31, 1953.

225. [Brand Book] *Official Brand Book and Supplement of the State of Arizona.* [Phoenix: Arizona Livestock Sanitary Board?], 1963. various paging, illus.
Includes all brands to April 5, 1963.

226. BRANDES, RAYMOND S. *Frank Hamilton Cushing: Pioneer Americanist.* Ann Arbor: University Microfilms, 1965. 250 pp.
A University of Arizona doctoral dissertation.

227. ————. *Frontier Military Posts of Arizona.* Globe, Arizona: Dale Stuart King, 1960. 94 pp., illus., plans.
Valuable information, wretchedly printed and designed. Extensive bibliographies.

228. ————. *A Guide to the Collections of the Arizona Pioneers' Historical Society.* [Tucson: The Society, 1961]. 93 pp.
Loose leaf, punched for a three-ring binder.

229. BRANDT, HERBERT. *Arizona and Its Bird Life*. Cleveland: Bird Research Foundation, 1951. 723 pp., illus.
Subtitle: "A naturalist's adventures with the nesting birds on the deserts, grasslands, foothills and mountains of southeastern Arizona."

230. BRANDT, RICHARD B. *Hopi Ethics, a Theoretical Analysis*. Chicago: University of Chicago Press, 1954. 398 pp.

231. BREED, WILLIAM J. *The Age of Dinosaurs in Northern Arizona*. Flagstaff: Museum of Northern Arizona, 1968. 44 pp., illus.
Drawings by Barton A. Wright.

232. BRENNAN, DANIEL J. *Geological Reconnaissance of Cienega Gap, Pima County, Arizona*. Ann Arbor: University Microfilms, 1957. 53 pp.
A University of Arizona doctoral dissertation.

233. BRENT, WILLIAM AND MILARDE BRENT. *The Hell Hole: The Yuma Prison Story*. Yuma: Southwest Printers, 1962. 61 pp., illus.

234. BRETERNITZ, DAVID A. *An Appraisal of Tree-Ring Dated Pottery in the Southwest*. Tucson: University of Arizona Press, 1966. (Anthropological Papers of the University of Arizona no. 10) 128 pp., tables.
Slightly revised and shortened version of his Ph.D. dissertation.

235. ———. *Archaeological Investigations in Turkey Cave (NA 2520) Navajo National Monument, 1963*. Flagstaff: Northern Arizona Society of Science and Art, 1969. (Museum of Northern Arizona Technical Series no. 8) 26 pp., illus., tables, diags.

236. ———. *Excavations at Nantack Village, Point of Pines, Arizona*. Tucson: [University of Arizona], 1959. (Anthropological Papers of the University of Arizona no. 1) 77 pp., illus., tables.

237. ———. *Excavations at Three Sites in the Verde Valley, Arizona*. Flagstaff: Northern Arizona Society of Science and Art, 1960. (Museum of Northern Arizona Bulletin, no. 34) 29 pp., illus., diags., tables.

238. BREW, DOUGLAS C. *Stratigraphy of the Naco Formation (Pennsylvanian) in Central Arizona*. Ann Arbor: University Microfilms, 1966. 230 pp.
A Cornell University doctoral dissertation.

239. BRIGGS, LLOYD V. *Arizona and New Mexico, 1882; California 1886; Mexico, 1891*. New York: Argonaut Press Ltd. for University Microfilms, 1966. 282 pp., illus.
Tombstone, Tucson, Apache wars; apparently based on diaries. Originally privately printed in 1932.

240. Briggs, P. C. *Ground-Water Conditions in McMullen Valley, Maricopa, Yuma and Yavapai Counties, Arizona.* Phoenix: Arizona State Land Department, 1969. (Water-Resources Report no. 40) 31 pp., maps, tables.

241. ———. *Ground-Water Conditions in the Ranegras Plain, Yuma County, Arizona.* Phoenix: Arizona State Land Department, 1969. (Water-Resources Report no. 41) 28 pp., tables, maps.

242. ——— and L. L. Werho. *Infiltration and Recharge from the Flow of April 1965 in the Salt River near Phoenix, Arizona.* Phoenix: Arizona State Land Department, 1966. (Water-Resources Report no. 29) 12 pp., illus., diags.

243. Brinckerhoff, Sidney B. and Odie B. Faulk. *Lancers for the King.* Phoenix: Arizona Historical Foundation, 1965. 128 pp., illus., maps.
     Subtitle: "A study of the frontier military system of northern New Spain, with a translation of the Royal Regulations of 1772." Foreword by Kieran McCarty, O.F.M.

244. Brisbin, Bryce J. *Marketing Problems of the Arizona Lumber Industry.* Ann Arbor: University Microfilms, 1967. 264 pp.
     A University of Southern California doctoral dissertation.

245. Brittan, Margaret R. *A Probability Model for Integration of Glen Canyon Dam into the Colorado River System.* Ann Arbor: University Microfilms, 1961. 201 pp.
     A University of Colorado doctoral dissertation.

246. Brodrick, Harold J. *Agatized Rainbows, a Story of the Petrified Forest.* Petrified Forest Museum and Arizona State Highway Department, 1951. (Popular Series no. 3) 16 pp., illus.

247. Bromfield, Calvin S. and Andrew F. Shride. *Mineral Resources of the San Carlos Indian Reservation, Arizona.* Washington: U. S. Geological Survey, 1956. (Bulletin no. 1027-N) pp. 613–91, maps.

248. Brophy, Frank C. *Arizona Sketch Book; Fifty Historical Sketches.* Phoenix: Arizona-Messenger Printing, 1952. 310 pp., illus.

249. ———. *The Story of the Bank of Douglas and the Last Frontier.* [Phoenix: Bank of Douglas, 1955?]. 21 pp., illus.

250. Brower, David R. *Grand Canyon, the Threat Is Still Alive.* San Francisco: Sierra Club, 1967. 28 pp.
     A pamphlet opposing building of dams.

251. Brown, Chester J. and others. *Amphitheater School Survey, 1968.* [Tucson]: University of Arizona Bureau of Educational Research and Service, 1968. Various paging.

252. BROWN, ESTELLE A. *Stubborn Fool.* Caldwell, Idaho: Caxton Printers, 1952. 309 pp., illus.

> A teacher's experiences in the Indian Service, largely among the Pimas at Sacaton.

253. BROWN, STUART G. AND H. H. SCHUMANN. *Geohydrology and Water Utilization in the Willcox Basin, Graham and Cochise Counties, Arizona.* Washington: U. S. Geological Survey, 1969. (Water-Supply Paper no. 1859-F) 32 pp., tables, diags., maps.

254. ———— AND ————. *Geohydrology and Water Utilization in the Willcox Basin, Graham and Cochise Counties, Arizona.* Washington: U. S. Geological Survey, 1969. (Water-Supply Paper no. 1859-F) 32 pp., tables, diags., maps.

255. ———— AND OTHERS. *Basic Ground-Water Data of the Willcox Basin, Graham and Cochise Counties, Arizona.* Phoenix: Arizona State Land Department, 1963. (Water Resources Report no. 14) 93 pp., tables, maps.

256. ———— AND ————. *Water Resources of Fort Huachuca Military Reservation, Southeastern Arizona.* Washington: U. S. Geological Survey, 1966. (Water-Supply Paper no. 1819-D) 57 pp., tables, diags.

257. BROWNE, J. ROSS. *A Tour through Arizona, 1864, or Adventures in the Apache Country.* Tucson: Arizona Silhouettes, 1950. 292 pp., illus.

> First book issued by Silhouettes. A limited edition of 500 copies was followed by a trade edition. This is a facsimile of the 1869 edition which was titled *Adventures in the Apache Country* and contained notes on the silver region of Nevada not included here.

258. BRUGGE, DAVID M. *Long Ago in Navajoland.* Window Rock, Arizona: Navajo Tribal Museum, 1965. (Navajoland Publications series 6) 30 pp.

> Translations of early nineteenth-century Spanish documents.

259. ————. *Navajo Pottery and Ethnohistory.* Window Rock, Arizona: Navajo Tribal Museum, 1963. (Navajoland Publications series 2) 37 pp.

260. ———— AND OTHERS, COMPS. *Navajo Bibliography.* Window Rock, Arizona: The Navajo Tribe, 1967. (Navajoland Publications Series B) 291 pp.

> Includes references published in earlier bibliographies.

261. BRUNER, JOHN M. *An Analysis of Municipal Water Demand in the Phoenix Metropolitan Area.* Ann Arbor: University Microfilms, 1969. 201 pp.

> An Arizona State University doctoral dissertation.

262. BRYANT, DONALD G. *Intrusive Breccias and Associated Ore of the Warren (Bisbee) Mining District, Cochise County, Arizona.* Ann Arbor: University Microfilms, 1964. 347 pp.
A Stanford University doctoral dissertation.

263. BRYANT, DONALD L. *Stratigraphy of the Permian System in Southern Arizona.* Ann Arbor: University Microfilms, 1955. 224 pp.
A University of Arizona doctoral dissertation.

264. BRYNER, LEONID. *Geology of the South Comobabi Mountains and the Ko Vaya Hills, Pima County, Arizona.* Ann Arbor: University Microfilms, 1958. 181 pp.
A University of Arizona doctoral dissertation.

265. BRYSON, REID A. *The Annual March of Precipitation in Arizona, New Mexico, and Northwestern Mexico.* Tucson: University of Arizona Institute of Atmospheric Physics, 1957. (Technical Reports on the Meteorology and Climatology of Arid Regions no. 6) 24 pp., tables, diags.

266. ———. *Some Factors in Tucson Summer Rainfall.* Tucson: University of Arizona Institute of Atmospheric Physics, 1957. (Technical Reports on the Meteorology and Climatology of Arid Regions no. 4) 26 pp., tables, diags.

267. *Buckeye Union High School District: Report of Survey.* Tempe: Arizona State University, Bureau of Educational Research and Services, 1965. 283 pp., tables.

268. [Buckeye] *A Planning Report for Buckeye, Arizona.* [Phoenix]: Maricopa County Planning and Zoning Department, 1961. 42 pp., tables, diags., maps.

269. BUNKER, ROBERT AND JOHN ADAIR. *The First Look at Strangers.* New Brunswick, New Jersey: Rutgers University Press, 1959. 151 pp., illus.
Intercultural and communication problems of Papagos, Navajos, and Spanish-Americans.

270. BUOL, STANLEY W. *Calculated Actual and Potential Evapotranspiration in Arizona.* Tucson: University of Arizona Agricultural Experiment Station, 1964. (Technical Bulletin no. 162) 48 pp., tables, maps.
Water loss from the soil.

271. ———. *Soils of Arizona.* Tucson: University of Arizona Agricultural Experiment Station, 1966. (Technical Bulletin no. 171) 25 pp., illus., map in pocket.

272. BURGESS, OPIE R. *Bisbee Not So Long Ago.* San Antonio: Naylor, 1967. 179 pp., illus.
Bisbee 1879–1908; based on stories told by the author's mother.

273. BURNS, THOMAS A. *Ecology and Physiology of* Sceloporus Jarrovi *in the Graham Mountains, Arizona.* Ann Arbor: University Microfilms, 1969. 94 pp.
    An Arizona State University doctoral dissertation. Study of a lizard population.

274. BURRUS, ERNEST J. *Kino and the Cartography of Northwestern New Spain.* Tucson: Arizona Pioneers' Historical Society, 1965. 104 pp., illus., maps.
    Handsomely designed and printed by Lawton Kennedy and limited to 750 copies.

275. BURTON, JEFF. *Black Jack Christian, Outlaw.* Santa Fe: Press of the Territorian, 1967. (Number 14 of a Series of Western Americana) 42 pp.

276. BUTLER, GEORGE D., JR. *The Distribution and Host Plants of Leaf-Cutter Bees in Arizona.* Tucson: University of Arizona Agricultural Experiment Station, 1965. (Technical Bulletin no. 167) 19 pp.

277. —— AND FLOYD G. WERNER. *The Distribution and Host Plants of May Beetles in Arizona.* Tucson: University of Arizona Agricultural Experiment Station, 1961. (Technical Bulletin no. 147) 19 pp., maps.

278. —— AND OTHERS. *Melissodes Bees in Arizona Cotton Fields.* Tucson: University of Arizona Agricultural Experiment Station, 1960. (Technical Bulletin no. 139) 11 pp.

279. BUTT, PAUL D. *Branch Banking and Economic Growth in Arizona and New Mexico.* Albuquerque: University of New Mexico Bureau of Business Research, 1960. (New Mexico Studies in Business and Economics, no. 7) 39 pp., tables, maps.

280. *The Butterfield Overland Mail Across Arizona.* Tucson: Arizona Silhouettes, [1958]. 32 pp., illus., maps.
    Introduction and postal history by Eleanor Sloan; source material compiled by Yndia Moore.

281. CABEZA DE VACA, *see* NÚÑEZ CABEZA DE VACA.

282. CAIN, H. THOMAS. *Pima Indian Basketry.* Phoenix: Heard Museum of Anthropology and Primitive Arts, 1962. 40 pp., illus., maps.
    Photographs from the collection in the Heard Museum.

283. CALDWELL, WILLIAM N. *Arizona State Symbols and Constitution.* Phoenix: Symre Company, [1962?]. 60 pp., illus.
    Flag, flower, bird, seal, etc.

284. CALLAWAY, SYDNEY M. AND OTHERS. *Grandfather Stories of the Navahos.* Rough Rock, Arizona: Rough Rock Demonstration School, 1968. 77 pp., illus.

285. CAMERON, ROY E. *Algae of the Sonoran Desert in Arizona.* Ann Arbor: University Microfilms, 1961. 126 pp.
A University of Arizona doctoral dissertation.

286. CAMPBELL, ALBERT H. *Report upon the Pacific Wagon Roads.* [Fairfield, Washington]: Ye Galleon Press, 1969. 125 pp., 3 maps in pocket.
Reprint (facsimile enlarged) in 500 copies of 35th Congress, 2d Session, Senate Executive Document 36, Serial 984. Material on the El Paso to Fort Yuma road.

287. CAMPBELL, DAVE. *A Layman's Guide to Arizona's Public Schools.* Phoenix: The Author, 1965. 32 pp., diags.

288. CAMPBELL, GEORGE W., JR. *Pinal County Agriculture.* Tucson: Arizona Agricultural Extension Service, 1959. (Circular 269) 28 pp., illus., tables, maps.

289. CANNEY, F. C. AND OTHERS. *Mineral Resources of the Pine Mountain Primitive Area, Arizona.* Washington: U. S. Geological Survey, 1967. (Bulletin no. 1230-J) 45 pp., illus., tables, maps.
"An evaluation of the mineral potential of the area."

290. CANNON, HELEN L. *The Development of Botanical Methods of Prospecting for Uranium on the Colorado Plateau.* Washington: U. S. Geological Survey, 1960. (Bulletin no. 1085-A) 50 pp., illus., maps.

291. CARLSON, RAYMOND. *The Flowering Cactus.* New York: McGraw-Hill, 1954. 96 pp., illus.
Beautifully illustrated with color photographs by R. C. and Claire Meyer Proctor.

292. CARLSON, ROY L. *White Mountain Red Ware: a Stylistic Tradition in the Prehistoric Pottery of East Central Arizona.* Ann Arbor: University Microfilms, 1962. 314 pp.
A University of Arizona doctoral dissertation.

293. CARR, BOB. *A Night Ride in Arizona.* Verdi, Nevada: Sagebrush Press, 1968. 10 pp., illus.
Captain William H. Hardy, of Hardyville, pursues renegade Paiutes.

294. CARR, WILLIAM H. *Conservation Education Unlimited: The Arizona-Sonora Desert Museum.* New York: The Newcomen Society in North America, 1968. 24 pp., illus.

295. ———. *The Desert Speaks.* Tucson: Arizona-Sonora Desert Museum, 1956. (Educational Series no. 1) 49 pp., illus.
Subtitle: "The founding, building, and objectives of the Arizona-Sonora Desert Museum."

296. ———. *Tunnel in the Desert: An Underground Venture in Education.* Tucson: Arizona-Sonora Desert Museum, 1957. (Educational Series no. 2) 34 pp., illus.
About the museum's unique underground display.

297. CARR, WILLIAM H. *Water Street U. S. A.: The Watershed Exposition of the Arizona-Sonora Desert Museum.* Tucson: The Museum and the Charles Lathrop Pack Forestry Foundation, 1959. (Educational Series no. 3) 65 pp., illus.

298. CARSWELL, EVELYN M. *Trends in Educational Innovation in Arizona Elementary Schools Between 1960 and 1966.* Ann Arbor: University Microfilms, 1969. 160 pp.
    A University of Arizona doctoral dissertation.

299. CASADAY, LAUREN W. *Arizona — an Economic Report, 1953.* Tucson: University of Arizona Bureau of Business Research, 1953. (Special Studies no. 7) 94 pp., tables, diags.

300. ———. *Tucson as a Location for Small Industry.* Tucson: University of Arizona Bureau of Business Research, 1952. (Special Studies no. 4) 51 pp.

301. ———. *Yuma's Economy, City and County.* Tucson: University of Arizona Bureau of Business Research, 1953. (Special Studies no. 8) 40 pp., tables, maps, diags.

302. CASTETTER, EDWARD F. AND WILLIS H. BELL. *Yuman Indian Agriculture: Primitive Subsistence on the Lower Colorado and Gila Rivers.* [Albuquerque]: University of New Mexico Press, 1951. 274 pp., illus., maps.

303. CAVANAUGH, THOMAS A. AND DANNY SEIVERT. *Recreation Survey for Scottsdale, Arizona.* Tempe: Arizona State College, 1954. 21 pp., diags.

304. [Cave Creek] *A General Plan for the Desert Foothills Area of Cave Creek and Carefree, Arizona.* [Phoenix]: Maricopa County Planning Department, 1966. 31 pp., maps.

305. [Cave Creek] *A Planning Report for Cave Creek, Arizona.* [Phoenix]: Maricopa County Planning and Zoning Department, 1962. 40 pp., tables, maps.

306. [Census] *Federal Census — Territory of New Mexico and Territory of Arizona.* 89th Congress, 1st Session, Senate Document no. 13. Washington, 1965. 253 pp., tables.
    Subtitle: "Excerpts from the decennial federal census, 1860, for Arizona County in the Territory of New Mexico, the special territorial census of 1864 taken in Arizona, and decennial federal census, 1870 for the Territory of Arizona."

307. [Census] *Guide to Census Tracts, Tucson Standard Metropolitan Area, 1960.* Tucson: City-County Planning Dept., 1961. 15 pp., tables, maps.

308. [Census] *U. S. Census Bureau Tracts for Maricopa County with 1960 Population and Dwelling Count; a Statistical Base for Community Planning.* Phoenix: Maricopa County Planning and Zoning Department, 1961. 19 pp., tables, maps.

309. *The Central Arizona Project.* Hearings. 82nd Congress, 1st Session. House Committee on Interior and Insular Affairs. Washington, 1951. 862 pp. in 2 parts, maps.

310. *Central Arizona Project.* Hearing. 88th Congress, 2nd Session. House Committee on Interior and Insular Affairs. Washington, 1965. 143 pp., diags., maps.
     Hearing held at Phoenix November 9, 1964, on bills to authorize, construct, operate, and maintain.

311. *Central Arizona Project.* Hearings. 88th Congress, 2nd Session. Subcommittee on Irrigation and Reclamation, Committee on Interior and Insular Affairs, United States Senate. Washington, 1963–64. 757 pp.
     Hearings held August and October 1963 and April 1964 on bills to authorize, construct, and maintain.

312. *Central Arizona Project.* Hearings. 90th Congress, 1st Session. Subcommittee on Water and Power Resources, Committee on Interior and Insular Affairs, United States Senate. Washington, 1967. 762 pp., tables.
     On bills to authorize, construct, operate, and maintain.

313. CHAMBERLAIN, DELL. *Effects of Junior College Finance Plans in the United States on Potential Junior College Districts in Arizona.* Ann Arbor: University Microfilms, 1961. 144 pp.
     An Arizona State University doctoral dissertation.

314. *Chandler, Arizona; an Economic Survey.* Tempe: Arizona State University Bureau of Business Services, 1959. 47 pp., illus., tables, diags.

315. [Chandler] *A Comprehensive Plan for Chandler, Arizona.* [Phoenix]: Maricopa County Planning and Zoning Department, 1961. 2 vols. Tables, maps.
     Vol. 1, Population and Land Use.
     Vol. 2, Major Streets, Highways and Parking.

316. [Chandler] *A Study of the Schools of Chandler, Arizona.* Tucson. University of Arizona Bureau of School Services, 1961. 171 pp., illus., tables, maps.

317. *Changing Fortunes in Arizona Business Firms, 1963–1965.* Phoenix: Employment Security Commission of Arizona, Unemployment Compensation Division, 1968. 67 pp.

318. *Characteristics of the Navajo Work Force.* Phoenix: Arizona State Employment Service, 1956. 50 pp., tables, diags.

319. CHRISMAN, HARRY E. *Fifty Years on the Owl Hoot Trail: Jim Herron, the First Sheriff of No Man's Land, Oklahoma Territory.* From an original manuscript by Jim Herron. Chicago: Sage Books, 1969. 355 pp., illus.
    Fugitive from Kansas justice at twenty-eight, Herron spent most of the rest of his life in Arizona and Mexico.

320. CHRISTIAN, JANE M. *The Navajo, a People in Transition.* El Paso: Texas Western College Press, 1964–65. (Southwestern Studies vol. 2, nos. 3 and 4) 2 vols. Illus., maps.
    Social, economic, and cultural adjustments in recent decades.

321. CHRISTIANSON, LEE E. *Variation between Montane Populations of the Deer Mouse,* Peromyscus Maniculatus *(Rodentia Criceti-dae) in Southern Arizona.* Ann Arbor: University Microfilms, 1968. 88 pp.
    A University of Arizona doctoral dissertation.

322. *Civil Disorders, Lawlessness and Their Roots.* Research report prepared by the University of Arizona. Phoenix: Arizona Academy [1969]. 184 pp., tables.
    Fourteenth Arizona Town Hall, April 1969.

323. [Civil Rights] *Hearings before the United States Commission on Civil Rights, Phoenix, Arizona, February 2, 1962.* [Washington, 1962]. 149 pp., map.
    Excellent discussions and statements on racial discrimination, civil rights, and the problems of minority groups in Arizona.

324. CLARK, ART. *Ballad of a Laughing Mountain.* Photographed by Art Clark, text by Richard Snodgrass. Tempe: Counterpoint Productions, 1957. unpaged, illus.
    About Jerome. More pictures than text.

325. CLARK, LAVERNE H. *They Sang for Horses: The Impact of the Horse on Navajo and Apache Folklore.* Tucson: University of Arizona Press, 1966. 225 pp., illus.

326. CLARK, LLOYD. *Clark Biographical Reference, 1958.* [Phoenix: Lloyd Clark], 1958. unpaged.
    Brief sketches of persons living in or near Phoenix.

327. CLAVERAN ALONSO, RAMON. *Desert Grassland Mesquite and Fire.* Ann Arbor: University Microfilms, 1967. 182 pp.
    A University of Arizona doctoral dissertation.

328. CLELAND, ROBERT G. *A History of Phelps Dodge, 1834–1950.* New York: Knopf, 1952. 307 pp., illus.
    Good company history with much on the Arizona copper operations.

329. CLUM, JOHN P. *It All Happened in Tombstone*. Flagstaff, Arizona: Northland Press, 1965. 45 pp.
    Reprinted from the October 1929 *Arizona Historical Review*. Foreword and annotations by John D. Gilchriese.

330. COATES, DONALD R. AND ROBERT L. CUSHMAN. *Geology and Ground-Water Resources of the Douglas Basin, Arizona*. Washington: U. S. Geological Survey, 1955. (Water-Supply Paper no. 1354) 56 pp., maps, tables, diags.

331. COBLENTZ, STANTON A. *The Swallowing Wilderness: the Life of a Frontiersman, James Ohio Pattie*. New York: Thomas Yoseloff, 1961. 188 pp.
    A somewhat fictionalized retelling of the story that James Ohio told better in his own *Personal Narrative*.

332. [Cochise County] *Atlas of Cochise County*. [Phoenix]: Arizona State Highway Department, 1966. 42 sheets.
    Detailed road and street maps in a spiral binding.

333. COCKRUM, E. LENDELL. *The Recent Mammals of Arizona, Their Taxonomy and Distribution*. Tucson: University of Arizona Press, 1960. 276 pp., maps.
    Technical zoology. Distribution maps.

334. COFER, IRENE C. *The Lunch Tree*. Brooklyn: Theo. Gaus Sons, 1969. 210 pp., illus., map.
    Reminiscences of life in Kingman and Mohave County.

335. COLLIER, JOHN. *On the Gleaming Way*. Denver: Sage Books, 1962. 163 pp., illus.
    Subtitle: "Navajos, Eastern Pueblos, Zunis, Hopis, Apaches, and Their Land." Text originally published in 1949 with the title *Patterns and Ceremonials of the Indians of the Southwest* in a limited edition of distinguished format with handsome illustrations by Ira Moskowitz. In this undistinguished reissue the illustrations are replaced by indifferent photographs.

336. COLLINGS, M. R. *Throughfall for Summer Thunderstorms in a Juniper and Pinyon Woodland, Cibecue Ridge, Arizona*. Washington: U. S. Geological Survey, 1966. (Professional Paper 485-B) 13 pp., tables, diags.

337. ———— AND R. M. MYRICK. *Effects of Juniper and Pinyon Eradication on Streamflow from Corduroy Creek Basin, Arizona*. Washington: U. S. Geological Survey, 1966. (Professional Paper no. 491-B) 12 pp., tables, diags., maps.

338. COLLINS, HENRY H., JR. *Birds of Montezuma Castle and Tuzigoot National Monuments*. [Santa Fe?]: Southwestern Monuments Association, 1951. 13 pp., illus.

339. *Colorado River Basin Project.* Hearings. 90th Congress, 1st Session. Subcommittee on Irrigation and Reclamation of the Committee on Interior and Insular Affairs, House of Representatives. Washington, 1967–1968. 2 vols. Tables, maps.
    Hearings of March 1967 and January and February 1968.

340. *Colorado River Basin Project.* 89th Congress, 2nd Session, House Report no. 1849. [Washington, 1966?]. 157 pp., diags.

341. *Colorado River Development Within the State of Arizona; Colorado River Projects.* Prepared by Harza Engineering, Chicago. Phoenix: Arizona Power Authority, 1958. various paging, tables, maps, diags.
    At head of title: "Preliminary planning report."

342. *Colorado River Drainage Basin; Summary Report on Water Pollution.* Washington: U. S. Public Health Service, 1951. (Public Health Service Publication no. 110, Water Pollution Series no. 9) 46 pp., maps.

343. *Colorado River People and Places: A Catalogue of Books, Pamphlets, Maps and Manuscripts.* Introduction by C. Gregory Crampton. Scottsdale, Arizona: Guidon Books, 1969, 84 pp.
    Eight hundred forty-one items in an interesting and useful catalog. Many items not described in Farquhar.

344. *The Colorado River Region and John Wesley Powell.* Washington: U. S. Geological Survey, 1969. (Professional Paper no. 669), 145 pp., illus., tables, maps.
    Papers honoring the one-hundredth anniversary of Powell's exploration of the Colorado. Contents: "John Wesley Powell: Pioneer Statesman of Federal Science," by Mary C. Babbitt; "Stratified Rocks of the Grand Canyon," by Edwin D. McKee; "Geologic History of the Colorado River," by Charles B. Hunt; "The Rapids and the Pools — Grand Canyon," by Luna B. Leopold.

345. [Colorado River] *California and the Colorado River.* Los Angeles: Colorado River Association, 1954. 23 pp., illus.

346. [Colorado River] *The Lower Colorado River Basin Project.* 88th Congress, 2nd Session. Senate Report no. 1330. [Washington, 1964?]. 2 parts.
    Part two of 13 pages authorizes construction of the Central Arizona Project.

347. [Colorado River] *The Lower Colorado River Land Use Plan.* Washington: U. S. Department of the Interior, 1964. 187 pp., illus., maps.

348. [Colorado River] *Release of Colorado River Water.* Hearing. 87th Congress, 2nd Session. Subcommittee on Irrigation and Reclamation, Committee on Interior and Insular Affairs, United States Senate. Washington, 1962. 51 pp., table.
    Proposed release, for sluicing purposes, of water impounded in Lake Mead.

349. [Colorado River] *A Survey of the Recreational Resources of the Colorado River Basin.* Washington: National Park Service, 1950. 242 pp., illus., diags., maps.

350. COLTON, HAROLD S. *Black Sand: Prehistory in Northern Arizona.* Albuquerque: University of New Mexico Press, 1960. 132 pp., illus., maps.
A synthesis of the pre-history around the San Francisco Peaks and in adjacent areas.

351. ———. *Check List of Southwestern Pottery Types.* Flagstaff: Northern Arizona Society of Science and Art, 1955. (Museum of Northern Arizona Ceramic Series no. 2) 43 pp.
— revised edition, 1965. 55 pp.

352. ———. *Hopi Kachina Dolls, with a Key to Their Identification.* Revised edition. Albuquerque: University of New Mexico Press, 1959. 150 pp., illus.
Originally issued 1949. Color photos by Jack Breed.

353. ———. *Potsherds, an Introduction to the Study of Prehistoric Southwestern Ceramics and Their Use in Historical Reconstruction.* Flagstaff: Northern Arizona Society of Science and Art, 1953. (Museum of Northern Arizona Bulletin no. 25) 86 pp., illus.

354. ———. *Pottery Types of the Arizona Strip and Adjacent Areas in Utah and Nevada.* Flagstaff: Northern Arizona Society of Science and Art, 1952. (Museum of Northern Arizona Ceramic Series no. 1) 98 pp., illus.

355. ———. *Pottery Types of the Southwest.* Flagstaff: Northern Arizona Society of Science and Art, 1955–1958. (Museum of Northern Arizona Ceramic Series no. 3) unpaged, illus., maps.
Four parts published to 1958; no more published.

356. ———. *Precipitation about the San Francisco Peaks, Arizona.* Flagstaff: Northern Arizona Society of Science and Art, 1958. (Museum of Northern Arizona Technical Series no. 2) 18 pp., maps, tables.

357. COLTON, MARY-RUSSELL F. *Hopi Dyes.* Flagstaff: The Museum of Northern Arizona, 1965. (Museum of Northern Arizona Bulletin no. 41) 87 pp., illus.

358. COLYER, VINCENT. *Peace with the Apaches of New Mexico and Arizona: Report of Vincent Colyer, Member of Board of Indian Commissioners. 1871.* Tucson: Territorial Press, 1964.
Facsimile of the original issued by the Government Printing Office in 1872.

359. *Comprehensive Flood Control Program Report.* [Phoenix]: Maricopa County Flood Control District, 1963. 80 pp., tables, maps.

360. CONDIE, LE ROY. *The Effect of Cultural Difference in the Education of Navajo Indians.* [Albuquerque]: University of New Mexico College of Education, 1958. 119 pp.
   Prepared for the research study "Adjustment of Indian and Non-Indian Children in the Public Schools of New Mexico." Applies to all Navajos.

361. CONGDON, GEORGE K. *Navajo Indian Missions.* Compiled by Rev. and Mrs. Geo. K. Congdon. Window Rock, Arizona: Mission Press, 1955. 16 pp., illus.

362. CONNER, DANIEL E. *Joseph Reddeford Walker and the Arizona Adventure.* Edited by Donald J. Berthrong and Odessa Davenport. Norman: University of Oklahoma Press, 1956. 364 pp., illus.

363. CONROTTO, EUGENE L. *Lost Desert Bonanzas.* Palm Desert, California: Desert-Southwest Publishers, 1963. 278 pp., illus., maps.
   A condensation of articles on lost mines and buried treasure which appeared in *Desert* magazine from 1937 to 1962.

364. *Constitution and Bylaws of the Gila River Indian Community, Arizona.* Washington: U. S. Bureau of Indian Affairs, 1960. 15 pp.

365. *The Constitution of Occidente: The First Constitution of Arizona, Sonora, and Sinaloa (1825–1831).* Translated and edited by Odie B. Faulk. Tucson: Arizona Pioneers' Historical Society, 1967. (Arizona History Series no. 4) 53 pp.

366. *Construction Activity in Maricopa County, Arizona, 1951–1953.* Tempe: Arizona State College Bureau of Business Services, 1953. 35 pp., diags.

367. *Contributions to the Geology of Northern Arizona: Memorial to Major Brady.* Flagstaff: Northern Arizona Society of Science and Art, 1964. (Museum of Northern Arizona Bulletin no. 40) 71 pp., illus., maps, diags.
   Articles by various contributors.

368. CONVERSE, CHARLES D. *Alfalfa for Yuma Mesa.* Washington: U. S. Department of Agriculture, 1951. (Circular no. 897) 11 pp., illus.

369. COOK, L. DEAN. *Water Administration in Arizona: A Problem in Coordination.* Tempe: Arizona State University Institute of Public Administration, 1968. (Papers in Public Administration no. 15) 100 pp.

370. COOK, ROBERT L. *The Relationship of Selected Factors to the Success of Student Teachers at the University of Arizona.* Ann Arbor: University Microfilms, 1964. 173 pp.
   A University of Arizona doctoral dissertation.

371. COOKE, PHILIP ST. GEORGE. *The Conquest of New Mexico and California, an Historical & Personal Narrative.* Oakland, California: Biobooks, 1952. 165 pp., illus., map.

372. ————. *The Conquest of New Mexico and California, an Historical and Personal Narrative.* Albuquerque: Horn and Wallace, 1964. 307 pp., map.
> A facsimile of the 1878 edition with a foreword by Philip St. George Cook III.
> — another facsimile edition, Chicago: Rio Grande Press, 1964.

373. COOKRIDGE, E. H. *The Baron of Arizona.* New York: John Day, 1967. 304 pp., illus.
> Cookridge is the pseudonym of Edward Spiro. The book is about James Addison Reavis and the Peralta Grant.

374. COOLEY, M. E. *Stratigraphic Sections and Records of Springs in the Glen Canyon Region of Utah and Arizona.* Flagstaff: Northern Arizona Society of Science and Art, 1965. (Museum of Northern Arizona Technical Series no. 6) 140 pp., tables.

375. ———— AND OTHERS. *Regional Hydrogeology of the Navajo and Hopi Indian Reservations, Arizona, New Mexico, and Utah.* Washington: U. S. Geological Survey, 1969. (Professional Paper no. 521-A) 61 pp., tables, diags., maps.

376. COOMBS, L. MADISON. *Doorway Toward the Light: The Story of the Special Navajo Education Program.* [Washington?]: U. S. Bureau of Indian Affairs, 1962. 174 pp., illus.

377. COOPER, JAMES F. *The First Hundred Years: The History of Tucson School District 1, Tucson, Arizona, 1867–1967.* [Tucson: School District 1, 1968?]. 190 pp., illus.

378. COOPER, JOHN R. *Some Geologic Features of the Pima Mining District, Pima County, Arizona.* Washington: U. S. Geological Survey, 1960. (Bulletin no. 1112-C) pp. 63–103, illus., tables, maps.

379. ———— AND LEON T. SILVER. *Geology and Ore Deposits of the Dragoon Quadrangle, Cochise County, Arizona.* Washington: U. S. Geological Survey, 1964. (Professional Paper no. 416) 196 pp., illus., tables, maps, diags.

380. COPPLE, R. F. AND C. P. PASE. *A Vegetative Key to Some Common Arizona Range Grasses.* [Fort Collins, Colorado: Rocky Mountain Forest and Range Experiment Station?], 1967. (U. S. Forest Service Research Paper RM-27) 72 pp., illus.

381. CORBETT, PEARSON H. *Jacob Hamblin, the Peacemaker.* Salt Lake: Deseret Book Company, 1952. 538 pp.

382. CORBUSIER, WILLIAM T. *Verde to San Carlos.* Tucson: Dale Stuart King, 1968. [c. 1969] 310 pp., illus.
> Subtitle: "Reflections of a famous Army Surgeon and his observant family on the western frontier, 1869–1886." Only the deluxe first edition of 250 copies was issued in 1969.

383. CORLE, EDWIN. *The Gila, River of the Southwest.* New York: Rinehart, 1951. 402 pp., illus.
Illustrations by Ross Santee.

384. ———. *The Gila, River of the Southwest.* Lincoln: University of Nebraska Press, [196-?]. 402 pp., illus.
A facsimile of the 1951 edition, issued in paper covers.

385. CORMACK, CHARLES W. *Social Structure and Economic Production on an Arizona Indian Reservation.* Ann Arbor: University Microfilms, 1969. 639 pp.
A University of Arizona doctoral dissertation. The study was made on the Gila River Pima reservation.

386. CORNWELL, ROBERT C. *An Appraisal of the Business Administration Program at Northern Arizona University.* Ann Arbor: University Microfilms, 1968. 138 pp.
An Arizona State University doctoral dissertation.

387. *Correctional Services in Arizona, 1958.* New York: National Probation and Parole Association, 1958. various paging.

388. COSNER, OLIVER J. *Ground Water in the Wupatki and Sunset Crater National Monuments, Coconino County, Arizona.* Washington: U. S. Geological Survey, 1962. (Water-Supply Paper no. 1475-J) pp. 357–74, tables, maps.

389. [Cosulich, Bernice.] *Fifty Years of Growth in Tucson, 1903–1953.* Tucson: Southern Arizona Bank & Trust Company, 1953. 32 pp., illus.
Story of the bank and the city.

390. COSULICH, BERNICE. *Tucson.* Tucson: Arizona Silhouettes, 1953. 310 pp., illus., maps.
Chapters on the history of the Old Pueblo.

391. COTNER, MELVIN L. *Controlling Pinyon-Juniper.* Tucson: University of Arizona Agricultural Experiment Station, 1963. (Report no. 210) 28 pp., illus., tables, diags.

392. [Courts] *Report on Justice of the Peace Courts in Arizona.* Prepared by the Research Staff of the Arizona Legislative Council. Phoenix, 1958. 153 pp., tables.

393. COUTS, CAVE J. *Hepah, California! The Journal of Cave Johnson Couts from Monterey, Nuevo Leon, Mexico to Los Angeles, California During the Years 1848–1849.* Edited by Henry F. Dobyns. Tucson: Arizona Pioneers' Historical Society, 1961. 113 pp.
Seven hundred fifty copies designed and printed by Lawton Kennedy. The march went up the Santa Cruz Valley and followed the Gila Trail to the Yuma crossing.

394. Cox, Thomas J. *A Behavioral and Ecological Study of the Desert Pupfish* (Cyprinodon Maclarius) *in Quitobaquito Springs, Organ Pipe National Monument, Arizona.* Ann Arbor: University Microfilms, 1967. 102 pp.
A University of Arizona doctoral dissertation.

395. *Coyote Stories of the Navaho People.* Rough Rock, Arizona: Rough Rock Demonstration School, 1968. 141 pp., illus.

396. Cozzens, Samuel W. *The Marvellous Country; or, Three Years in Arizona and New Mexico, the Apaches' Home.* Minneapolis, Ross & Haines. 1967. 540 pp., illus.
A facsimile of the 1873 ? edition with an added index.

397. Crampton, C. Gregory. *Historical Sites in Glen Canyon, Mouth of San Juan River to Lee's Ferry.* Salt Lake City: University of Utah Press, 1960. (University of Utah Department of Anthropology, Anthropological Papers, no. 46) 130 pp., illus., maps.

398. ———. *Outline History of the Glen Canyon Region, 1776–1922.* Salt Lake City: University of Utah Press, 1959. (University of Utah Department of Anthropology, Anthropological Papers no. 42) 137 pp., illus., maps.

399. ———. *Standing Up Country: The Canyon Lands of Utah and Arizona.* New York and Salt Lake City: Alfred A. Knopf and University of Utah Press, in association with Amon Carter Museum of Western Art, 1964. 191 pp., illus, maps.

400. Creasey, Saville C. *General Geology of the Mammoth Quadrangle, Pinal County, Arizona.* Washington: U. S. Geological Survey, 1967. (Bulletin no. 1218) 94 pp., illus., maps.

401. ———. *Geology of the San Manuel Area, Pinal County, Arizona.* With a section on ore deposits by J. D. Pelletier and S. C. Creasey. Washington: U. S. Geological Survey, 1965. (Professional Paper no. 471) 64 pp., illus., tables, maps.

402. ——— and George L. Quick. *Copper Deposits of Part of Helvetia Mining District, Pima County, Arizona.* Washington: U. S. Geological Survey, 1955. (Bulletin no. 1027-F) pp. 301–23, maps.

403. Creer, Leland H. *The Activities of Jacob Hamblin in the Region of the Colorado.* Salt Lake City: University of Utah Press, 1958. (University of Utah Department of Anthropology, Anthropological Papers no. 33) 35 pp.
Issued in cover with no. 404 below.

404. CREER, LELAND H. *Mormon Towns in the Region of the Colorado.* Salt Lake City: University of Utah Press, 1958. (University of Utah Department of Anthropology, Anthropological Papers no. 32) 25 pp., map.
See note to item 403 above.

405. CREMONY, JOHN C. *Life Among the Apaches.* Tucson: Arizona Silhouettes, 1951. 322 pp., illus.
Facsimile of the edition of 1868, limited to 750 copies. Trade edition issued in 1954. Illustrations by William H. Bryant. Early and absorbing classic on the Apache tribes of Arizona.

406. ———. *Life Among the Apaches.* Glorieta, New Mexico: Rio Grande Press, 1969. 327 pp.
Slightly enlarged facsimile with new preface and index.

407. *Crime, Juvenile Delinquency, and Corrective Measures in Arizona.* Research report prepared by Arizona State College, Flagstaff. Phoenix: Arizona Academy, [1966]. 134 pp., tables, diags.
Eighth Arizona Town Hall, April 1966.

408. CRNKOVIC, JOHN K. *Anticipated Enrollment and Capital Outlay needs of Arizona Public Schools.* Ann Arbor: University Microfilms, 1961. 209 pp.
An Arizona State University doctoral dissertation.

409. CROW, JOHN E. *Discrimination, Poverty and the Negro: Arizona in the National Context.* Tucson: University of Arizona Press, 1968. (Institute of Government Research, Arizona Government Studies no. 5) 53 pp.

410. CRUMRINE, LYNNE S. *The Phonology of Arizona Yaqui with Texts.* Tucson: University of Arizona Press, 1961. (Anthropological Papers of the University of Arizona no. 5) 43 pp.

411. CUMMINGS, BYRON. *First Inhabitants of Arizona and the Southwest.* Tucson: Cummings Publications Council, 1953. 251 pp., illus., maps, tables.
Prehistoric Indians of the region.

412. ———. *Indians I Have Known.* Tucson: Arizona Silhouettes, 1952. 55 pp., illus.
Navajos and some Apaches.

413. CUMMINGS, JOSEPH B. AND THOMAS M. ROMSLO. *Investigation of Twin Buttes Copper Mines, Pima County, Arizona.* [Pittsburgh]: U. S. Bureau of Mines, 1950. (Report of Investigations no. 4732) 12 pp., maps.

414. CUMMINGS, VIOLET M. *Along Navajo Trails.* Washington, D. C.: Review and Herald Publishing Assn., 1964. 189 pp., illus.
About Veda Scholder and the work of the Adventist missionaries in the Four Corners region.

415. CUSHING, FRANK H. *The Nation of the Willows.* Flagstaff, Arizona: Northland Press, 1965. 75 pp.
   The nation is the Havasupai tribe. The account is reprinted from *Atlantic Monthly* of 1882, volume 50, pp. 362–74, 541–59, the issues for September and October.

416. DAANE, KENNETH E. *The Economic Implications of the Regional Park System in Maricopa County.* Tempe: Arizona State University Bureau of Business Services, 1964. 52 pp., tables, maps.

417. DAIFUKU, HIROSHI. *Jeddito 264: A Report on the Excavation of a Basket Maker III-Pueblo I Site in Northeastern Arizona with a Review of Some Current Theories in Southwestern Archaeology.* Cambridge, Massachusetts: Peabody Museum, 1961. (Peabody Papers, vol. 33, no. 1, Reports of the Awatovi Expedition no. 7) 86 pp., illus., diags., maps.

418. DALE, V. B. *Mining, Milling and Smelting Methods, San Manuel Copper Corp., Pinal County, Ariz.* [Washington]: U. S. Bureau of Mines, [1962]. (Information Circular no. 8104) 45 pp., illus., maps, tables, diags.

419. ———. *Tungsten Deposits of Gila, Yavapai and Mohave Counties, Ariz.* [Washington]: U. S. Bureau of Mines, [1961] (Information Circular no. 8078) 104 pp., tables, maps, diags.

420. ——— AND OTHERS. *Tungsten Deposits of Cochise, Pima, and Santa Cruz Counties, Ariz.* [Washington]: U. S. Bureau of Mines, 1960. (Report of Investigations no. 5650) 132 pp., diags., maps.

421. DALTON, PATRICK D., JR. *Ecology of the Creosotebush, Larrea Tridentata (DC.) Cov.* Ann Arbor: University Microfilms, 1962. 170 pp.
   A University of Arizona doctoral dissertation.

422. DAMMANN, ARTHUR E. *Some Factors Affecting the Distribution of Sympatric Species of Rattlesnakes (Genus Crotalus) in Arizona.* Ann Arbor: University Microfilms, 1961. 105 pp.
   A University of Michigan doctoral dissertation.

423. DANSON, EDWARD B. *An Archaeological Survey of West Central New Mexico and East Central Arizona.* Cambridge, Massachusetts: Peabody Museum, 1957. (Peabody Papers, v. 44, no. 1) 133 pp., illus., tables.

424. DARBY, WILLIAM J. AND OTHERS. *A Study of the Dietary Background and Nutriture of the Navajo Indian.* Philadelphia: Wistar Institute of Anatomy and Biology, 1956. 85 pp., tables.
   Issued as a supplement to the *Journal of Nutrition,* volume 60, November 1956.

425. DARE, WILBERT L. *Uranium Mining in the Lukachukai Mountains, Apache County, Ariz., Kerr-McGee Oil Industries, Inc.* [Washington]: U. S. Bureau of Mines, [1961]. (Information Circular no. 8011) 30 pp., illus., maps.

426. ———— AND OTHERS. *Uranium Mining on the Colorado Plateau.* [Pittsburgh]: U. S. Bureau of Mines, 1955. (Information Circular no. 7726) 60 pp., illus., tables.

427. DARLING, MARILYN L. *Structure and Productivity of a Pinyon-Juniper Woodland in Northern Arizona.* Ann Arbor: University Microfilms, 1967. 188 pp.
      A Duke University doctoral dissertation.

428. DAVIS, BRITTON. *The Truth About Geronimo.* Chicago: Lakeside Press, 1951. (Lakeside Classics no. 49) 380 pp., illus.
      Originally issued by Yale in 1929. This edition contains a 45-page historical introduction by M. M. Quaife.

429. ————. *The Truth about Geronimo.* New Haven: Yale University Press, 1963. 253 pp., illus.
      Paperbound facsimile of the original text of the 1929 edition with a new introduction by Robert M. Utley and with the illustrations regrouped.

430. DAVIS, G. E. AND OTHERS. *Geohydrologic Data in the Navajo and Hopi Indian Reservations, Arizona, New Mexico and Utah.* Tucson: Arizona State Land Department? 1963–1966. (Water Resources Report no. 12) 5 parts, maps, tables.
      Prepared by the U.S. Geological Survey in cooperation with the Navajo Tribe and given a Water Resources Report designation.

431. DAVIS, RICHARD N. *History of Dairying in Arizona.* Tucson: University of Arizona Agricultural Experiment Station, 1959. 111 pp., illus., tables.
      Issued 1955 as Experiment Station Report no. 171. Only minor changes in the 1959 edition.

432. DAVIS, WILLIAM C. *Values of Hunting and Fishing in Arizona, 1960.* Tucson: University of Arizona Bureau of Business and Public Research, 1962. (Special Studies no. 21) 61 pp., illus., tables.
      ". . . considers not merely the economic value . . . but also the social values inherent in hunting and fishing in our increasingly urban society."

433. ————. *Values of Hunting and Fishing in Arizona in 1965.* Prepared for Arizona Game and Fish Department. [Tucson]: University of Arizona, 1967. 91 pp., illus., tables.

434. *Dawn on the Desert: An Arizona Saga of People, Power, Progress.* [Phoenix: Arizona Public Service Co.,], 1961. 41 pp., illus.
      A book commemorating the seventy-fifth anniversary of the Arizona Public Service Company, and giving the history of public utilities in the Salt River Valley.

435. DAY, ARDEN D. *Small Grain Varieties for Arizona.* Tucson: University of Arizona Agricultural Experiment Station, 1954. (Report no. 114) 15 pp., tables.

436. DAY, JERRY AND STEVE GALLIZIOLI. *Boom and Bust: The Story of the Chiricahua Whitetail Deer.* [Phoenix: Arizona Game and Fish Department, 1967?]. 12 pp., illus.

437. DEAN, JEFFREY S. *Chronological Analysis of Tsegi Phase Sites in Northeast Arizona.* Ann Arbor: University Microfilms, 1967. 779 pp.
     A University of Arizona doctoral dissertation.

438. ————. *Chronological Analysis of Tsegi Phase Sites in Northeast Arizona.* Tucson: University of Arizona Press, 1969. (Papers of the Laboratory of Tree-Ring Research, no. 3) 207 pp., illus., tables, diags.
     A revision of the author's dissertation.

439. DEAN, KARL C. AND OTHERS. *Concentration of Oxide Ores from Vicinity of Winkelman, Pinal County, Arizona.* [Pittsburgh]: U. S. Bureau of Mines, 1952. (Report of Investigations no. 4848) 21 pp.

440. DEAVER, CHESTER F. AND HORACE S. HASKELL. *Pinyon Resources: Distribution of Pinyon* (Pinus Edulis), *Yield and Resin Potentialities, Navajo-Hopi Reservations, Arizona-Utah.* Tucson: University of Arizona Press, 1955. 37 pp., maps, tables.
     Though University of Arizona Press had appeared earlier as a joint imprint, this was the first publication to carry its sole imprint.

441. DEDERA, DON. *A Mile in His Moccasins.* Phoenix: McGrew Printing & Lithographing Co., 1960. 342 pp., illus.
     Brief Arizona sketches reprinted from the author's column in the *Arizona Republic.*

442. DEEVER, R. MERWIN AND HAROLD E. MOORE. *Design for Lifetime Learning in a Dynamic Social Structure; Education 1980 A. D.* Tempe: Arizona State University Bureau of Educational Research and Services, 1968. 148 pp., illus., tables, diags.
     Subtitle: "A study of education potential in the Litchfield Park area of Arizona."

443. ... *Defense Production Facilities in Arizona.* [Phoenix]: Arizona State Employment Service, 1951–52. 3 vols. and supplements.

444. DE GRAZIA, ETTORE T. *Arizona South.* Tucson: De Grazia Studios, [1950?]. unpaged, illus.
     Papago and Yaqui Indians. Illustrated, as are the others following with color prints by De Grazia. First of the Arizona South series.

445. ————. *The Blue Lady; a Desert Fantasy of Papago Land.* Tucson: De Grazia Studios, 1957. (Arizona South Book no. V) unpaged, illus.

446. DE GRAZIA, ETTORE T. *De Grazia Paints the Yaqui Easter.* Tucson: University of Arizona Press, 1968. 92 pp., illus.
Paintings of the Easter ceremonials as performed in the Yaqui villages of southern Arizona and northern New Mexico.

447. ————. *The Flute Player.* Tucson: De Grazia Studios, 1952. (Arizona South Book no. II) unpaged, illus.
A fantasy inspired by Hohokam pottery designs.

448. ————. *Mission in the Santa Catalinas.* Tucson: De Grazia Studios, 1951. (Arizona South Book no. III) unpaged, illus.

449. ————. *Padre Nuestro.* Tucson: De Grazia Studios, 1953. (Arizona South Book no. IV) unpaged, illus.

450. DEKENS, CAMIEL. *Riverman, Desertman: Recollections of Camiel Dekens as told to Tom Patterson.* Riverside, California: Press-Enterprise Co., 1962. 111 pp., illus.
Mostly Blythe and the Palo Verde Valley but with some interesting sidelights on the Lower Colorado River.

451. DELLENBAUGH, FREDERICK S. *A Canyon Voyage.* New Haven: Yale University Press, 1962. 277 pp., illus., map.
Subtitle: "The narrative of the second Powell expedition down the Green-Colorado River from Wyoming, and the explorations on land in the years 1871 and 1872." Originally published in 1908.

452. ————. *The Romance of the Colorado River.* Chicago: Rio Grande Press, 1962. 399 pp., illus.
A facsimile of the original of 1904.

453. DENIS, E. E. *Ground-Water Conditions in the Waterman Wash Area, Maricopa and Pinal Counties, Arizona.* Phoenix: Arizona State Land Department, 1968. (Water Resources Report no. 37) 23 pp.

454. DENNIS, ROBERT E. AND ARDEN D. DAY. *Growing Wheat in Arizona.* Tucson: Cooperative Extension Service and University of Arizona Agricultural Experiment Station, 1964. (Bulletin A-32) 19 pp., illus.

455. DENNIS, WAYNE. *The Hopi Child.* New York: Science Editions, John Wiley & Sons, 1965. 200 pp., illus.
Originally published by the University of Virginia Institute for Research in Social Sciences in 1940. In this reprint edition four journal articles by Dennis have been added as an appendix of 40 pages following page 197.

456. DENTON, JOHN H. AND JOHN F. GOODSON. *Legal Aspects of Doing Business in Arizona.* Tucson: University of Arizona Bureau of Business and Public Research, 1961. (Special Studies no. 19) 88 pp.

457. DERBY, GEORGE H. *Derby's Report on Opening the Colorado, 1850–1851.* Edited with an introduction by Odie B. Faulk. Albuquerque: University of New Mexico Press, 1969. 54 pp., illus., folding map.
Reprint of Senate Executive Document, 32d Congress, 1st Session, 1852. The expedition determined the navigability of the lower river.

458. DE ROOS, ROBERT. *Monument Valley.* Flagstaff, Arizona: The Northland Press, 1965. 24 pp., illus.
Subtitle: "An exploration of a red-rock land where the desert becomes magic and wonder."

459. DEROSS, ROSE M. *Adventures of Georgie White, TV's "Woman of the Rivers."* Palm Desert, California: Desert Magazine, 1958. 84 pp., illus., maps.
Boating on the Colorado.

460. *Desert Survival: Basic Information for Anyone Traveling in the Sonoran Desert.* Phoenix: Maricopa County-City of Phoenix Civil Defense Joint Council, 1958. 20 pp.

461. DES JARDINS, ROBERT B. *The Distribution of Clouds at Tucson, Arizona, with Respect to Type, Amount, and Time of Observation.* Tucson: University of Arizona Institute of Atmospheric Physics, 1958. (Scientific Report no. 6) 52 pp., tables, diags.

462. DEVEREUX, GEORGE. *Mohave Ethnopsychiatry and Suicide: The Psychiatric Knowledge and the Psychic Disturbances of an Indian Tribe.* Washington: U. S. Bureau of American Ethnology, 1961. (Bulletin no. 175) 586 pp.
Reprinted in 1969 by the Smithsonian Institution Press.

463. DEVINE, LOTTIE C. *"Es Verdad" or "It Is True."* Coolidge, Arizona: Coolidge Shopper Printing & Publishing Co., 1964. 88 pp., illus.
Turn-of-the century life in Florence.

464. DEVNER, KAY. *Backward Through a Bottle.* Tucson: The Author, 1964. 55 pp., illus.
Old towns, ruins, bottles and other glass in southern Arizona.

465. DEXTER, EARLE F. *Doors Toward the Sunrise.* New York: Friendship Press, 1955. 116 pp., illus.
Protestant missions among the Indians, especially a work camp in the Navajo country.

466. DINGMAN, ROSS E. *Variation in Selected Populations of Pocket Gophers* (Thomomys Bottae) *of the Lower Colorado River.* Ann Arbor: University Microfilms, 1967. 134 pp.
A University of Arizona doctoral dissertation.

467. DINGMAN, VERA I. *The First 500.* New York: Carlton Press, 1969.
93 pp.
Experiences operating a home for unwanted children near Mesa.

468. DINGS, McCLELLAND G. *The Wallapai Mining District, Cerbat Mountains, Mohave County, Arizona.* Washington: U. S. Geological Survey, 1951. (Bulletin no. 978-E) pp. 123–163, maps.

469. DiPESO, CHARLES C. *The Babocomari Village Site on the Babocomari River, Southeastern Arizona.* Dragoon, Arizona: Amerind Foundation, 1951. (Publication no. 5) 248 pp., illus., tables, maps.

470. ———. *The Reeve Ruin of Southeastern Arizona.* Dragoon, Arizona: Amerind Foundation, 1958. (Publication no. 8) 189 pp., illus., tables, maps.
A ruin in the middle San Pedro Valley.

471. ———. *The Sobaipuri Indians of the Upper San Pedro Valley, Southeastern Arizona.* Ann Arbor: University Microfilms, 1953. 304 pp.
A University of Arizona doctoral dissertation.

472. ———. *The Sobaipuri Indians of the Upper San Pedro River Valley, Southeastern Arizona.* Dragoon, Arizona: Amerind Foundation, 1953. (Publication no. 6) 285 pp., illus., tables, maps.
Arthur Woodward, Rex and Virginia Gerald, collaborators.

473. ———. *The Upper Pima of San Cayetano del Tumacacori; An Archaeohistorical Reconstruction of the Ootam of Pimería Alta.* Dragoon, Arizona: Amerind Foundation, 1956. (Publication no. 7) 589 pp., illus., tables, maps, diags.

474. *A Directory of Libraries and Library Resources in the Tucson Area and Southeastern Arizona.* Tucson: Tucson Area Library Council, 1969. 64 pp.

475. *Directory of Officials of Cities and Towns in Arizona.* Phoenix: Arizona Municipal League, 1953–
Annual. Title varies slightly.

476. *The Discovery of Rainbow Bridge: The Natural Bridges of Utah, and the Discovery of Betatakin.* Tucson: Cummings Publication Council, 1959. (Bulletin no. 1) 46 pp., illus.

477. *Disturnell's Treaty Map.* Santa Fe: Stagecoach Press, 1965. 20 pp., map.
A facsimile reproduction of the 1847 map which was used to fix the southwest boundary between Mexico and the United States after the treaty of Guadalupe Hidalgo. Issued folded and bound with the accompanying text by Jack Rittenhouse of the Stagecoach Press and rolled in a cardboard tube with the text in green paper wrappers.

478. DITZLER, ROBERT E. *The Indian People of Arizona.* New York: Vantage Press, 1967. 177 pp.
A brief chapter on each of the state's tribes.

479. DIXON, KEITH A. *Archaeological Objectives and Artifact Sorting Techniques; a Re-examination of the Snaketown Sequence.* [Missoula, Montana?]: Western States Branch, American Anthropological Association, 1956. (Western Anthropology no. 3) 33 pp.

480. ————. *Hidden House, a Cliff Ruin in Sycamore Canyon, Central Arizona.* Flagstaff: Northern Arizona Society of Science and Art, 1956. (Museum of Northern Arizona Bulletin no. 29) 90 pp., illus.

481. *Do Agricultural Problems Threaten Arizona's Total Economy?* Research report prepared by the University of Arizona. Phoenix: Arizona Academy, [1967?]. 173 pp., tables, diags.
Tenth Arizona Town Hall, April 1967.

482. DOAN, MAY C. *I Wouldn't Trade These Yesterdays.* Edited by Andrew Wallace. Tucson: Arizona Pioneers' Historical Society, 1966. 38 pp., illus.
Reminiscences of Yuma and Silverbell.

483. DOBYNS, HENRY F. *Lance Ho!: Containment of the Western Apaches by the Royal Spanish Garrison at Tucson.* Lima, Peru: Editorial Estudios Andinos, 1964. 47 pp.

484. ————. *Papagos in the Cotton Fields, 1950.* [Tucson? 1950?]. 140 pp., illus., maps.
". . . a report on the role of one Southwestern Indian tribe in the cotton harvest on Anglo-owned irrigated lands near its tribal reserves."

485. ————. *Pioneering Christians Among the Perishing Indians of Tucson.* Lima, Peru: Editorial Estudios Andinos, 1962. 36 pp.

486. ————. *University of Arizona Indian Ruin.* Chicago: Inner Creations, 1953. 20 pp., illus.

487. ———— AND ROBERT C. EULER. *The Ghost Dance of 1889 among the Pai Indians of Northwestern Arizona.* Prescott, Arizona: Prescott College Press, 1967. (Prescott College Studies in Anthropology no. 1) 67 pp., illus., map.

488. DOCKSTADER, FREDERICK J. *The Kachina and the White Man: A Study of the Influences of White Culture on the Hopi Kachina Cult.* Bloomfield Hills, Michigan: Cranbrook Institute of Science, 1954. (Bulletin no. 35) 185 pp., illus.

489. DODGE, FRED. *Under Cover for Wells Fargo: The Unvarnished Recollections of Fred Dodge.* Edited by Carolyn Lake. Boston: Houghton Mifflin, 1969. 280 pp., illus.
Part I covers Dodge's experiences in Tombstone from 1879 to 1888.

490. DODGE, NATT N. *Flowers of the Southwest Deserts.* Santa Fe: Southwestern Monuments Association, 1951. (Popular Series no. 4) 112 pp., illus.

    A second edition, 1952; a third, 1954; and a fourth, 1958. Slight revisions.

491. ———. *100 Desert Wildflowers in Natural Color.* Globe, Arizona: Southwestern Monuments Association, 1963. unpaged, illus.

    Quite good photographs, brief descriptions. Almost qualifies as the book we have been wanting for years.

492. ———. *100 Roadside Wildflowers of Southwest Uplands in Natural Color.* Globe, Arizona: Southwest Monuments Association, 1967. (Popular Series no. 12) unpaged, illus.

493. ———. *Saguaro National Monument, Arizona.* Washington: National Park Service, 1957. (Natural History Handbook Series no. 4) 64 pp., illus.

494. ——— AND HERBERT S. ZIM. *The American Southwest: A Guide to the Wide Open Spaces.* New York: Simon and Schuster, 1955. 160 pp., illus.

    Pocket guide to Indians, scenery, wildlife, profusely and surprisingly well illustrated in color.

495. DODGE, RICHARD A. *Investigations into the Ecological Relationships of Ponderosa Pine in Southeast Arizona.* Ann Arbor: University Microfilms, 1963. 131 pp.

    A University of Arizona doctoral dissertation.

496. DONALDSON, MARION G. *An Appraisal of the Arizona Education Association and Its Contribution to the Improvement of Public Education in Arizona.* Ann Arbor: University Microfilms, 1959. 362 pp.

    A University of Arizona doctoral dissertation.

497. [Douglas] *Basic Data Studies for Community Planning.* [Phoenix?]: Van Cleeve Associates, 1963–64. 6 parts, tables, maps.

    Part 1, Location, history, land use, resources.
    Part 2, Population, economics, housing.
    Part 3, Community facilities.
    Part 4, Streets, thoroughfares, public utilities.
    Part 5, Commercial districts, industrial development.
    Part 6, Douglas general plan.
    Title varies.

498. DOWNS, JAMES F. *Animal Husbandry in Navajo Society and Culture.* Berkeley and Los Angeles: University of California Press, 1964. (University of California Publications in Anthropology, vol. 1) 104 pp., charts.

499. DOZIER, EDWARD P. *Hano, a Tewa Indian Community in Arizona.* New York: Holt, Rinehart and Winston, 1966. (Case Studies in Cultural Anthropology) 104 pp., illus.

500. ――――. *The Hopi-Tewa of Arizona.* Berkeley: University of California Press, 1954. (Publications in American Archaeology and Ethnology vol. 44, no. 3) pp. 259–376, illus., maps.

501. DUKE, ALTON. *Arizona Gem Fields.* Yuma: Southwest Printers, 1956. 116 pp., illus., maps.

502. DUMOND, JACK W. *An Analysis of School Board Policy Decisions in Selected Arizona Public School Districts as they Relate to Community Pressure.* Ann Arbor: University Microfilms, 1964. 122 pp.
A University of Arizona doctoral dissertation.

503. DUNBAR, DAVID L. *Economic Feasibility of a Petroleum Refinery in Arizona.* Phoenix: Arizona Development Board, [1961]. 13 pp., tables.

504. DUNBIER, ROGER. *The Sonoran Desert, Its Geography, Economy, and People.* Tucson: University of Arizona Press, 1968. 426 pp., illus., maps.
Every aspect of the desert north and south of the Mexican border examined with clarity and in detail. Excellent maps and illustrations.

505. DUNNING, CHARLES H. AND EDWARD H. PEPLOW, JR. *Rock to Riches.* Phoenix: Southwest Publishing Company, 1959. 406 pp., illus., maps.
The story of mining in Arizona. Much information on individual mines.

506. ―――― AND ――――. *Silver, from Spanish Missions to Space Age Missiles.* Pasadena, California: Hicks Publishing Corporation, 1966. 199 pp., illus., maps.
Brief information on Arizona mines listed alphabetically.

507. DURBIN, CAROLYN B. *History of Tucson Medical Center.* [Tucson?], 1965. unpaged, illus.

508. DUTTON, BERTHA P. *Navajo Weaving Today.* Santa Fe: Museum of New Mexico Press, 1961. 43 pp., illus.

509. ――――, ed. *Pocket Handbook; Indians of the Southwest.* Santa Fe: New Mexico Association on Indian Affairs, 1958. 104 pp., illus.
Formerly published as *New Mexico Indians,* 1948.

510. EARLE, W. HUBERT. *Cacti of the Southwest: Arizona, Western New Mexico, Southern Colorado, Southern Utah, Southern Nevada, Eastern California.* [Phoenix?]: Arizona Cactus and Native Flora Society, 1963. (Desert Botanical Garden Science Bulletin no. 4) 112 pp., illus.

511. EASON, NICHOLAS J. *Fort Verde: An Era of Men and Courage.* Camp Verde, Arizona: Fort Verde Museum Society, 1966. 17 pp., illus.
     Printed at the Northland Press.

512. EATON, JERRY. *The State We're In.* Phoenix: Southwest Publishing Co., [1965]. 253 pp., illus.
     Amusingly written vignettes of Arizona persons, places and things. Entertaining but inconsequential.

513. ECCLESTON, ROBERT. *Overland to California on the Southwestern Trail, 1849.* Edited by George P. Hammond and Edward H. Howes. Berkeley: University of California Press, 1950. (Bancroft Library Publications no. 2) 256 pp., maps.
     Seven hundred fifty copies printed by the Westgate Press for Friends of the Bancroft Library.

514. *Echoes of the Past: Tales of Old Yavapai.* [Prescott?]: Yavapai Cow Belles, 1955. 159 pp., illus.
     Spine is lettered vol. 1.

515. *Echoes of the Past: Tales of Old Yavapai.* Volume 2. Edited by Robert C. Stevens. Prescott, Arizona: Yavapai Cowbelles Inc., 1964. 312 pp., illus.
     More brief chapters on Yavapai County history.

516. *Economic Data for Equal Employment Opportunity Program, Phoenix, Arizona, 1968.* U. S. Bureau of Reclamation, Region 3, [1968?]. 130 pp., maps.

517. *Economic Impact of the Proposed Interstate Program in the Tucson Area.* Phoenix: Planning Corporation of America, 1957. 54 pp., illus.
     Prepared for the Arizona Highway Department.

518. *Economic Impact of the Proposed Interstate Program on the Phoenix Area.* Phoenix: Planning Corporation of America, 1957. 57 pp., illus.
     Prepared for the Arizona Highway Department.

519. *Economic Planning and Development.* Research report prepared by Arizona State University, Tempe. Phoenix: Arizona Academy, [1969]. 174 pp., tables.
     Fifteenth Arizona Town Hall, October 1969.

520. *Economic Study of Alternative Proposals for the Construction of Route I-10 between Phoenix and Brenda, Arizona.* [Phoenix]: Stanley Womer Associates, 1958. 120 pp., tables, maps.
     Prepared for the Arizona Highway Department.

521. *The Economy of Arizona.* Phoenix: Employment Security Commission of Arizona, 1950. 41 pp., tables.
     Analysis of population, labor, industry, employment trends, and economic outlook as affecting unemployment insurance costs.

522. *The Economy of Arizona.* [Phoenix?]: Employment Security Commission of Arizona, 1964. 72 pp., tables, diags.
Subtitle: "A review of Arizona's population, labor force, industries and economic outlook, February, 1964." Prepared by experts of the University of Arizona, Arizona State University, and the Valley National Bank.

523. EDLUND, V. E. AND R. S. LANG. *Sintering and Smeltering Manganese Concentrates from Maggie Canyon Ore, Artillery Mountains Area, Ariz.* [Washington]: U. S. Bureau of Mines, 1962. (Report of Investigations no. 5939) 27 pp., tables, diags.

524. [Education] *Elementary and High School Education in Arizona.* Research report prepared by Arizona State College, Flagstaff. Phoenix: Arizona Academy, [1964?]. 194 pp., tables, diags.
Third Arizona Town Hall, April, 1964.

525. [Education] *Philosophies of Education in Arizona High Schools.* By the Committee on a Philosophy of Education for Arizona High Schools. Tempe: Arizona State College Bookstore, 1958. 43 pp.

526. [Education] *A Report on a Study of the Public School System of Arizona.* [Chicago]: Griffenhagen & Associates, 1952. 3 vols., tables.

527. [Education] *State-Controlled Higher Education in Arizona.* Report of a Survey authorized . . . by the Board of Regents . . . prepared under the . . . Division of Higher Education . . . Office of Education. [Phoenix?]: The Board of Regents of the University and State Colleges of Arizona, 1954. 288 pp., tables.

528. EGGAN, FREDERICK R. *Social Organization of the Western Pueblos.* Chicago: University of Chicago Press, 1950. 373 pp., diags.
The Hopi and the Western New Mexico Pueblos.

529. EISELEIN, EDDIE B. *Water for Weststate, U. S. A.: The Association in the Politics of Water Resource Development.* Ann Arbor: University Microfilms, 1969. 296 pp.
A University of Arizona doctoral dissertation. Weststate is Arizona thinly disguised.

530. ELKINS, D. A. *Estimated Cost of Exploiting Enriched Hard Manganese Ore from the Maggie Canyon Deposit, Artillery Mountains Region, Mohave County, Ariz.* [Washington]: U. S. Bureau of Mines, 1964. (Report of Investigations no. 6438) 78 pp., tables.

531. ELLIOTT, WALLACE W. & Co. *A Reprint of the History of Arizona Territory, Showing Its Resources and Advantages.* Flagstaff, Arizona: Northland Press, 1964. 322 pp., illus., loose map.
A facsimile reprint of the original of 1884 published by Elliott in San Francisco. There is an introduction by Douglas D. Martin. After 13 unnumbered facsimile pages of the original, page numbering begins with 26. Edition limited to 350 copies.

532. ELLISON, GLENN R. *Cowboys Under the Mogollon Rim.* Tucson: University of Arizona Press, 1968. 274 pp., illus.
Reminiscences in cowboy vernacular.

533. ELMER, CARLOS. *Carlos Elmer's Arizona: Color Photography by Carlos and Frank Elmer from the pages of Arizona Highways Magazine.* Scottsdale: The Author, 1967. unpaged., illus.
Reissued 1968 and 1969 with slight variations.

534. [Eloy] *Comprehensive Plan, Eloy, Arizona, December, 1969.* Phoenix: R. W. Beck and Associates, 1969. unpaged, tables, maps, diags.

535. ELY, SIMS. *The Lost Dutchman Mine.* New York: William Morrow, 1953. 178 pp.
Subtitle: "The fabulous story of the seven-decade search for the hidden treasure in the Superstition Mountains of Arizona."

536. EMBRY, CARLOS B. *America's Concentration Camps: The Facts about Our Indian Reservations Today.* New York: David McKay, 1956. 242 pp.

537. EMORY, WILLIAM H. *Lieutenant Emory Reports.* Edited by Ross Calvin. Albuquerque: University of New Mexico Press, 1951. 208 pp., maps.
Reprint of Emory's *Notes of a Military Reconnoissance* of 1848. The account of his march with the Army of the West over the Gila Trail has been called the first scientific description of the Southwest.

538. [Employment] *Your Local Employment Office.* [Phoenix]: Arizona State Employment Service, 1952. 61 pp., illus., diags.

539. ERICKSON, CLARENCE E. *Sunset Sportsman's Atlas, Colorado River and Lake Mead: Boating, Fishing, Exploring.* Menlo Park, California: Lane Publishing Company, 1952. 32 pp., maps.
Issued in a waterproof plastic case.

540. ERICKSON, MELVIN C. *An Analysis of the Activities of Parent-Teacher Associations in the State of Arizona.* Ann Arbor: University Microfilms, 1961. 304 pp.
An Arizona State University doctoral dissertation.

541. ERICKSON, ROLFE C. *Petrology and Geochemistry of the Dos Cabezas Mountains, Cochise County, Arizona.* Ann Arbor: University Microfilms, 1969. 480 pp.
A University of Arizona doctoral dissertation.

542. ERIE, LEONARD J. AND OTHERS. *Consumptive Use of Water by Crops in Arizona.* Tucson: University of Arizona Agricultural Experiment Station, 1965. (Technical Bulletin no. 169) 41 pp., diags.

543. ERWIN, ALLEN A. *The Southwest of John H. Slaughter, 1841–1922*. Glendale, California: Arthur H. Clark Co., 1965. 368 pp., illus., map.
Subtitle: "Pioneer Cattleman and Trail-driver of Texas, the Pecos, and Arizona and Sheriff of Tombstone."

544. EULER, ROBERT C. *An Archaeological Survey of the South Rim of Walnut Canyon National Monument, Arizona*. Flagstaff: Arizona State College, 1964. (Anthropological Papers no. 1) 15 pp., illus., tables.
Printed by the Northland Press.

545. ———. *Walapai Culture-History*. Ann Arbor: University Microfilms, 1959. 296 pp.
A University of New Mexico doctoral dissertation.

546. EVENSEN, JAMES MILLARD. *Geology of the Central Portion of the Agua Fria Mining District, Yavapai County, Arizona*. Ann Arbor: University Microfilms, 1969. 168 pp.
A University of Arizona doctoral dissertation.

547. *Expanded Services to Arizona Reservation Indians*. Phoenix: Arizona State Employment Service, 1952–
Annual. Title varies: current title, "Manpower Services to Arizona Indians."

548. EZELL, PAUL H. *The Hispanic Acculturation of the Gila River Pimas*. Ann Arbor: University Microfilms, 1956. 460 pp.
A University of Arizona doctoral dissertation.

549. ———. *The Hispanic Acculturation of the Gila River Pimas*. [Menasha, Wisconsin?]: American Anthropological Association, 1961. (Memoir no. 90) 171 pp., illus., maps.
Based on the dissertation cited above.

550. ———. *The Maricopas: An Identification from Documentary Sources*. Tucson: University of Arizona Press, 1963. (Anthropological Papers no. 6) 29 pp., maps.

551. *A Factful and Colorful Guide to Phoenix and the Valley of the Sun*. Phoenix: Jim Sexton, 1955. 32 pp., illus.

552. FAICK, JOHN N. *Geology of the Ord Mine, Mazatzal Mountains, Quicksilver District, Arizona*. Washington: U. S. Geological Survey, 1958. (Bulletin no. 1042-R) pp. 685–98, maps.

553. FAIR, CHARLES L. *Geology of the Fresnal Canyon Area, Baboquivari Mountains, Pima County, Arizona*. Ann Arbor: University Microfilms, 1966. 111 pp.
A University of Arizona doctoral dissertation.

554. FAIRCHILD, HURLSTONE. *An Artist's Notebook: Selected Sketches from Studies Made at the Grand Canyon.* Hollywood: Homer H. Boelter, 1950. 32 pp., illus.
Pictures and poems.

555. FANNIN, PAUL AND OTHERS. *The Office of the Governor in Arizona.* Tempe: Arizona State University Bureau of Government Research, 1964. (Public Affairs Series no. 7) 24 pp., 1 folding chart.

556. FARNHAM, LLOYD L. AND L. A. STEWART. *Manganese Deposits of Western Arizona.* [Pittsburgh]: U. S. Bureau of Mines, 1958. (Information Circular no. 7843) 87 pp., illus., maps.

557. ———— AND OTHERS. *Manganese Deposits of Eastern Arizona.* [Washington]: U. S. Bureau of Mines, [1961]. (Information Circular no. 7990) 178 pp., illus., maps.

558. FARNSWORTH, HARRIETT. *Remnants of the Old West.* San Antonio: The Naylor Co., 1965. 139 pp., illus.
Verde Valley, Yavapai cowboys, Jerome.

559. FARQUHAR, FRANCIS P. *The Books of the Colorado River & the Grand Canyon; a Selective Bibliography.* Los Angeles: Glen Dawson, 1953. (Early California Travel Series no. 12) 75 pp.
An annotated and readable bibliography.

560. FARRIS, MARTIN T. AND WILLIAM S. PETERS. *Arizona Transportation.* Tempe: Arizona State University Bureau of Business Services, 1961. 52 pp., tables.
Roads, rail, and air.

561. FAULK, ODIE B. *Arizona's State Historical Society, Its History and Leaders, and Its Services to the Public.* Tucson: Arizona Pioneers' Historical Society, 1966. 43 pp., illus.

562. ————. *The Geronimo Campaign.* New York: Oxford University Press, 1969. 245 pp., illus.

563. ————. *Land of Many Frontiers: A History of the American Southwest.* New York: Oxford University Press, 1968. 358 pp.

564. ————. *Too Far North . . . Too Far South.* Los Angeles: Westernlore Press, 1967. (Great West and Indian Series no. 35) 186 pp., illus., maps.
The controversial Bartlett boundary survey and the Gadsden Purchase.

565. FEENEY, FRANCIS H. *The Incredible Story of Arizona, or How the Original Baby State Achieved Adolescence.* [no place, no date]. 40 pp.
A brief satirical look at things Arizonan from travel to the damned water problem.

566. FERDON, EDWIN N., JR. *A Trial Survey of Mexican Southwestern Architectural Parallels.* Santa Fe: School of American Research. 1955. (Monograph no. 21) 35 pp.
Mexican-like features in the buildings of the Anasazi and Hohokam.

567. FERGUSSON, ERNA. *Dancing Gods: Indian Ceremonials of New Mexico and Arizona.* Albuquerque: University of New Mexico Press, 1957. 276 pp., illus.
Facsimile reprint of the original published by Knopf in 1931.

568. FETH, J. H. AND J. D. HEM. *Reconnaissance of Headwater Springs in the Gila River Drainage Basin, Arizona.* Washington: U. S. Geological Survey, 1963 (Water-Supply Paper no. 1619-H) 54 pp., tables, maps.

569. FETTERHOFF, WILLARD M. *Federal Land Grants to the State of Arizona for Common Schools.* Ann Arbor: University Microfilms, 1962. 155 pp.
A University of Denver doctoral dissertation.

570. FEWKES, JESSE WALTER. *Hopi Katcinas Drawn by Native Artists.* Chicago: Rio Grande Press, 1962.
A facsimile reprint of part of the twenty-first annual report of the Bureau of American Ethnology, 1903. Pagination and placement of the plates varies from the original. Color reproduction is inferior.

571. FIERMAN, FLOYD S. *Some Early Jewish Settlers on the Southwestern Frontier.* El Paso: Texas Western Press, 1960. 58 pp., illus.
The Lesinsky, Solomon, and Freudenthal families. Edition limited to 250 copies. Typography by Carl Hertzog.

572. FIGUHR, RICHARD A. *The Development and Student Appraisal of the Educational Administration Program at Arizona State University.* Ann Arbor: University Microfilms, 1965. 140 pp.
An Arizona State University doctoral dissertation.

573. FILLO, P. V. *Manganese Mining and Milling Methods and Costs, Mohave Mining and Milling Co., Maricopa County, Ariz.* [Washington]: U. S. Bureau of Mines, [1963]. (Information Circular no. 8144) 29 pp., illus., tables, maps.

574. FINNELL, TOMMY L. AND OTHERS. *Mineral Resources of the Mount Baldy Primitive Area, Arizona.* Washington: U. S. Geological Survey, 1967. (Bulletin no. 1230-H) 14 pp., tables, maps.
"An evaluation of the mineral potential of the area."

575. *The First 3 Years of Arizona Western College, Yuma, Arizona, 1963–1966.* [Yuma, 1966]. 47 pp., illus., tables.

576. FISHER, RALPH A., SR. *The Guide to Javelina.* San Antonio: Naylor, 1957. 208 pp., illus.
Hunting experiences.

577. FISHLER, STANLEY A. *In the Beginning: A Navaho Creation Myth.* Salt Lake City: University of Utah Press, 1953. (University of Utah Department of Anthropology, Anthropological Papers no. 13) 130 pp.

578. FLAGG, ARTHUR L. *Mineralogical Journeys in Arizona.* Scottsdale, Arizona: Fred H. Bitner, 1958. 93 pp., illus., maps.

579. *Flagstaff, the Trading Center of Northern Arizona.* Flagstaff: Flagstaff Chamber of Commerce, [1951?]. 16 pp., maps.
     An industrial survey.

580. [Flagstaff] *The General Development Plan for McMillan Heights: A Part of the Master Plan for Flagstaff.* [Scottsdale?: Van Cleve Associates], 1962. 19 pp., maps.

581. FLAKE, O. D. *William J. Flake, Pioneer — Colonizer.* [no place, 1966?]. 197 pp., illus.
     Founding of and life in Snowflake and the Mormon communities of east-central Arizona.

582. FLEMING, WESLEY B. *Migratory Waterfowl in Arizona; a Management Study.* Phoenix: Arizona Game and Fish Department, 1959. (Wildlife Bulletin no. 5) 74 pp., illus., tables, maps.

583. FLETCHER, COLIN. *The Man Who Walked Through Time.* New York: Alfred A. Knopf, 1967. 239 pp., illus., map.
     The first trip afoot through Grand Canyon from Havasupai to Point Imperial. The arid challenge, the solitude, the awesome beauty, and ultimate peace vividly described.

584. FLOCKER, WILLIAM J. *The Absorption of Radioactive Strontium by Certain Crop Plants as Influenced by the Chemical Properties of Some Arizona Soils.* Ann Arbor: University Microfilms, 1955. 125 pp.
     A University of Arizona doctoral dissertation.

585. FOLKNER, JOSEPH S. *Landscaping Arizona Homes.* Tucson: University of Arizona Agricultural Experiment Station, 1958. (Report no. 166) 24 pp., illus.

586. ———— AND ROBERT F. CHARLES, JR. *Native Trees and Shrubs for Landscape Use in Southern Arizona.* Tucson: University of Arizona Agricultural Experiment Station and Cooperative Extension Service, 1964. (Bulletin no A-29) 15 pp., tables, illus.

587. FONTANA, BERNARD L. *Assimilative Change: A Papago Indian Case Study.* Ann Arbor: University Microfilms, 1960. 279 pp.
     A University of Arizona doctoral dissertation.

588. ————. *Biography of a Desert Church: The Story of Mission San Xavier del Bac.* Tucson: The Westerners, 1961. (The Smoke Signal, no. 3) 20 pp., illus.

589. ——— AND OTHERS. *Papago Indian Pottery.* Seattle: University of Washington Press, 1962. (American Ethnological Society Monograph no. 37) 163 pp., illus.

590. *For the Dean: Essays in Anthropology in Honor of Byron Cummings on His Eighty-Ninth Birthday, September 20, 1950.* Tucson and Santa Fe: Hohokam Museums Association and Southwestern Monuments Association, 1950. 318 pp., illus.

591. FORBES, JACK D. *Apache, Navaho and Spaniard.* Norman: University of Oklahoma Press, 1960. 304 pp., illus., maps.
Traces the history of the Southern Athapascans and their relations with other Indians and the Spanish from about 1535 to 1698.

592. ———. *Apache, Navaho, and Spaniard: A History of the Southern Athapaskans and Their Relations with the Spanish Empire, 1540–1698.* Ann Arbor: University Microfilms, 1962. 459 pp.
A University of Southern California doctoral dissertation.

593. ———. *Warriors of the Colorado: The Yumas of the Quechan Nation and Their Neighbors.* Norman: University of Oklahoma Press, 1965. 378 pp., illus., maps.

594. FORBES, ROBERT H. *Crabb's Filibustering Expedition into Sonora, 1857.* Tucson: Arizona Silhouettes, 1952. 60 pp., illus.
Edition limited to 650 copies.

595. [Forests] *An Analysis of Forest Products Potential in Arizona.* Phoenix: Arizona Development Board, [1960?]. 19 pp., illus., tables, maps.

596. FORREST, EARLE R. *Arizona's Dark and Bloody Ground.* Revised and enlarged edition. Caldwell, Idaho: Caxton Printers, 1950. 382 pp., illus.
The notorious and bloody Graham-Tewksbury feud which took place in the Tonto Basin's Pleasant Valley. First edition published in 1936.

597. ———. *Missions and Pueblos of the Old Southwest.* Chicago: Rio Grande Press, 1962. 386 pp., illus.
Originally published in 1929. Covers New Mexico and Arizona.

598. ———. *The Snake Dance of the Hopi Indians.* Los Angeles: Westernlore Press, 1961. 172 pp., illus.
Illustrated with excellent photographs taken by the author in 1906, 1907, and 1908 before cameras were banned at the ceremonies.

599. *Fort Bowie, Ariz.* Hearing. 88th Congress, 2nd Session. Subcommittee on Public Lands of Committee on Interior and Insular Affairs, United States Senate. Washington, 1964. 13 pp.
Hearings on its establishment as a historical monument.

600. [Fort Huachuca] *Guide to Fort Huachuca.* Second edition. Sierra Vista, Arizona: Pearce Publishers, 1959. 52 pp.
     Brief history of the fort; directory, recreation.

601. *42 Years of Distinguished Service: Senator Carl Hayden.* Phoenix: Democratic State Central Committee, 1954. 20 pp., illus.

602. FOSTER, KENNETH E. *Navajo Sandpaintings.* Window Rock, Arizona: Navajo Tribal Museum, 1964. (Navajoland Publications Series 3) 34 pp., illus.

603. *Four Corners Regional Development Study Program.* Baltimore: Westinghouse Electric Corporation Systems Operations, 1969. various paging, tables, maps.
     Subtitle: "A study of development guidelines including the analysis of economic potential and the concept of a new town for the Four Corners Region."

604. FOWLER, DON D. AND OTHERS. *The Glen Canyon Archeological Survey.* Parts I and II. Edited by Charles E. Dibble. Salt Lake City: University of Utah Press, 1959. (University of Utah Department of Anthropology, Anthropological Papers no. 39) 707 pp., illus., tables, maps.

605. ———— AND ————. *John Wesley Powell and the Anthropology of the Canyon Country.* Washington: U. S. Geological Survey, 1969. (Professional Paper 670) 30 pp., illus., maps.
     Subtitle: "A description of John Wesley Powell's anthropological fieldwork, the archeology of the Canyon Country, and extracts from Powell's notes on the origins, customs, practices, and beliefs of the Indians of that area."

606. FOWLIE, JACK A. *The Snakes of Arizona.* Fallbrook, California: Azul Quinta Press, 1965. 164 pp., illus., maps.
     Subtitle: "Their derivation, speciation, distribution, description, and habits; a study in evolutionary herpeto-zoogeographic phylogenetic ecology."

607. FOX, THERON, COMP. *Arizona Treasure Hunters Ghost Town Guide.* San Jose, California: The Author, [1964]. 24 pp., illus., maps.
     Most of the text and a folding map in the pocket are taken from Rand McNally's *Indexed Map of the World* for 1881.

608. FRANKE, PAUL. *They Plowed up Hell in Old Cochise.* Douglas, Arizona: Douglas Climate Club, 1950. 58 pp., illus.

609. FRASER, JAMES. *Cattle Brands in Arizona: A Bibliography of Published Territorial and State Brand Registration Books.* Flagstaff, Arizona: Northland Press, 1968. 45 pp., illus.
     One thousand copies printed of this unusually handsome book.

610. FRAZER, WILLIAM J. *Changing Patterns of Land Utilization Within the Salt River Valley of Arizona.* Ann Arbor: University Microfilms, 1959. 390 pp.
     A University of Michigan doctoral dissertation.

611. FREEMAN, ARTIE E. *Pioneers of the Trail: Reminiscences of the Old West.* New York: Greenwich Book Publishers, 1959. 27 pp.
     Very brief reminiscences of Columbus R. Freeman set down by his wife. Cattle ranching and a few other things in Cochise and Pinal counties.

612. FREESTONE, JOHN W. *I Remember.* Glendale, California: Arthur H. Clark Co., 1963. 85 pp., illus.
     Slight, interesting reminiscences of northern Arizona and of the Safford area about 1900. One hundred copies printed.

613. FRENZEL, CARROLL W. *The Low-Level Wind Field at Phoenix and Tucson.* Tucson: University of Arizona Institute of Atmospheric Physics, 1961. (Scientific Report no. 17) 45 pp., tables, diags.
     Daily wind movements and air pollution.

614. FRINK, MAURICE. *Fort Defiance and the Navajos.* Boulder, Colorado: Pruett Press, 1968. 124 pp.
     History with a chapter on today and tomorrow. Excellent illustrations.

615. FRISBIE, CHARLOTTE J. *Kinaaldá: A Study of the Navaho Girl's Puberty Ceremony.* Middletown, Connecticut: Wesleyan University Press, 1967. 437 pp., illus.
     The ceremony and especially its music.

616. FRONTAIN, DICK. *San Xavier del Bac, a Living Mission.* Tucson: Los Amigos, 1968. 40 pp., illus.
     Many photographs by the author and a chapter, "An Architect Views San Xavier del Bac," by Tucson architect Arthur Brown.

617. FROST, KENNETH R., JR. AND K. C. HAMILTON. *Report on the Wellton-Mohawk Salt Cedar Clearing Studies.* Tucson: University of Arizona Agricultural Experiment Station, 1960. (Report no. 193) 54 pp., illus., tables, map.

618. FUCHS, JAMES R. *A History of Williams, Arizona, 1876–1915.* Tucson: University of Arizona, 1955. (Social Science Bulletin no. 23) 168 pp., illus.

619. FULBRIGHT, TOM. *Cow-Country Counselor.* New York: Exposition Press, 1968. 196 pp.
     Forty years of legal practice in the Pinal County seat of Florence.

620. FULLER, WALLACE H. *Effect of Kind of Phosphate . . . on Phosphorus Absorption by Crops Grown on Arizona Calcareous Soil.* Tucson: University of Arizona Agricultural Experiment Station, 1953. (Technical Bulletin no. 128) pp. 235–55, tables.

621. ———— AND OTHERS. *The Influence of Soil Aggregate Stabilizers on Stand, Composition, and Yield of Crops on Calcareous Soils of Southern Arizona.* Tucson: University of Arizona Agricultural Experiment Station, 1953. (Technical Bulletin no. 129) pp. 257–80, illus., diags.

622. FUNNELL, JOHN E. AND E. J. WOLFE. *Compendium on Nonmetallic Minerals of Arizona.* San Antonio, Texas: Southwest Research Institute for Arizona Public Service Co., 1964. 374 pp., tables, maps.

623. GAINES, XERPHA M. *An Annotated Catalogue of Glen Canyon Plants.* Flagstaff: Northern Arizona Society of Science and Art, 1960. (Museum of Northern Arizona Technical Series no. 4) 18 pp.

624. GALBRAITH, FREDERIC W. AND DANIEL J. BRENNAN. *Minerals of Arizona.* 3rd edition revised. Tucson: University of Arizona Press, 1959. (Physical Science Bulletin no. 4) 116 pp.
  Reissued 1960 by the University of Arizona Press, but not in series.

625. GALE, ROBERT E. *The Geology of Mission Copper Mine, Pima Mining District, Arizona.* Ann Arbor: University Microfilms, 1965. 176 pp.
  A Stanford University doctoral dissertation.

626. GALLIZIOLI, STEVE. *Quail Research in Arizona.* [Phoenix: Arizona Game and Fish Department, 1965?]. 11 pp., illus.

627. GÁLVEZ, BERNARDO DE. *Instructions for Governing the Interior Provinces of New Spain, 1786.* Translated and edited by Donald E. Worcester. Berkeley, California: The Quivira Society, 1951. (Publications vol. 12) 150 pp.
  Spanish and English texts; 500 copies issued.

628. GAMBLE, FELTON O. *Your Grand Canyon Adventure Guide: 7 Exciting Ways to Enjoy Grand Canyon.* Flagstaff, Arizona: KC Publications, 1968. 72 pp., illus., maps.

629. GANZHORN, JOHN W. *I've Killed Men; An Epic of Early Arizona.* New York: Devin-Adair, 1959. 256 pp., illus.
  First published in London in 1940. Reminiscences of life in Tombstone in its heyday and later in Tucson and along the Mexican border.

630. GARBER, PAUL N. *The Gadsden Treaty.* Gloucester, Massachusetts: Peter Smith, 1959. 222 pp.
  Reprint in 300 copies of a work originally published in 1923.

631. GARCÉS, FRANCISCO. *Diario de Exploraciones en Arizona y California en los Años de 1775 y 1776.* Mexico: Universidad Nacional Autónoma de México, Instituto de Investigaciones Históricos, 1968. (Cuadernos, Serie Documental, numero 6) 103 pp., maps.
  Spanish version of the following item but lacks the appendices.

632. ———. *A Record of Travels in Arizona and California, 1775–1776.* New translation edited by John Galvin. San Francisco: John Howell — Books, 1965. 113 pp., illus., maps.
  The Gila Trail, the Colorado valley, and the visit to the Hopi country.

633. GARDNER, ERLE STANLEY. *Hunting Lost Mines by Helicopter.* New York: William Morrow, 1965. 287 pp., illus., maps.
    The Lost Dutchman and the Lost Nummel mines.

634. GARTH, JOHN S. *Butterflies of Grand Canyon National Park.* Grand Canyon: Grand Canyon Natural History Association, 1950. (Bulletin no. 11) 52 pp., illus., maps.

635. GATES, GERALD O. *Ecology of the Iguanid Lizard* Urosaurus graciosus *in Arizona.* Ann Arbor: University Microfilms, 1964. 270 pp.
    A University of Arizona doctoral dissertation.

636. GATEWOOD, JOSEPH S. AND OTHERS. *Use of Water by Bottom-Land Vegetation in Lower Safford Valley, Arizona.* Washington: U. S. Geological Survey, 1950. (Water-Supply Paper no. 1103) 210 pp., illus., tables, maps.

637. GAVASCI, ANNA T. *Uranium Emplacement at Garnet Ridge, Arizona.* Ann Arbor: University Microfilms, 1969. 88 pp.
    A Columbia University doctoral dissertation.

638. *Gearing Arizona's Communities to Orderly Growth.* Research report prepared by Arizona State University, Tempe. Phoenix: Arizona Academy, [1965?]. 151 pp., diags.
    Sixth Arizona Town Hall, April 1965.

639. GENTRY, CURT. *The Killer Mountains: A Search for the Legendary Lost Dutchman Mine.* New York: New American Library, 1968. 212 pp., illus., maps.

640. *Geochronology, with Special Reference to Southwestern United States.* Edited by Terah L. Smiley. Tucson: University of Arizona Press, 1955. (Physical Science Bulletin no. 2) 200 pp., illus., diags.

641. *Geohydrologic Data in the Navajo and Hopi Indian Reservations, Arizona, New Mexico, and Utah.* Phoenix: Arizona State Land Dept., 1963–64. (Water-Resources Report no. 12) 3 parts.
    Various authors.

642. *Geological Symposium of the Four Corners Region....* [Durango, Colorado?]: Four Corners Geological Society, [1952?]. 145 pp., illus., maps, diags.

643. [Geology] *Contributions to the Geology of Northern Arizona: Memorial to Major Brady.* Flagstaff: Northern Arizona Society of Science and Art, 1964. (Museum of Northern Arizona Bulletin no. 40) 71 pp., illus., maps, diags.

644. [Geology] *Guide Book for Field Trip Excursions in Southern Arizona.* Tucson: [Arizona Geological Society], 1952. 150 pp., illus., maps.
    Prepared for the Cordilleran Section meetings of the Geological Society of America, April 1952.

645. [Geology] *Guidebook of the Black Mesa Basin, Northeastern Arizona.* [Socorro]: New Mexico Geological Society, [1959?]. 205 pp., illus., maps, diags.

646. [Geology] *Guidebook of the South and West Sides of the San Juan Basin, New Mexico and Arizona.* Socorro: [New Mexico Geological Society?], 1951. 167 pp., illus., maps.

647. [Geology] *Southern Arizona Guidebook II; Combined with the 2nd Annual Arizona Geological Society Digest.* Tucson: [Arizona Geological Society?], 1959. 290 pp., illus., maps.

    Title pages, or lack thereof, on these guidebooks, give bibliographers nightmares. One assumes that number I is item 644, since this was also prepared for a meeting of the Cordilleran Section of the Geological Society of America in 1959.

648. [Geology] *Southern Arizona Guidebook III, 1968.* Edited by Spencer R. Titley. Tucson: [Arizona Geological Society?], 1968. 354 pp.

    Prepared for the annual meeting, Cordilleran Section, Geological Society of America.

649. GERRARD, THOMAS A. *Environmental Studies of the Fort Apache Member, Supai Formation (Permian), East-Central Arizona.* Ann Arbor: University Microfilms, 1964. 208 pp.

    A University of Arizona doctoral dissertation.

650. GETSINGER, FLOYD R. *Rockhound Primer of Arizona.* [Phoenix]: Arizona Development Board, [1956?]. 59 pp., illus., tables.

    A helpful handbook for the beginner with some illustrations in color.

651. GETTY, HARRY T. *The San Carlos Indian Cattle Industry.* Tucson: University of Arizona Press, 1963. [Anthropological Papers of the University of Arizona, no. 7] 87 pp., illus., tables, maps.

652. [Gila Bend] *A Planning Report for Gila Bend, Arizona.* [Phoenix]: Maricopa County Planning and Zoning Department, 1960. 39 pp., tables, maps.

653. *Gila County, Arizona, Industrial and Commercial Summary.* [Phoenix?]: Gila County Chambers of Commerce and Arizona Development Board, [1963]. 32 pp., tables.

654. [Gila County] *Atlas of Gila County.* [Phoenix]: Arizona State Highway Department, 1961. 12 sheets.

    Detailed road and street maps.

655. [Gila County] *Economic Survey of Gila County.* Tempe: Arizona State College Bureau of Business Services, 1955. (Arizona Counties Economic Survey Series no. 5) 163 pp., maps, tables, diags.

656. *Gila River and Tributaries Downstream from Painted Rock Reservoir, Arizona.* 87th Congress, 2nd Session, Senate Document no. 116. Washington, 1962. 98 pp., tables, maps.
   Flood control. Issued also in a departmental edition.

657. *Gila River and Tributaries in the Vicinity of Tucson, Arizona.* 86th Congress, 2nd Session, Senate Document no. 116. Washington, 1960. 72 pp., tables, maps.
   Issued also in a Defense Department edition.

658. *Gila River, Arizona, Camelsback Reservoir.* 87th Congress, 2nd Session, Senate Document no. 127. Washington, 1962. 112 pp.
   Flood control. Issued also in a Defense Department edition.

659. [Gilbert] *A Plan for Gilbert, Arizona.* [Phoenix]: Maricopa County Planning and Zoning Department, 1960. 48 pp., tables, maps.

660. GILBERTSON, ROBERT L. AND JERRY MCHENRY. *Check List and Host Index for Arizona Rust Fungi.* Tucson: University of Arizona Agricultural Experiment Station, 1969. (Technical Bulletin no. 186) 40 pp.

661. GILKEY, MILLARD M. AND ROBERT T. BECKMAN. *Water Requirements and Uses in Arizona Mineral Industries.* [Washington]: U. S. Bureau of Mines, [1963]. (Information Circular no. 8162) 97 pp., illus., tables, maps, diags.

662. GILLENWATER, VIRGIL M. AND OTHERS. *The Verde Valley Survey, 1953.* [Tucson?], 1953. 69 pp., tables, maps.
   School survey.

663. GILLERMAN, ELLIOT. *Geology of the Central Peloncillo Mountains, Hidalgo County, New Mexico and Cochise County, Arizona.* Socorro: New Mexico State Bureau of Mines and Mineral Resources, 1958. (Bulletin no. 57) 152 pp., illus., maps.

664. GILLESPIE, J. B. AND OTHERS. *Basic Hydrologic Data of the Hualapai, Sacramento, and Big Sandy Valleys, Mohave County, Arizona.* Phoenix: Arizona State Land Department, 1966. (Water-Resources Report no. 26) 39 pp., tables, maps, diags.

665. GILLULY, JAMES. *General Geology of Central Cochise County, Arizona.* Washington: U. S. Geological Survey, 1956. (Professional Paper no. 281) 169 pp., illus., maps.

666. ———— AND OTHERS. *Late Paleozoic Stratigraphy of Central Cochise County, Arizona.* Washington: U. S. Geological Survey, 1954. (Professional Paper no. 266) 49 pp., maps, diags.

667. GILPIN, LAURA. *The Enduring Navaho.* Austin: University of Texas Press, 1968. 263 pp., illus.
   Interesting text based on the author's experiences, but it is her splendid photographs which give this volume its distinction.

668. GLADEN, FRANK H., JR. *An Historical Survey of Public Land and Public Education in the State of Arizona from 1863 to 1960.* Ann Arbor: University Microfilms, 1962. 472 pp.
     A University of Arizona doctoral dissertation.

669. GLADWIN, HAROLD S. *A History of the Ancient Southwest.* Portland, Maine: Bond Wheelwright, 1957. 383 pp., illus., maps.

670. ———— AND OTHERS. *Excavations at Snaketown: Material Culture.* Tucson: University of Arizona Press for the Arizona State Museum, 1965. 305 pp., illus., maps, diags., tables.
     A reprint of the original of 1938 which was no. 25 in the series of Medallion Papers issued by Gila Pueblo.

671. [Glendale] *City of Glendale 1985 Development Plan.* [Phoenix and Denver]: Holland & Rubin and Ken R. White Co., 1966–1967. 3 unnumbered parts; illus., tables, diags., maps.
     Report on the central business district. Report on land use. General plan, without subtitle.

672. [Glendale] *School Housing for Our Children.* [Glendale, Arizona], 1950. 206 pp., illus., maps, tables, diags.
     Irving R. Melbo, director of survey.

673. *Glossary of Common Medical Terms (English to Navajo).* Window Rock, Arizona: Office of Indian Affairs, 1956. 23 pp.

674. GOETZ, CHARLES E. *A Prophet with Honor: The Fred Tuttle Colter Story.* [Phoenix?: The Author?], 1965. 91 pp., maps, diags.
     Story of the man and his efforts to bring water from the Colorado to central Arizona.

675. GOFF, JOHN S. *Arizona Civilization.* Phoenix: Hooper Publishing Corp., 1968. 185 pp., illus., maps.

676. *Gold Placers and Placering in Arizona.* Tucson: University of Arizona Press, 1961. (Arizona Bureau of Mines Bulletin no. 168) 124 pp., illus., tables, maps.
     A "thorough modification" of material which appeared in bulletins no. 142 and 160.

677. GOLDEN, GERTRUDE. *Red Moon Called Me: Memoirs of a Schoolteacher in the Government Indian Service.* San Antonio: Naylor, 1954. 211 pp., illus.
     About half deals with Yuma and Fort Defiance in the first decades of this century.

678. GOLDWATER, BARRY M. *The Face of Arizona.* [Phoenix: F. P. Middleton, 1964]. 14 pp. and 50 plates.
     A folio volume of Goldwater photographs; a limited edition of 1,000 copies.

679. ————. *People and Places.* Text and photographs by Barry Goldwater. New York: Random House, 1967. 86 pp., illus.
     A collection of Goldwater's photographs with comment.

680. —— AND BYRON HARVEY. *The Goldwater Kachina Doll Collection.* Tempe: Arizona Historical Foundation for the Heard Museum, 1969. 27 pp., illus.

681. GOODMAN, DAVID M. *Apaches as Prisoners of War, 1886–1894.* Ann Arbor: University Microfilms, 1969. 241 pp.
A Texas Christian University doctoral dissertation.

682. ——. *Arizona Odyssey: Bibliographic Adventures in Nineteenth-Century Magazines.* Tempe: Arizona Historical Foundation, 1969. 360 pp., illus.
Useful bibliography of articles in nineteenth-century periodicals, many of them obscure and forgotten.

683. ——. *A Western Panorama, 1849–1875: the Travels, Writings and Influence of J. Ross Browne* . . . . Glendale, California: Arthur H. Clark, 1966. 328 pp., illus., maps.

684. GOODWIN, GRENVILLE. *The Social Organization of the Western Apache.* Tucson: University of Arizona Press, 1969. 701 pp.
A slightly enlarged facsimile of the original edition of 1942 with a new introduction by Keith Basso.

685. [Goodyear Farms] *The Story of Goodyear Farms.* Akron, Ohio: Goodyear Tire & Rubber Company, 1953. 44 pp., illus.

686. GOOSSEN, IRVY W. *Navajo Made Easier: A Course in Conversational Navajo.* Salina Springs, Chinle, Arizona: Navajo Book Shelf, 1967. 271 pp.

687. ——. *Navajo Made Easier: A Course in Conversational Navajo.* Flagstaff, Arizona: Northland Press, 1967. 271 pp.

688. GORNITZ, VIVIEN M. *Mineralization, Alteration and Mechanism of Emplacement, Orphan Ore Deposit, Grand Canyon, Arizona.* Ann Arbor: University Microfilms, 1969. 196 pp.
A Columbia University doctoral dissertation.

689. GOULD, FRANK W. *Grasses of Southwestern United States.* Tucson: University of Arizona, 1951. (Biological Science Bulletin no. 7) 343 pp., illus.

690. *Government in Arizona.* Washington: U. S. Bureau of the Census, 1959. (1957 Census of Governments, vol. 6, no. 2) 33 pp., tables.
Financial tables relating to local government.

691. *Government in Arizona.* Washington: U. S. Bureau of the Census, 1964. (Census of Governments, 1962, vol. 7, no. 3) 51 pp., tables.

692. [Graham County] *Atlas of Graham County.* [Phoenix]: Arizona State Highway Department, 1965. 23 sheets.
Detailed road and street maps in a spiral binding.

693. [Graham County] *Economic Study of Graham County.* Edited by Charles A. Wothke and Wilson H. Yarbrough. Tempe: Arizona State College Bureau of Business Services, 1953. (Arizona Counties Survey Series no. 1) 98 pp., tables, maps, diags.

694. [Granger, Byrd H.] *The Authentic History of Scottsdale, Arizona, since 1891.* Scottsdale: Scottsdale Convention and News Bureau, [1956]. unpaged, illus.

695. GRANGER, BYRD H. *Grand Canyon Place Names.* Tucson: University of Arizona Press, 1960. 26 pp., map.
    Reprinted, with omission of pronunciation and map references, from *Arizona Place Names.* See next item.

696. ———. *Will C. Barnes' Arizona Place Names.* Revised and enlarged by Byrd H. Granger. Tucson: University of Arizona Press, 1960. 519 pp., illus., maps.

697. GRANGER, HARRY C. AND ROBERT B. RAUP. *Geology of Uranium Deposits in the Dripping Spring Quartzite, Gila County, Arizona.* Washington: U. S. Geological Survey, 1969. (Professional Paper no. 595) 108 pp., illus., maps, tables, diags.

698. ——— AND ———. *Reconnaissance Study of Uranium Deposits in Arizona.* Washington: U. S. Geological Survey, 1962. (Bulletin no. 1147-A) 54 pp., maps, diags.

699. ——— AND ———. *Stratigraphy of the Dripping Spring Quartzite, Southeastern Arizona.* Washington: U. S. Geological Survey, 1964. (Bulletin no. 1168) 119 pp., illus., tables, maps.

700. ——— AND ———. *Uranium Deposits in the Dripping Spring Quartzite, Gila County, Arizona.* Washington: U. S. Geological Survey, 1959. (Bulletin no. 1046-P) pp. 415–86, illus., maps.

701. GRANT, JACK. *Trail Dust and Gun Smoke: Factual Stories of a Cowboy's Life.* New York: Vantage Press, 1965. 122 pp.
    Cowpunching and other things in the first two decades of the century and mostly in southern Arizona.

702. GRAY, ANDREW B. *Survey of a Route on the 32nd Parallel for the Texas Western Railroad, 1854: The A. B. Gray Report and Including the Reminiscences of Peter R. Brady Who Accompanied the Expedition.* Edited by L. R. Bailey. Los Angeles: Westernlore Press, 1963. 240 pp., illus.
    Shreveport to San Diego. This is the first appearance of Brady's reminiscences in book form. Though written after the event they are far more interesting than Gray's narrative.

703. GRAY, IRVING B. *Nature and Origin of the Moenkopi-Shinarump Hiatus in Monument Valley, Arizona and Utah.* Ann Arbor: University Microfilms, 1962. 127 pp.
    A University of Arizona doctoral dissertation.

704. GRAY, ROBERT S. *Late Cenozoic Geology in the San Pedro Valley Near St. David, Arizona.* Tucson: University of Arizona Geochronology Laboratories, 1965. (Interim Research Report no. 8) 32 pp., illus., maps, tables.

705. ———. *Late Cenozoic Sediments in the San Pedro Valley near St. David, Arizona.* Ann Arbor: University Microfilms, 1965. 268 pp. A University of Arizona doctoral dissertation.

706. GREEN, CHRISTINE R. *Arizona Statewide Rainfall.* Tucson: University of Arizona Institute of Atmospheric Physics, 1959. (Technical Reports on the Meteorology and Climatology of Arid Regions no. 7) 8 pp., appendices.

707. ———. *Distribution of Rainfall in Arizona.* Tucson: University of Arizona Institute of Atmospheric Physics, 1964. (Technical Reports on the Meteorology and Climatology of Arid Regions no. 13) 17 pp., tables, diags.

708. ———. *Heating and Cooling Degree-Day Characteristics in Arizona.* [Tucson]: University of Arizona Institute of Atmospheric Physics, 1962. (Technical Reports on the Meteorology and Climatology of Arid Regions no. 10) 64 pp., tables, diags.

709. ———. *Probabilities of Drought and Rainy Periods for Selected Points in the Southwestern United States.* Tucson: University of Arizona Institute of Atmospheric Physics, 1960. (Technical Reports on the Meteorology and Climatology of Arid Regions, no. 8) 4 pp. and 24 diags.

710. ———. *Seasonal Precipitation and Temperature Data for Selected Arizona Stations.* Tucson: University of Arizona Institute of Atmospheric Physics, 1964. (Technical Reports on the Meteorology and Climatology of Arid Regions no. 12) 42 pp., tables, maps, diags.

711. ———. *Summer Rainy Days in Arizona.* Tucson: University of Arizona Institute of Atmospheric Physics, 1963. (Technical Reports on the Meteorology and Climatology of Arid Regions no. 11) 61 pp., tables, diags.
    Descriptive study of daily summer rainfall. No attempt to explain results physically.

712. ——— AND WILLIAM D. SELLERS, eds. *Arizona Climate.* Tucson: University of Arizona Press, 1964. 503 pp., tables, maps.
    Introductory material and detailed statistics by station. A revised edition of the same title edited by Sellers, 1960, which see.

713. GREEN, ROBERT B. *On the Arkansas Route to California in 1849: The Journal of Robert B. Green of Lewisburg, Pennsylvania.* Edited by J. Orin Oliphant. Lewisburg, Pennsylvania: Bucknell University Press, 1955. 87 pp.
    They followed the Gila Trail. Three hundred fifty copies of a first printing and 300 of a second.

714. GREENBERG, NORMAN C. *Administrative Problems Related to Integration of Navajo Indians in Public Education.* Ann Arbor: University Microfilms, 1963. 148 pp.
A University of Colorado doctoral dissertation.

715. GREENE, JONATHAN H. *A Desperado in Arizona, 1858–1860, or, the Life, Trial, Death, and Confession of Samuel H. Calhoun, the Soldier-Murderer.* Santa Fe: Stagecoach Press, 1964. 89 pp., illus.
Important for its picture of the mines before the Civil War.

716. GREENFIELD, CURTIS O. *A Study of the Teacher Tenure Law in Arizona.* Ann Arbor: University Microfilms, 1962. 405 pp.
A University of Southern California doctoral dissertation.

717. [Greenlee County] *Atlas of Greenlee County.* [Phoenix]: Arizona State Highway Department, 1965. 11 sheets.
Detailed road and street maps in a spiral binding.

718. GREEVER, WILLIAM S. *Arid Domain; The Santa Fe Railway and Its Western Land Grant.* Stanford: Stanford University Press, 1954. 184 pp., maps.

719. GREGORY, HERBERT E. *Geology and Geography of the Zion Park Region, Utah and Arizona.* Washington: U. S. Geological Survey, 1950. (Professional Paper no. 220) 200 pp., illus., maps.

720. GRESSINGER, A. W. *Charles D. Poston, Sunland Seer.* Globe, Arizona: Dale Stuart King, 1961. 212 pp., illus.
A biography which quotes extensively from Poston's writings.

721. GRIFFITH, A. KINNEY. *Mickey Free, Manhunter.* Caldwell, Idaho: Caxton Printers, 1969. 239 pp., illus.

722. [Griswold, J. F.?] *Salt River Project.* [Phoenix: Salt River Valley Water Users Association?], 1960. 33 pp., illus., maps.
Subtitle: "A United States reclamation project operated by Salt River Project Agricultural Improvement and Power District and Salt River Valley Water Users' Association." Major facts briefly told.

723. GULLEY, MARY L. *My Mystery Castle.* Culver City, California: Murray & Gee, 1952. 294 pp., illus.
About the strange structure at the base of the mountains south of Phoenix by the girl who inherited it.

724. GUMERMAN, GEORGE J., III. *The Archaeology of the Hopi Buttes District, Arizona.* Ann Arbor: University Microfilms, 1969. 460 pp.
A University of Arizona doctoral dissertation.

725. GUSTAFSON, ALBURN M. *A History of Teacher Certification in Arizona.* Ann Arbor: University Microfilms, 1955. 557 pp.
A University of Arizona doctoral dissertation.

726. GUTENBERG, ARTHUR W. *The Economics of the Evaporative Cooler Industry in the Southwestern United States.* Ann Arbor: University Microfilms, 1956. 285 pp.
A Stanford University doctoral dissertation.

727. ———. *Retail Trade Survey.* Tempe: Arizona State College Bureau of Business Services, 1955. (Miscellaneous Papers no. 4) 26 pp., tables.
Survey of Phoenix.

728. ——— AND OTHERS. *Economic Impact of Relocation of Highway 86 on Willcox-Bowie-San Simon.* [Phoenix: Arizona State Highway Department, 1957]. 33 pp., tables.

729. GUTHRIE, MELVIN G. *A Study of Conditions and Services in School Libraries in the State of Arizona.* Tempe: Arizona State University Bureau of Educational and Research Services, 1968. 247 pp., tables.
A supplementary report to the *Arizona Library Survey* by Grace T. Stevenson, intended to be used as a basis for library development in the state.

730. [Hackenberg, Robert A.] *A Brief History of the Gila River Reservation.* Tucson: University of Arizona, Department of Anthropology, [1955]. 94 pp.
One hundred copies mimeographed and distributed at the Sacaton Education Conference, 1955.

731. HACKENBERG, ROBERT A. *Economic and Political Change Among the Gila River Pima Indians.* Tucson: University of Arizona Bureau of Ethnic Research, 1955. 177, 3 pp.
A classified, mimeographed report to the John Hay Whitney Foundation, declassified in 1968.

732. ———. *Indian Administration and Social Change.* Ann Arbor: University Microfilms, 1962. 505 pp.
A Cornell University doctoral dissertation. A study of the Gila River Pima-Maricopa Indian community.

733. ———. *A Navajo Population Register; Preliminary Considerations.* [Tucson: University of Arizona Bureau of Ethnic Research], 1964. 28 pp.

734. ———. *Papago Population Study, Research Methods and Preliminary Results.* Tucson: University of Arizona Bureau of Ethnic Research, 1961. 177 pp., tables.
Subtitle: "A report prepared for the National Cancer Institute by the Bureau of Ethnic Research, Department of Anthropology, University of Arizona."

735. HAGAN, MAXINE W. *An Educational History of the Pima and Papago Peoples from the Mid-Seventeenth Century to the Mid-Twentieth Century.* Ann Arbor: University Microfilms, 1959. 331 pp.
    A University of Arizona doctoral dissertation.

736. HAGGERSON, NELSON L. AND DEL WEBBER. *Social Studies in Arizona Secondary Schools.* Tempe: Arizona State University Bureau of Educational Research and Services, 1963. (Research and Services Bulletin no. 13) 43 pp., tables.

737. HAILE, BERARD. *Legend of the Ghostway Ritual in the Male Branch of Shootingway, Part 1. Suckingway, Its Legend and Practice, Part 2.* Saint Michaels, Arizona: Saint Michaels Press, 1950. 372 pp., illus.

738. ———. *Property Concepts of the Navaho Indians.* Washington: Catholic University of America Press, 1954. (Anthropology Series no. 17) 56 pp.

739. ———. *A Stem Vocabulary of the Navaho Language.* Saint Michaels, Arizona: Saint Michaels Press, 1950–51. 2 vols.

740. HALE, KENNETH L. *A Papago Grammar.* Ann Arbor: University Microfilms, 1959. 188 pp.
    An Indiana University doctoral dissertation.

741. HALL, DICK WICK. *Dick Wick Hall: Stories from the Salome Sun by Arizona's Most Famous Humorist.* Collected by Frances Dorothy Nutt. Flagstaff, Arizona: Northland Press, 1968. 136 pp.

742. HALL, SHARLOT. *Poems of a Ranch Woman.* Posthumously compiled by Joseph Mackenzie with biography by Charles F. Parker. Prescott, Arizona: Sharlot Hall Historical Society, 1953. 154 pp., illus.
    Listed here for the biography of Miss Hall.

743. HALLORAN, ARTHUR F. *The Mammals of Navajoland.* Window Rock, Arizona: Navajo Tribal Museum, 1964 (Navajoland Publications Series 4) 23 pp.

744. HAMILL, LLOYD AND ROSE HAMILL. *Hamill's Tombstone Picture Gallery.* Glendale, California: Western Americana Press, 1960. 23 pp., illus.
    Excellent photographs, brief history of the town (more Earps and Clantons, of course), and tours of the area.

745. HAMILTON, JOYCE. *White Water: The Colorado Jet Boat Expedition of 1960.* Christchurch, New Zealand: Carton Press, 1963. 259 pp., illus.
    The first *up*-river run, made in power boats.

746. HAMILTON, KEITH C. AND H. F. ARLE. *Weeds of Crops in Southern Arizona.* Tucson: University of Arizona Agricultural Experiment Station, 1958. (Bulletin no. 296) 64 pp., illus.

747. HAMILTON, PATRICK. *The Resources of Arizona.* [Tucson: Piñon Press of Arizona, 1966]. 120 pp.
A facsimile reprint of the second edition of 1881. It was, as its original title page says, "a manual of reliable information concerning the territory." A most peculiar piece of book-making, without title page of its own and with the introduction and index preceding the facsimile title.

748. HANNAU, HANS W. *Arizona.* [Munich, Germany: Wilhelm Andermann Verlag] distributed by Doubleday, Garden City, New York, [1967?]. 61 pp., illus.
Brief travel information and 30 pages of color plates.

749. HANNUM, ALBERTA. *Paint the Wind.* New York: Viking, 1958. 206 pp., illus.
About the Navajo artist Beatien Yazz. A sequel to *Spin a Silver Dollar.*

750. HANSON, HIRAM S. *Petrography and Structure of the Leatherwood Quartz Diorite, Santa Catalina Mountains, Pima County, Arizona.* Ann Arbor: University Microfilms, 1966. 125 pp.
A University of Arizona doctoral dissertation.

751. HARBECK, GUY E. AND OTHERS. *Water-Loss Investigations: Lake Mead Studies.* Washington: U. S. Geological Survey, 1958. (Professional Paper no. 298) 100 pp., illus., tables, diags.

752. HARDT, WILLIAM F. AND OTHERS. *Basic Ground-Water Data for Western Pinal County, Arizona.* Phoenix: Arizona State Land Department, 1964. (Water Resources Report no. 18) 59 pp., tables, maps.

753. HARDWICK, WILLIAM R. *Block-Caving Copper Mining Methods and Costs at the Miami Mine, Miami Copper Company, Gila County, Ariz.* [Washington]: U.S. Bureau of Mines, [1965]. (Information Circular no. 8271) 96 pp., illus., tables, maps.

754. ———. *Block-Caving Mining Methods and Costs, Bagdad Mine ... Yavapai County, Arizona.* [Pittsburgh]: U. S. Bureau of Mines, 1959. (Information Circular no. 7890) 28 pp., tables, maps.

755. ———. *Mining Methods and Costs, Inspiration Consolidated Copper Co., Open-Pit Mine, Gila County, Ariz.* [Washington]: U. S. Bureau of Mines, [1963]. (Information Circular no. 8154) 65 pp., illus., tables, maps, diags.

756. HARDWICK, WILLIAM R. *Open-Pit Copper Mining and Concentrating Methods and Costs, Silver Bell Unit, American Smelting and Refining Co., Pima County, Ariz.* [Washington]: U. S. Bureau of Mines, [1963]. (Information Circular no. 8153) 72 pp., illus., maps, table, diags.

757. ———. *Open-Pit Copper Mining Methods at New Cornelia Branch, Phelps Dodge Corp., Pima County, Ariz.* [Washington]: U. S. Bureau of Mines, [1960]. (Information Circular no. 7938) 83 pp., illus., tables, maps.

758. ———. *Open-Pit Copper Mining Methods, Morenci Branch, Phelps Dodge Corp., Greenlee County, Ariz.* [Washington]: U. S. Bureau of Mines, 1959. (Information Circular no. 7911) 67 pp., illus., maps, diags.

759. ——— AND E. L. JONES. *Open-Pit Copper Mining Methods and Costs at the Bagdad Copper Corp., Yavapai County, Ariz.* [Washington]: U. S. Bureau of Mines, 1959. (Information Circular no. 7929) 30 pp., illus., tables, maps.

760. ——— AND JOE SIERAKOSKI. *Mining Methods and Practices at the Johnson Camp Copper-Zinc Mine . . . Cochise County, Arizona.* [Pittsburgh]: U. S. Bureau of Mines, 1957. (Information Circular no. 7788) 27 pp., illus., maps, tables.

761. ——— AND M. M. STOVER. *Open-Pit Copper Mining Methods and Practices, Copper Cities Division, Miami Copper Co., Gila County, Ariz.* [Washington]: U. S. Bureau of Mines, [1960]. (Information Circular no. 7985) 52 pp., illus., tables, maps.

762. HARRER, C. M. *Reconnaissance of Iron Resources in Arizona.* [Washington]: U. S. Bureau of Mines, [1964]. (Information Circular no. 8236) 204 pp., illus., tables, maps.

763. HARRIS, BENJAMIN B. *The Gila Trail: The Texas Argonauts and the California Gold Rush.* Edited by Richard H. Dillon. Norman: University of Oklahoma Press, 1960. 175 pp., illus., map.
Reminiscences of an overland journey 1849.

764. HARRIS, WILLIAM H. *A Study of the Physical Education Programs for Men at the State Institutions of Higher Learning in Arizona.* Ann Arbor: University Microfilms, 1958. 228 pp.
A University of Kentucky doctoral dissertation.

765. HARSHBARGER, JOHN W. *Water Resources of Chuska Mountains Area, Navajo Indian Reservation, Arizona and New Mexico.* Washington: U. S. Geological Survey, 1954. (Circular no. 308) 16 pp., illus., maps.

766. ——— AND OTHERS. *Arizona Water.* Washington: U. S. Geological Survey, 1966. (Water-Supply Paper no. 1648) 85 pp., illus., maps, diags.
A popular account.

767. ———— AND OTHERS. *Stratigraphy of the Uppermost Triassic and the Jurassic Rocks of the Navajo Country.* Washington: U. S. Geological Survey, 1957. (Professional Paper no. 291) 74 pp., illus., maps.

768. HARVEY, BYRON AND SUZANNE DE BERGE. *Hopi Miniature Baskets.* Phoenix: Arequipa Press, 1969. 41 pp., illus.
    Limited to 500 copies.

769. HARVILL, RICHARD A. *Arizona; Its University's Contribution to the Southwest.* New York: Newcomen Society, 1953. 32 pp., illus.

770. ————. *Arizona: la Contribución de la Universidad hacia el Suroeste.* Versión Española de Renato Rosaldo. Tucson: University of Arizona Press, 1960. 31 pp., illus.
    Translation of preceding item.

771. [Harvill] *Inauguration of Richard Anderson Harvill as President of the University.* Tucson: University of Arizona Press, 1955. (General Bulletin no. 17) 76 pp., illus.

772. HARWARD, NAOMI. *Socio-Economic and Other Variations Related to Rehabilitation of Mexican Americans in Arizona.* Tempe: Arizona State University, 1969. 90 pp.
    "This study was made to increase understanding of the Mexican American rehabilitant in Arizona, his unique characteristics and needs, and his adjustment to vocational rehabilitation."

773. HASTINGS, JAMES R. *Historical Changes in the Vegetation of a Desert Region.* Ann Arbor: University Microfilms, 1963. 499 pp.
    A University of Arizona doctoral dissertation. The area is the San Pedro and Santa Cruz valleys and south in Sonora.

774. ———— AND RAYMOND M. TURNER. *The Changing Mile: An Ecological Study of Vegetation Change with Time in the Lower Mile of an Arid and Semiarid Region.* Tucson: University of Arizona Press, 1965. 317 pp., illus., maps.
    Mostly central Arizona south of Tucson but with some locations in northern Sonora.

775. HATTICH, WILLIAM. *Pioneer Magic.* New York: Vantage Press, 1964. 73 pp., illus.
    Inconsequential reminiscences of Tombstone and other Arizona places and things.

776. [Haugh, Solanus, Father] *Papago, the Desert People.* No publisher, [1958?]. unpaged, illus.
    Splendid photographs with simple accompanying text.

777. ————. *Papago, the Desert People.* [Oakland, California: The Franciscan Missions, 1961?]. 48 pp., illus.
    New edition with revised text and added illustrations.

778. HAURY, EMIL W. *The Stratigraphy and Archaeology of Ventana Cave, Arizona.* Tucson and Albuquerque: The University of Arizona Press and the University of New Mexico Press, 1950. 599 pp., illus., tables, maps.
      Collaborators: Kirk Bryan, Edwin H. Colbert, Norman E. Gabel, Clara Lee Tanner, and T. F. Buehrer.

779. HAVENS, RICHARD AND KARL C. DEAN. *Chemical Stabilization of the Uranium Tailings at Tuba City, Arizona.* [Washington]: U. S. Bureau of Mines, 1969. (Report of Investigations no. 7288) 12 pp., illus.

780. HAYDEN, CARL T., comp. *A History of the Pima Indians and the San Carlos Irrigation Project.* 89th Congress, 1st Session, Senate Document no. 11. Washington, 1965. 94 pp.
      Compiled in 1924.

781. [Hayden, Carl T.] *Tributes to Honorable Carl Hayden, Senator from Arizona, to Commemorate the Occasion of His Fiftieth Anniversary of Congressional Service, February 19, 1962.* 87th Congress, 2nd Session, Senate Document 76. Washington, 1962. 137 pp.

782. HAYDEN, JULIAN D. *Excavations, 1940, at University Indian Ruin, Tucson, Arizona.* Globe, Arizona: Southwestern Monuments Association, 1957. (Technical Series vol. 5) 234 pp., illus., plans, diags.

783. [Hayden-Winkelman] Despain, I. Dale. *General Plan, Hayden-Winkelman, Arizona.* 1961. 65 pp., maps.

784. HAYES, JESS G. *". . . And Then There Were None . . .": A Long-buried Chapter in Apache History.* Globe: The Author, 1965. 18 pp., illus.
      The story behind the hanging in December 1889 of Gon-shay-ee and four other Apaches and of Nah-deiz-az, the killer of Lieutenant Mott.

785. ———. *Apache Vengeance; True Story of the Apache Kid.* Albuquerque: University of New Mexico Press, 1954. 185 pp., illus.

786. ———. *Boots and Bullets: The Life and Times of John W. Wentworth.* Tucson: University of Arizona Press, 1967. 139 pp., illus.
      The experiences of a probate judge, clerk of the Board of Supervisors, and U. S. Commissioner in Globe and Gila County from the 1880s to the 1930s.

787. ———. *Sheriff Thompson's Day — Turbulence in the Arizona Territory.* Tucson: University of Arizona Press, 1968. 190 pp., illus.
      The career of a Gila County sheriff, some of it based on the author's recollections.

788. HAYES, PHILIP T. AND EDWIN R. LANDIS. *Paleozoic Stratigraphy of the Southern Part of the Mule Mountains, Arizona.* Washington: U. S. Geological Survey, 1965. (Bulletin no. 1201-F) 43 pp., maps.

789. HAZEN, SCOTT W. *Statistical Analysis of Churn-Drill and Diamond-Drill Sample Data from the San Manuel Copper Mine, Arizona.* [Washington]: U. S. Bureau of Mines, 1963. (Report of Investigations no. 6216) 124 pp., tables, maps, diags.

790. HEADLEY, JOSEPH C. *The Economics of Forage Harvesting in Arizona.* Tucson: University of Arizona Agricultural Experiment Station, 1957. (Report no. 163) 22 pp., tables, diags.

791. HEALD, WELDON F. *Arizona Scenic Guide.* Susanville, California: Scenic Guides, 1962. 60 pp., illus., maps.

792. ———. *Sky Island.* Princeton, New Jersey: Van Nostrand, 1967. 166 pp., illus.
      Natural history of the Chiricahua Mountains where the author made his home for many years, set down with affection and enthusiasm.

793. HEGEMANN, ELIZABETH COMPTON. *Navaho Silver.* Los Angeles: Southwest Museum, 1962. (Southwest Museum Leaflets no. 29) 31 pp., illus.
      Reprinted from *Masterkey,* volume 36, April–June and July–September 1962.

794. ———. *Navaho Trading Days.* Albuquerque: University of New Mexico Press, 1963. 388 pp., illus.
      Experiences on the reservation, especially at the Shonto trading post. Profusely illustrated with remarkable photographs by the author.

795. HEINDL, LEOPOLD A. *Cenozoic Alluvial Deposits of the Upper Gila River Area, New Mexico and Arizona.* Ann Arbor: University Microfilms, 1958. 300 pp.
      A University of Arizona doctoral dissertation.

796. ———. *Cenozoic Geology in the Mammoth Area, Pinal County, Arizona.* Washington: U. S. Geological Survey, 1963. (Bulletin no. 1141-E) 41 pp., maps.

797. ———. *Mesozoic Formations in the Comobabi and Roskruge Mountains, Papago Indian Reservation, Arizona.* Washington: U. S. Geological Survey, 1965. (Bulletin no. 1194-H) 15 pp., maps.

798. ——— AND C. A. ARMSTRONG. *Geology and Ground-Water Conditions in the Gila Bend Indian Reservation, Maricopa County, Arizona.* Washington: U. S. Geological Survey, 1963. (Water-Supply Paper no. 1647-A) 48 pp., illus., tables, maps.

799. HEINDL, LEOPOLD A. AND O. J. COSNER. *Hydrologic Data and Drillers' Logs, Papago Indian Reservation, Arizona.* Tucson: Arizona State Land Department, 1961. (Water Resources Report no. 9) 116 pp., tables.

800. —— AND C. L. FAIR. *Mesozoic (?) Rocks in the Baboquivari Mountains, Papago Indian Reservation, Arizona.* Washington: U. S. Geological Survey, 1965. (Bulletin no. 1194-I) 12 pp., map.

801. —— AND R. A. McCULLOUGH. *Geology and the Availability of Water in the Lower Bonita Creek Area, Graham County, Arizona.* Washington: U.S. Geological Survey, 1961. (Water-Supply Paper no. 1589) 56 pp., tables, diags., map.

802. —— AND NATALIE D. WHITE. *Hydrologic and Drill-Hole Data, San Xavier Indian Reservation and Vicinity, Pima County, Arizona.* Phoenix: Arizona State Land Department, 1965. (Water Resources Report no. 20) 48 pp., tables, maps.

803. HEINRICH, E. WILLIAM. *Some Rare-Earth Mineral Deposits in Mohave County, Arizona.* Tucson: University of Arizona Press, 1960. (Arizona Bureau of Mines Bulletin no. 167, Mineral Technology Series no. 51) 22 pp., illus., tables.

804. HELY, ALLEN G. *Lower Colorado River Water Supply — Its Magnitude and Distribution.* Washington: U. S. Geological Survey, 1969. (Professional Paper no. 486-D) 54 pp., maps, tables, diags.

805. —— AND EUGENE L. PECK. *Precipitation, Runoff and Water Loss in the Lower Colorado River–Salton Sea Area.* Washington: U. S. Geological Survey, 1964. (Professional Paper no. 486-B) 16 pp., maps.

806. HEM, JOHN D. *Quality of Water of the Gila River Basin above Coolidge Dam, Arizona.* Washington: U. S. Geological Survey, 1950. (Water-Supply Paper no. 1104) 230 pp., tables.

807. HENDERSON, PATRICK C. *The Public Domain in Arizona: 1863–1891.* Ann Arbor: University Microfilms, 1966. 276 pp.
A University of New Mexico doctoral dissertation.

808. HENDERSON, RANDALL. *Sun, Sand and Solitude: Vignettes from the Notebook of a Veteran Desert Reporter.* Los Angeles: Westernlore Press, 1968. 206 pp., illus.
Pleasant for reading or browsing. Enough Arizona to merit its inclusion here.

809. HENDERSON, RONALD W. *Environmental Stimulation and Intellectual Development of Mexican-American Children: an Exploratory Study.* Ann Arbor: University Microfilms, 1966. 240 pp.
A University of Arizona doctoral dissertation. The children studied were from Tucson elementary schools.

810. HENDERSON, WILLIAM L. *Public Finance in Navajo County, the Towns of Holbrook and Snowflake and the City of Show Low, Arizona.* Tucson: University of Arizona Bureau of Business and Public Research, 1964. 41 pp., tables, diags.

811. HENDRICKS, E. L. AND OTHERS. *Progress Report on Use of Water by Riparian Vegetation, Cottonwood Wash, Arizona.* Washington: U. S. Geological Survey, 1960. (Circular no. 434) 11 pp., tables.

812. HENNACY, AMMON. *Autobiography of a Catholic Anarchist.* New York: Catholic Worker Books, 1954. 314 pp.
The author has lived in or near Phoenix.

813. HENSON, PAULINE. *Founding a Wilderness Capital: Prescott, A. T. 1864.* Flagstaff, Arizona: Northland Press, 1965. 261 pp., illus., map.

814. HESTER, JAMES J. *Early Navajo Migrations and Acculturation in the Southwest.* Ann Arbor: University Microfilms, 1961. 495 pp.
A University of Arizona doctoral dissertation.

815. ————. *Early Navajo Migrations and Acculturation in the Southwest.* Santa Fe: Museum of New Mexico Press, 1962. (Museum of New Mexico Papers in Anthropology no. 6) 138 pp., illus., tables, maps.
A slightly abbreviated version of the dissertation listed above.

816. HETMANN, FREDERIK *see* KIRSCH, HANS CHRISTIAN

817. HEVLY, RICHARD H. *Pollen Analysis of Quaternary Archaeological and Lacustrine Sediments from the Colorado Plateau.* Ann Arbor: University Microfilms, 1964. 150 pp.
A University of Arizona doctoral dissertation. Covers Arizona north of the Mogollon Rim.

818. HICKS, FREDERIC N. *Ecological Aspects of Aboriginal Culture in the Western Yuman Area.* Ann Arbor: University Microfilms, 1963. 391 pp.
A University of California, Los Angeles, doctoral dissertation.

819. *Higher Education in Arizona.* Research report prepared by the State Universities of Arizona . . . . Phoenix: Arizona Academy, [1966]. 233 pp., tables, diags.
Ninth Arizona Town Hall, October 1966.

820. *Higher Education in Arizona, the Next Decade: Recommendations of Arizona Board of Regents, September 1966.* No place, no publisher, 1966. 19 pp., diags.

821. *A Highway Related Economic Survey, Casa Grande, Coolidge, Florence, Mesa and Surrounding Areas.* [Phoenix]: Arizona Highway Department, 1960. 81 pp., tables, diags., maps.

822. HILGEMAN, ROBERT H. AND DAVID R. RODNEY. *Commercial Citrus Production in Arizona.* Tucson: University of Arizona Agricultural Experiment Station and Cooperative Extension Service, 1961. (Special Report no. 7) 30 pp., illus., diags.

823. ———— AND CLIFTON W. VAN HORN. *Citrus Growing in Arizona.* Tucson: University of Arizona Agricultural Experiment Station, 1954. (Bulletin no. 258) 36 pp., illus., tables, diags.

824. HILL, JAMES S. *A Statistical Handbook for the Desert Grapefruit Industry.* Tucson: University of Arizona Agricultural Experiment Station, 1963. (Report no. 220) 54 pp., tables, diags.

825. ———— AND OTHERS. *Some Economic Aspects of the Arizona Citrus Industry.* Tucson: University of Arizona Agricultural Experiment Station, 1965. (Technical Bulletin no. 168) 42 pp., tables.

826. HILTON, WILLIAM H. *Sketches in the Southwest and Mexico, 1858–1877.* Introduction and notes by Carey S. Bliss. Los Angeles: Dawson's Book Shop, 1963. unpaged, illus.
    Delightful and historically important drawings from a collection at the Huntington Library. A beautiful book from the Plantain Press.

827. HILZINGER, J. GEORGE. *Treasure Land, a Story.* Glorieta, New Mexico: Rio Grande Press, 1969. 160 pp., illus., maps.
    Arizona and particularly Tucson and Nogales as they were in 1879, some of it written with tongue in cheek. Facsimile of the 1897 edition with added illustrations of Tucson in the 1960s and an index.

828. HINE, ROBERT V. *Bartlett's West: Drawing the Mexican Boundary.* New Haven: Yale University Press for the Amon Carter Museum, Fort Worth, 1968. 135 pp., illus., map.
    Hine furnishes an able account of Bartlett and the experiences of the boundary commission, but it is the reproductions of Bartlett's drawings that make the book outstanding.

829. HINTON, HARWOOD P., ed. *A Comprehensive Index to the* Arizona Historical Review. Tucson: University of Arizona, 1969. 116 pp.
    The *Review* was published between 1928 and 1936. The index is exhaustive.

830. HINTON, RICHARD J. *Arizona Ghost Trails.* Fort Davis, Texas: Frontier Book Co., 1969. lx pp.
    Reprint of the first 60 pages of the Appendix to Hinton's *The Hand-Book to Arizona,* 1878, giving general information on minerals and transportation including tables of distances.

831. ————. *The Hand-Book to Arizona; Its Resources, History, Towns, Mines, Ruins and Scenery.* Tucson: Arizona Silhouettes, 1954. 431 pp. and appendices, illus., tables, maps.
    Facsimile of the original edition of 1878. Limited to 1000 numbered copies.

832. ————. *1000 Old Arizona Mines.* Toyahville, Texas: Frontier Book Company, 1962. 126 pp., illus., maps.

A facsimile reprint of pages 77–167 of Hinton's *Hand-Book to Arizona* (San Francisco, 1878) with the addition of poorly reproduced and unrelated photographs from the Rose-Bartholomew collection.

833. HISLOP, HERBERT R. *An Englishman's Arizona: The Ranching Letters of Herbert R. Hislop, 1876–1878.* Introduction by Bernard L. Fontana. Tucson: Overland Press, 1965. 74 pp., illus.

Five hundred and ten copies printed by Carl Hertzog. Hislop and the Vails were early owners of the Empire Ranch near Sonoita.

834. HJALMARSON, H. W. AND E. S. DAVIDSON. *Anticipated Changes in the Flow Regimen Caused by the Addition of Water to the East Verde River, Arizona.* Phoenix: Arizona State Land Department, 1966. (Water-Resources Report no. 28) 10 pp., map, diags.

835. HOBSON, RICHARD. *Navaho Acquisitive Values.* Cambridge, Massachusetts: Peabody Museum, 1954. (Peabody Papers, vol. 42, no. 3) 37 pp.

836. HOCHDERFFER, GEORGE. *Flagstaff Whoa! The Autobiography of a Western Pioneer.* Flagstaff: Museum of Northern Arizona, 1965. 171 pp., illus.

Printed at the Northland Press.

837. HODGE, CARLE AND WILLIAM S. KING. *Indians and the Law: An Analysis of Tribal Governments and Tribal Courts in Arizona.* Appendix on tribal jurisdiction by Jerry Angle. Tucson: University of Arizona Bureau of Ethnic Research, 1958. 99 pp., tables.

838. HODGE, GENE MEANY. *The Kachinas Are Coming: Pueblo Indian Kachina Dolls with Related Folktales.* Flagstaff, Arizona: Northland Press, 1967. 129 pp., illus.

Facsimile of the 1936 edition.

839. HODGE, HIRAM C. *Arizona As It Was.* Chicago: Rio Grande Press, 1962. 273 pp., map.

Issued first in 1877 with the title *Arizona As It Is.* A facsimile reprint.

840. HODGE, WILLIAM H. *The Albuquerque Navahos.* Ann Arbor: University Microfilms, 1967. 227 pp.

A Brandeis University doctoral dissertation.

841. ————. *The Albuquerque Navajos.* Tucson: University of Arizona Press, 1969. (Anthropological Papers of the University of Arizona, no. 11) 76 pp., maps.

Based on the author's dissertation listed above.

842. HOFFMEISTER, DONALD F. AND WOODROW W. GOODPASTER. *The Mammals of the Huachuca Mountains, Southeastern, Arizona.* Urbana: University of Illinois Press, 1954. (Illinois Biological Monographs vol. 24, no. 1) 152 pp., illus., tables.

843. HOGAN, RAY. *Johnny Ringo: Gentleman Outlaw.* London: John Long, 1964. 192 pp.
Fictionalized biography.

844. HOLMES, GEORGE H., JR. *Investigation of Beryllium Deposits in the Northern Virgin Mountains of Clark County, Nev., and Mohave County, Ariz.* [Washington]: U. S. Bureau of Mines, 1964. (Report of Investigations no. 6572) 30 pp., tables, diags.

845. HOOK, RALPH C., JR. *Pinal County Tourism Study: Basic Data.* Prepared for the Pinal County Development Board. Tempe: Arizona State University Bureau of Business Services, 1961. 28 pp., tables.

846. ———— AND JACK KEKAR. *Basic Economic Data, Tempe, Arizona.* Tempe: Arizona State University, Bureau of Business Research and Services, 1965. 18 pp., tables, maps, diags.

847. ———— AND PAUL D. SIMKINS. *Recent Migrations to Arizona.* [Tempe]: Arizona State University Bureau of Business Services, 1959. 17 pp., tables, diags.

848. *Hopi Customs, Folklore, and Ceremonies.* Flagstaff: Northern Arizona Society of Science and Art, 1954. (Museum of Northern Arizona Reprint Series no. 4) 79 pp., illus.
Articles reprinted from *Museum Notes* and *Plateau.*

849. *Hopi Hearings, July 15–30, 1955.* [Phoenix]: Bureau of Indian Affairs, Phoenix Area Office, [1955?]. 412 pp.
Hearings by a team appointed by the Commissioner of Indian Affairs.

850. *Hopi History.* Flagstaff: Northern Arizona Society of Science and Art, 1951. (Museum of Northern Arizona Reprint Series no. 2) 57 pp., illus., maps.

851. *Hopi Indian Agriculture and Food.* Flagstaff: Northern Arizona Society of Science and Art, 1954. (Museum of Northern Arizona Reprint Series no. 5) 26 pp., illus., maps.

852. *Hopi Indian Arts and Crafts.* Flagstaff: Northern Arizona Society of Science and Art, 1951. (Museum of Northern Arizona Reprint Series no. 3) 102 pp., illus.
This and items 850 and 851 are articles reprinted from *Museum Notes* and *Plateau.*

853. HOPKINS, ERNEST J. *Financing the Frontier: A Fifty Year History of the Valley National Bank.* Phoenix: Arizona Printers, 1950. 271 pp., illus.

854. ———— AND ALFRED THOMAS, JR. *The Arizona State University Story.* Phoenix: Southwest Publishing Co., 1960. 305 pp., illus.

855. HORN, TOM. *Life of Tom Horn, Government Scout and Interpreter, Written by Himself, Together with His Letters and Statements by His Friends: a Vindication.* Introduction by Dean Krakel. Norman: University of Oklahoma Press, 1964. 277 pp.
Originally issued in Denver in 1904.

856. HORNADAY, WILLIAM T. *Campfires on Desert and Lava.* New York: Arno Press, 1967. 366 pp., illus., maps.
Facsimile of the 1908 edition, except that the color plates of the original are here reproduced in black and white. A volume in the Abercrombie & Fitch Library.

857. HOROWITZ, WAYNE S. *Occupational Licensing in Arizona.* Tempe: Arizona State University Bureau of Government Research, 1966. (Research Study no. 10) 64 pp., tables.

858. HOWELL, PAUL W. *The Cenozoic Geology of the Chetoh Country, Arizona and New Mexico.* Ann Arbor: University Microfilms, 1959. 329 pp.
A University of Arizona doctoral dissertation.

859. HOWES, PAUL G. *The Giant Cactus Forest and Its World.* New York: Duell, Sloan and Pearce, 1954. 258 pp., illus.
A biological study of the saguaro country.

860. [Huachuca City] *Background Studies for Planning, Huachuca City, Arizona.* Scottsdale, Arizona: Van Cleve Associates, 1968. 36 pp., tables, maps.

861. [Huachuca City] *Community Development Plan, Huachuca City, Arizona.* Scottsdale, Arizona: Van Cleve Associates, 1968. 37 pp., tables, maps.

862. HUDDLE, JOHN W. AND ERNEST DOBROVOLNY. *Devonian and Mississippian Rocks of Central Arizona.* Washington: U. S. Geological Survey, 1952. (Professional Paper no. 233-D) pp. 67–112, illus., maps.

863. HUFF, LYMAN C. AND OTHERS. *Mineral Resources of the Sycamore Canyon Primitive Area, Arizona.* Washington: U. S. Geological Survey, 1966. (Bulletin no. 1230-F) 19 pp., maps, diags.
This is the canyon in Coconino and Yavapai counties.

864. HUGHES, J. DONALD. *The Story of Man at Grand Canyon.* Flagstaff: KC Publications, 1967. (Grand Canyon Natural History Association Bulletin no. 14) 195 pp., illus.
Indians, Spaniards, American explorers, pioneers, tourists.

865. HUGHSTON, CAROLINE M. *Old Fort Lowell.* Tucson: Arizona Silhouettes, 1964. unpaged, illus.
A reissue of the original pamphlet of 1911.

866. HUMPHREY, ROBERT R. *Arizona Range Grasses, Their Description, Forage Value and Management.* Tucson: University of Arizona Agricultural Experiment Station, 1958. (Bulletin 298) 104 pp., illus.

Enlarged revision of item 874.

867. ———. *Arizona Range Resources II, Yavapai County; a Study in Range Condition.* Tucson: University of Arizona Agricultural Experiment Station, 1950. (Bulletin no. 229) 55 pp., illus., map.

868. ———. *The Desert Grassland; A History of Vegetational Change and an Analysis of Causes.* Tucson: University of Arizona Agricultural Experiment Station, 1959. (Bulletin no. 299) 62 pp., illus.

Reprinted from *The Botanical Review,* vol. 24, April, 1958.

869. ———. *The Desert Grassland: A History of Vegetational Change and an Analysis of Causes.* [Tucson]: University of Arizona Press, [1968?]. 74 pp., illus.

A slight revision of preceding item, with some additional illustrations.

870. ———. *Forage Production on Arizona Ranges III, Mohave County; a Study in Range Condition.* Tucson: University of Arizona Agricultural Experiment Station, 1953. (Bulletin no. 244) 79 pp., illus., map.

871. ———. *Forage Production on Arizona Ranges IV, Coconino, Navajo, Apache Counties; a Study in Range Condition.* Tucson: University of Arizona Agricultural Experiment Station, 1955. (Bulletin no. 266) 84 pp., illus., maps.

872. ———. *Forage Production on Arizona Ranges V, Pima, Pinal and Santa Cruz Counties.* Tucson: University of Arizona Agricultural Experiment Station, 1960. (Bulletin no. 302) 137 pp., illus., maps.

873. ———, comp. *Your Range — Its Management.* Tucson: Arizona Agricultural Extension Service and Agricultural Experiment Station, 1959. (Special Report, no. 2) 35 pp., illus.

874. ——— AND OTHERS. *Common Arizona Range Grasses, Their Description, Forage Value and Management.* Tucson: University of Arizona Agricultural Experiment Station, 1952. (Bulletin no. 243) 102 pp., illus.

875. HUNGERFORD, CHARLES R. *The Factors Affecting the Breeding of Gambel's Quail,* Lophortyx Gambelli Gambelli *Gambel, in Arizona.* Ann Arbor: University Microfilms, 1960. 103 pp.

A University of Arizona doctoral dissertation.

876. HUNT, CHARLES B. *Cenozoic Geology of the Colorado Plateau.* Washington: U. S. Geological Survey, 1956. (Professional Paper no. 279) 99 pp., illus., maps.

877. HUNT, FRAZIER. *Cap Mossman, Last of the Great Cowmen.* New York: Hastings House, 1951. 277 pp., illus.
Illustrations by Ross Santee.

878. HUNTER, ZENA M. *The Story of the Colorado River.* Garden City, New York: Doubleday, 1960. 64 pp., illus.
Prepared with the cooperation of the American Geographical Society. Popularly written.

879. ILIFF, FLORA G. *People of the Blue Water: My Adventures among the Walapai and Havasupai Indians.* New York: Harper, 1954. 271 pp., illus.

880. *Indian Affairs and the Indian Reorganization Act, the Twenty Year Record.* Edited by William H. Kelly. Tucson: University of Arizona, 1954. 39 pp.
Symposium at the 1953 meeting of the American Anthropological Association, Tucson. Participants: Allan Harper, John Collier, Theodore Haas, Clarence Wesley, Clyde Kluckhohn, Joseph Garry.

881. *Indian Education and the Classroom Teacher.* Edited by Robert A. Roessel, Jr. [Tempe]: Arizona State University Indian Education Center, 1961. 317 pp., illus.
Cover title. "Material prepared by members of a graduate workshop in Indian education."

882. *Indians in Non-Indian Communities: A Survey of Navajo and Hopi Indians . . . .* [Window Rock, Arizona?: U. S. Indian Service], 1953.

883. *Indians of Arizona.* Washington: U. S. Bureau of Indian Affairs, 1966. 24 pp., illus.
Brief background and current conditions among the tribes. A good introduction.

884. [Indians] *Tribal Directory.* [Phoenix]: Arizona Commission of Indian Affairs, 1962. 27 pp.
Officials, council members, committees.

885. *Industrial Development in Arizona, Manufacturing, 1966–1968.* Phoenix: Employment Security Commission of Arizona, 1969. 77 pp., tables.
Supplemented by a report for 1969 issued in October of that year, 30 pp.

886. *Industrial Zoning in Arizona.* Prepared by the Bureau of Business Services, Arizona State College. Phoenix: Arizona Development Board, 1955. 72 pp., maps.

887. INMAN, DEE. *Don't Fence Me In: Life of a Teacher in a Navajo School Hogan.* New York: Exposition Press, 1955. 167 pp., illus.

888. *Inside Phoenix.* The Arizona Republic and the Phoenix Gazette. 1954–. illus., tables, maps.

    An annual report on buying habits of Phoenix families expanded to include a wide variety of statistics. A supplement, *Profiles,* has been published since 1968, and presents "a demographic look at the area's consumer households . . . ."

889. *Intermountain Union List of Serials: Part I, Periodicals.* Prepared under the editorial direction of Donald W. Johnson and Larry Larason. Tempe: Arizona State Library Association, 1969. 793 pp.

    Includes holdings of thirteen Arizona and two Nevada libraries. Part II, to include all serials scheduled for 1970 publication.

890. *Interstate Compact Defining the Boundary Between the States of Arizona and California.* [Sacramento?: California Office of State Printing, 1965]. 195 pp., illus., maps.

891. *The Invisible Minority: Report of the NEA-Tucson Survey on the Teaching of Spanish to the Spanish Speaking.* Washington: National Education Association, 1966. 39 pp.

892. IRERI, DUNSTAN. *California-Arizona Economic Interdependence and Their Water Use Patterns.* Ann Arbor: University Microfilms, 1967. 235 pp.

    A University of California, Davis, doctoral dissertation.

893. ITULE, BRUCE. *John Clum's Tombstone Epitaph.* Tombstone, Arizona: Tombstone Epitaph, 1969. 32 pp., illus.

894. IVES, JOSEPH C. *Report upon the Colorado River of the West.* New York: Da Capo Press, 1969. various paging, illus., maps.

    A facsimile reprint of House Executive Document 90, 36th Congress, 1st Session, 1861. This was Ives' report on his exploration of the river in 1857 and 1858.

895. ———. *Steamboat up the Colorado.* From the journal of Lieutenant Joseph Christmas Ives, United States Topographical Engineers, 1857–1858. Edited by Alexander L. Crosby. Boston: Little, Brown, 1965. 112 pp., illus.

    Ives' account condensed.

896. JACKSON, EARL. *Tumacacori's Yesterdays.* Santa Fe: Southwestern Monuments Association, 1951. (Popular Series no. 6) 96 pp., illus.

897. ——— AND SALLIE P. VAN VALKENBURGH. *Montezuma Castle Archeology, Part I.* Globe, Arizona: Southwestern Monuments Association, 1954. (Technical Series vol. 3, part 1) 86 pp., illus., tables.

    Appendix by Katharine Bartlett. For part 2 see item 960.

898. JAEGER, EDMUND C. *The North American Deserts.* Stanford: Stanford University Press, 1957. 308 pp., illus.

899. JAHNS, PATRICIA. *The Frontier World of Doc Holliday, Faro Dealer from Dallas to Deadwood.* New York: Hastings House, 1957. 305 pp.

900. JAHNS, RICHARD H. *Pegmatite Deposits of the White Picacho District, Maricopa and Yavapai Counties, Arizona.* Tucson: University of Arizona, 1952. (Arizona Bureau of Mines Bulletin no. 162) 105 pp., illus., maps.

901. JAMES, MILO S. AND OTHERS. *Physical Land Conditions in the Fredonia Soil Conservation District, Arizona.* Tucson: University of Arizona Agricultural Experiment Station, 1950. (Bulletin no. 231) 19 pp., illus., map.

902. JEFFERS, JO. *Ranch Wife.* Garden City, New York: Doubleday, 1964. 273 pp., illus.
Illustrations by Ross Santee.

903. JEFFREY, JOHN M. *Adobe and Iron: The Story of the Arizona Territorial Prison.* La Jolla, California: Prospect Avenue Press, 1969. 113 pp., illus.

904. JEMMETT, JOE P. *Geology of the Northern Plomosa Mountain Range, Yuma County, Arizona.* Ann Arbor: University Microfilms, 1966. 169 pp.
A University of Arizona doctoral dissertation.

905. JENKINS, MINNIE B. *Girl from Williamsburg.* Richmond, Virginia: Dietz Press, 1951. 343 pp., illus.
Teaching among the Navajos and Mohaves in the early years of this century.

906. JENNINGS, JAMES R. *The Freight Rolled.* San Antonio: Naylor, 1969. 99 pp., illus.
Freighting in northern Arizona at the turn of the century.

907. JEROME, STANLEY E. *Reconnaissance Geologic Study of the Black Canyon Schist Belt, Bradshaw Mountains, Yavapai and Maricopa Counties, Arizona.* Ann Arbor: University Microfilms, 1957. 160 pp.
A University of Utah doctoral dissertation.

908. JETT, STEPHEN C. *Tourism in the Navajo Country: Resources and Planning.* Window Rock, Arizona: The Navajo Tribe, 1967. 184 pp., maps.
A somewhat updated reprinting of the author's doctoral dissertation of the same title published by University Microfilms in 1964.

909. ———— AND OTHERS. *Navajo Wildlands: "As Long As the Rivers Shall Run." Photographs by Philip Hyde.* San Francisco: Sierra Club, 1967. (Exhibit Format Series no. 14) 160 pp., illus., map.

910. JOHANSEN, H. C. *Directory of Arizona Labor Unions, 1958.* Phoenix: Arizona State Employment Service, 1958. various paging.

911. JOHNSON, ALFRED E. *The Development of Western Pueblo Culture.* Ann Arbor: University Microfilms, 1966. 124 pp.
A University of Arizona doctoral dissertation. The area is southeast Arizona and southwest New Mexico.

912. —— AND WILLIAM WASLEY. *Pottery and Artifact Provenience Data from Sites in the Painted Rocks Reservoir, Western Arizona.* Madison: Society for American Archaeology and University of Wisconsin Press, 1961. (Archives of Archaeology no. 18) 52 pp. on two microcards.

913. JOHNSON, BRODERICK H. *Navaho Education at Rough Rock.* Rough Rock, Arizona: Rough Rock Demonstration School, 1968. 212 pp., illus.

914. JOHNSON, GEORGE H. AND JOHN H. SOULÉ. *Measurements of Surface Subsidence, San Manuel Mine, Pinal County, Arizona.* [Washington]: U. S. Bureau of Mines, 1963. (Report of Investigations no. 6204) 36 pp., illus., maps, diags.

915. JOHNSON, H. CYRIL. *Scenic Guide to Arizona.* Susanville, California: The Author, 1957. 56 pp., illus., maps.

916. JOHNSON, PHILLIP W. *Water in the Coconino Sandstone for the Snowflake-Hay Hollow Area, Navajo County, Arizona.* Washington: U. S. Geological Survey, 1962. (Water-Supply Paper no. 1539-S) 46 pp., illus., maps, tables.

917. —— AND R. B. SANDERSON. *Spring Flow into the Colorado River, Lees Ferry to Lake Mead, Arizona.* Phoenix: Arizona State Land Department, 1968. (Water-Resources Report no. 34) 26 pp., tables, diags.

918. JOHNSTON, DENIS F. *An Analysis of Sources of Information on the Population of the Navajo.* Washington: U. S. Bureau of American Ethnology, 1966. (Bulletin 197) 220 pp., tables, maps.
A revision of the author's doctoral dissertation presented to the American University in 1961 and published by University Microfilms.

919. JONES, DANIEL W. *Forty Years among the Indians: a True Yet Thrilling Narrative of the Author's Experiences among the Natives.* Los Angeles: Westernlore Press, 1960. 378 pp.
Edition limited to 1000 copies. The experiences of a Mormon peacemaker among western tribes including those in Arizona. Originally published in 1890.

920. JONES, DOUGLAS M. *Economic Aspects of Agricultural Use of Colorado River Water in Yuma County, Arizona.* Ann Arbor: University Microfilms, 1969. 128 pp.
A University of Arizona doctoral dissertation.

921. JONES, LOUIS T. *Highlights of Puebloland.* San Antonio: Naylor, 1968. 107 pp., illus.
A rather superficial look at some aspects of Pueblo and Navajo culture.

922. JONES, RICHARD D. *An Analysis of Papago Communities, 1900–1920.* Ann Arbor: University Microfilms, 1969. 651 pp.
A University of Arizona doctoral dissertation. ". . . attempts to make explicit the meaning of community, as commonly understood in social science and to apply this definition to Papago culture in order to identify and describe various types of Papago communities." Abstract. The period covered is 1900 to 1920.

923. JONES, STANLEY A. *The Arizona-Sonora Desert Museum.* Photographs by Richard Jepperson. [Tucson]: Sun Country Publications, 1965. 32 pp., illus.
Brief text and over 100 color photographs.

924. ———. *Arizona's Future, Nineteen Hundred and Sixty-four.* Phoenix: Republican State Committee of Arizona, 1964. 240 pp., illus.
County by county survey, many colored illustrations.

925. ———. *Spectacular Lake Powell.* Photographs by Richard Jepperson. Tucson: Sun Country Publications, [1967]. 40 pp.
Color photographs, brief text.

926. JORDAN, GILBERT L. *An Evaluation of Pelleted Seeds for Seeding Arizona Rangelands.* Tucson: University of Arizona Agricultural Experiment Station, 1967. (Technical Bulletin no. 183) 32 pp., tables, illus.

927. JUDD, B. IRA. *Principal Forage Plants of Southwestern Ranges.* [Fort Collins, Colorado]: U. S. Forest Service, Rocky Mountain Forest and Range Experiment Station, 1962 (Station Paper no. 69). 93 pp., illus.
Chiefly Arizona and New Mexico.

928. JUDD, NEIL M. *Men Met along the Trail: Adventures in Archaeology.* Norman: University of Oklahoma Press, 1968. 162 pp., illus.
Autobiography.

929. *Junior College Survey of Cochise County.* Tempe: Arizona State University, 1961. 70 pp., tables, diags.

930. *Junior College Survey of Pinal County.* Tucson: University of Arizona Bureau of School Services, 1963. 67 pp., maps, tables, diags.

931. *Junior Colleges for Maricopa County.* Tempe: Arizona Educational Consultants, 1963. 66 pp., tables, diags.

932. [Junior Colleges] *Report of the Junior College Survey Committee to the Twenty-Fourth Legislature.* Phoenix, 1958. 93 pp., tables.

933. JUSTICE, KEITH E. *Ecological and Genetical Studies of Evolutionary Forces Acting on Desert Populations of* Mus Musculus. Tucson: Arizona-Sonora Desert Museum, 1962. 68 pp., illus., tables, diags. Technical.

934. *Juvenile Deliquency among Indians.* 84th Congress, 1st Session. Senate Judiciary Committee. Committee Print. Washington, 1955. 239 pp.
    Interim report.

935. *Juvenile Delinquency (Indians).* Hearings. 84th Congress, 1st Session, Senate Judiciary Committee, Subcommittee to Investigate Juvenile Delinquency. Washington, 1955. 479 pp.
    Relates in part to Arizona Indians.

936. *Juvenile Delinquency (Plural Marriages).* Hearings. 84th Congress, 1st Session. Senate Judiciary Committee. Subcommittee to Investigate Juvenile Delinquency. Washington, 1955. 135 pp.
    Hearings held at Phoenix and at Short Creek.

937. [Juvenile Delinquency] *Report of Juvenile Delinquency Study Committee to Legislative Council, State of Arizona.* [Phoenix?], 1954. 40, xxii pp.

938. KAIGLER, CLAYTON O. AND OTHERS. *Arizona Cotton Production Survey, 1959–1960.* [Phoenix?]: Employment Security Commission of Arizona, [1961?]. 87 pp., illus., tables.

939. KALT, WILLIAM D., JR. *Awake the Copper Ghosts! The History of Banner Mining Company and the Treasure of Twin Buttes.* [Tucson?]: Banner Mining Company, 1968. 99 pp., illus.
    For private distribution only.

940. KAM, WILLIAM. *Geology and Ground-Water Resources of the McMullen Valley, Maricopa, Yavapai, and Yuma Counties, Arizona.* Phoenix: Arizona State Land Department, 1961. (Water Resources Report no. 8) 72 pp., illus., tables, maps.

941. ———— AND OTHERS. *Basic Ground-Water Data for Western Salt River Valley, Maricopa County, Arizona.* Phoenix: Arizona State Land Department, 1966. (Water-Resources Report no. 27) 72 pp., maps, tables, diags.

942. KAUT, CHARLES R. *The Western Apache Clan System, Its Origin and Development.* Albuquerque: University of New Mexico Press, 1957. (Publications in Anthropology no. 9) 99 pp., illus.
    The Western Apache as defined here are the tribes which settled on the upper drainage of the Salt and Gila rivers in Arizona.

943. KEARNEY, THOMAS H. AND ROBERT H. PEEBLES. *Arizona Flora.* Berkeley: University of California Press, 1951. 1032 pp., illus. Based on the authors' *Flowering Plants and Ferns of Arizona.* (U. S. Department of Agriculture Miscellaneous Publication no. 432, 1942.)

944. ———— AND ————. *Arizona Flora.* Second edition with supplement by John Thomas Howell, Elizabeth McClintock, and collaborators. Berkeley: University of California Press, 1960. 1085 pp., illus.
The basic text of 1032 pp. remains unchanged.

945. KEARNS, FRANK W. *A Preliminary Study of Tourist Expenditures in Arizona.* Tempe: Arizona State University Bureau of Business Research and Services, 1968. (Arizona Industry Reports no. 7) 44 pp., tables.

946. KELEHER, WILLIAM A. *Turmoil in New Mexico, 1846–1868.* Santa Fe: Rydal Press, 1952. 534 pp.
Contains much on Arizona — California Column, Apaches and Navajos, the Long Walk.

947. KELLEY, VINCENT C. *Regional Tectonics of the Colorado Plateau and Relationship to the Origin and Distribution of Uranium.* Albuquerque: University of New Mexico Press, 1935. (Publications in Geology no. 5) 120 pp., illus., maps.

948. KELLY, LAWRENCE C. *The Navajos and Federal Policy, 1913–1935.* Ann Arbor: University Microfilms, 1962. 423 pp.
A University of New Mexico doctoral dissertation.

949. ————. *The Navajo Indians and Federal Indian Policy, 1900–1935.* Tucson: University of Arizona Press, 1968. 221 pp., tables, maps.
A revision of the author's doctoral dissertation.

950. KELLY, ROGER E. AND JOHN O. CRAMER. *American Indians in Small Cities: A Survey of Urban Acculturation in Two Northern Arizona Communities.* Flagstaff: Northern Arizona University Department of Rehabilitation, 1966. (Rehabilitation Monographs no. 1) 90 pp., illus., maps.
Indians living in Flagstaff and Winslow.

951. KELLY, WILLIAM H. *The Changing Role of the Indian in Arizona.* Tucson: University of Arizona Agricultural Extension Service, 1958. (Circular 263) 26 pp., illus., tables, maps.

952. ————. *Indians of the Southwest; a Survey of Indian Tribes and Indian Administration in Arizona.* Tucson: University of Arizona Bureau of Ethnic Research, 1953. 129 pp.
First annual report of the Bureau. After the 2nd (item 995) series was discontinued.

953. KELLY, WILLIAM H. *The Papago Indians of Arizona, a Population & Economic Study.* Tucson: University of Arizona Bureau of Ethnic Research, 1963. 129 pp., tables, maps.

954. ———. *A Study of Southern Arizona School-Age Indian Children, 1966–1967.* Tucson: University of Arizona Bureau of Ethnic Research, 1967. 38 pp.

955. KELSO, PAUL. *A Decade of Council-Manager Government in Phoenix.* [Phoenix]: City Council, 1960. 66 pp.

956. ———. *State Budget Preparation in Arizona: Fifty-two Years of Legislative Budget Making.* Tucson: University of Arizona Press, 1964. (Institute of Government Research, Arizona Government Studies no. 1) 30 pp.

957. KENNEDY, MARGUERITE W. *My Home on the Range.* Boston: Little, Brown, 1951. 341 pp., illus.
Southern Arizona ranch life.

958. KENNEDY, MARY J. *Tales of a Trader's Wife (Life on the Navajo Indian Reservation) 1913–1938.* Albuquerque?: [The Author], 1965. 61 pp., illus.

959. KENT, KATE P. *The Cultivation and Weaving of Cotton in the Prehistoric Southwestern United States.* Philadelphia: American Philosophic Society, 1957. (Transactions of the American Philosophic Society, new series, vol. 47, part 3.) pp. 457–732, illus., tables, maps.

960. ———. *Montezuma Castle Archeology, Part 2, Textiles.* Globe, Arizona: Southwestern Monuments Association, 1955. (Technical Series vol. 3, part 2) 102 pp., illus., diags.
For part 1 see item 897.

961. ———. *The Story of Navaho Weaving.* Phoenix: Heard Museum of Anthropology and Primitive Arts, 1961. 47 pp., illus., maps.
Handsomely illustrated with color photographs of blankets from the Heard Museum collection.

962. KERBY, ROBERT L. *The Confederate Invasion of New Mexico and Arizona, 1861–1862.* Los Angeles: Westernlore Press, 159 pp., illus., maps.
Limited edition of 850 copies.

963. KESTER, GERALD AND OTHERS. *Soil Survey of the Holbrook-Show Low Area, Arizona.* Washington: U. S. Department of Agriculture, Soil Conservation Service, and University of Arizona Agricultural Experiment Station, [1964]. (1956 Series, no. 22) 79 pp., illus., tables, maps.

964. KEW, GEORGE. *DeGrazia in Chiaroscuro.* Tucson: Photocenter, 1963. unpaged, illus.
Photographs. No text.

965. KEYTON, CLARA Z. *Tourist Camp Pioneering Experiences.* Chicago: Adams Press, 1960. 152 pp.
Operating a tourist camp 1925–1940 in a northern Arizona town designated as "Adobeville." Disjointed and repetitious.

966. KHALAF, JASSIM M. *The Water Resources of the Lower Colorado River Basin.* Chicago: [University of Chicago], 1951. (Department of Geography, Research Paper no. 22) 2 vols., illus., maps.

967. KIDWELL, RICHARD A. *An Investigation of Selected Factors Related to Drop-Out Students in the College of Business and Public Administration, University of Arizona, with Implications for Terminal Business Education.* Ann Arbor: University Microfilms, 1959.
A title like this could only belong to a doctoral dissertation. This one was committed at the University of Arizona.

968. KIERSCH, GEORGE A. AND OTHERS. *Mineral Resources, Navajo-Hopi Reservations, Arizona-Utah.* Tucson: University of Arizona Press, 1955–56. 3 vols.

969. KILLIAN, J. L. *Common Reptiles of Arizona.* [Phoenix]: Arizona Game and Fish Department, [1954]. 16 pp., illus.
Popular pamphlet.

970. KIMBER, BENJAMIN J. *Grand Canyon Deeps; Words Written by Mortals and Immortals.* Modesto, California: Roadrunner Guidebooks and Research, 1960. 64 pp., illus.
Fine black-and-white photographs with quotations from writings on the canyon.

971. KING, JEFF. *Where the Two Came to Their Father: A Navaho War Ceremonial.* Text and paintings recorded by Maud Oakes; commentary by Joseph Campbell. Second edition. Princeton: Princeton University Press, 1969. (Bollingen Series no. 1) 55 pp., 18 loose plates.
Originally issued by Pantheon Books in 1943. In the present edition the text has been rearranged, revised, and reset and the plates have been reduced in size.

972. *Kingman-Needles Power Contracts.* Hearings. 84th Congress, 1st Session. Senate Interior and Insular Affairs Committee. Washington, 1955. 144 pp.

973. KINO, EUSEBIO FRANCISCO. *Correspondencia del P. Kino con los Generales de la Compañiá de Jesús, 1682–1707.* Mexico: Editorial Jus, 1961. (Testimonia Historica, num. 5) 95 pp.
All the extant correspondence with the Generals of the Society of Jesus; 300 copies printed.

974. ———. *Kino Escribe a la Duquesa: Correspondencia del P. Eusebio Francisco Kino con la Duquesa de Aveiro y Otros Documentos.* Por Ernest J. Burrus, S. J. Madrid, José Porrúa Turanzas, 1964. (Colección Chimalistac no. 18) 536 pp., illus., maps.

975. KINO, EUSEBIO FRANCISCO. *Kino Reports to Headquarters; Correspondence of Eusebio F. Kino, S. J. from New Spain with Rome.* Edited and translated by Ernest J. Burrus, S. J. Rome: Institutum Historicum Societatis Jesu, 1954. 135 pp., supplement of 12 plates, maps.

976. ⸺. *Kino Writes to the Duchess: Letters of Eusebio Francisco Kino, S. J., to the Duchess of Aveiro.* Translated and edited by Ernest J. Burrus, S. J. Rome and St. Louis: Jesuit Historical Institute, 1965. (Sources and Studies for the History of the Americas, vol. 1) 290 pp., illus., maps.
    A translation of the letters in item 974, with the text of the non-Spanish letters but omitting the other documents in the Madrid edition.

977. ⸺. *Kino's Plan for the Development of Pimería Alta, Arizona & Upper California: A Report to the Mexican Viceroy.* Translated and annotated by Ernest J. Burrus, S. J. Tucson: Arizona Pioneers' Historical Society, 1961. 70 pp.
    Five hundred copies.

978. *Kino, a Commemoration.* Tucson: Arizona Pioneers' Historical Society, 1961. unpaged, illus.
    "A Short Assessment" by Patricia P. Paylore, bibliography by Donald M. Powell, and sketches by Ted De Grazia. Commemorative booklet issued for the 1961 Arizona Historical Convention.

979. [Kino] *Acceptance of the Statue of Eusebio Francisco Kino Presented by the State of Arizona.* 89th Congress, 1st Session, House Document no. 158. Washington, 1965. 47 pp., illus.
    Proceedings in the rotunda of the Capitol on February 14, 1965. Contains an address by Ernest J. Burrus, "Kino's Vision of the Future."

980. KIPP, J. B. *The Colorado River.* Los Angeles: Muir Dawson, 1950. 7 pp.
    Reprint of a newspaper account of James White's raft voyage; 180 copies issued.

981. KIRSCH, HANS CHRISTIAN. *Die Spur der Navahos: Leben und Geschichte eines indianischen Volkes.* Recklinghausen, Germany: Georg Bitter Verlag, 1969. 146 pp., illus.

982. KISTER, L. R. AND W. F. HARDT. *Salinity of the Ground Water in Western Pinal County, Arizona.* Washington: U. S. Geological Survey, 1966. (Bulletin no. 1819-E) 21 pp., maps, diags.

983. *Kitt Peak National Observatory.* Tucson, 1960. unpaged, illus., maps.
    Pamphlet for the visitor.

984. *Kitt Peak National Observatory.* Tucson: [The Observatory?], 1965. unpaged.
    Handsome illustrated booklet explaining the functions of the observatory.

985. KLAH, HASTEEN. *Myth of Mountain Chant.* Told by Hasteen Klah, and *Beauty Chant.* Told by Hasteen Gahni. Recorded and retold by Mary C. Wheelwright. Santa Fe: Museum of Navajo Ceremonial Art, 1951. (Bulletin no. 5) 22 pp.

986. KLINCK, RICHARD E. *Land of Room Enough and Time Enough.* Albuquerque: University of New Mexico Press, 1953. 135 pp., illus.
    All about Monument Valley.

987. KLUCKHOHN, CLYDE. *Navaho Witchcraft.* Boston: Beacon Press, [1962]. 254 pp.
    Originally published in 1944 as vol. 22, no. 2 of the Papers of the Peabody Museum at Harvard.

988. ———. *The Ramah Navaho.* Washington: U. S. Bureau of American Ethnology, 1966. (Bulletin no. 196, Anthropological Papers no. 79) pp. 327–77; tables.

989. ———. *To the Foot of the Rainbow.* Glorieta, New Mexico: Rio Grande Press, 1967. 276 pp.
    Subtitle: "A tale of twenty-five hundred miles of wandering on horseback through the Southwest enchanted land." A facsimile of the 1927 original without the illustrations.

990. ——— AND DOROTHEA LEIGHTON. *The Navaho.* Revised ed. Revisions by Lucy H. Wales and Richard Kluckhohn. Garden City, New York: Doubleday, 1962. 355 pp., illus.
    A Doubleday Anchor paperback published in cooperation with the American Museum of Natural History. Originally published in 1946.

991. KNEALE, ALBERT H. *Indian Agent.* Caldwell, Idaho: Caxton Printers, 1950. 429 pp., illus., maps.
    Deals, in part, with the Navajos and Pimas.

992. KNIPE, THEODORE. *The Javelina in Arizona: a Research and Management Study.* Phoenix: Arizona Game and Fish Department, [1957]. (Wildlife Bulletin no. 2) 96 pp., illus., maps, diags.

993. *Know Your County.* Phoenix: League of Women Voters of Phoenix, 1953. unpaged.
    Primer of Maricopa County government. Revised occasionally.

994. KNOWLTON, CLARK S., ed. *Indian and Spanish American Adjustments to Arid and Semiarid Environments.* Lubbock: Texas Technological College, 1964. (Committee on Desert and Arid Zone Research, Contribution no. 7) 89 pp., illus., maps, diags.
    Papers presented at a symposium of the American Association for the Advancement of Science. Contains material on Pima, Navajo, and Apache land use.

995. KRAUS, BERTRAM S. *Indian Health in Arizona: a Study of Health Conditions among Central and Southern Arizona Indians*. Tucson: University of Arizona Bureau of Ethnic Research, 1954. 164 pp., illus., tables, maps, diags.
      Bonnie M. Jones, collaborator. Covers only reservations under jurisdiction of the Phoenix Area Office Bureau of Indian Affairs. Second and last report of the bureau. See item 952.

996. KRIEGER, MEDORA H. *Geology of the Prescott and Paulden Quadrangles, Arizona*. Washington: U. S. Geological Survey, 1965. (Professional Paper no. 467) 127 pp., illus., tables, maps, diags.

997. KROEBER, ALFRED L. AND MICHAEL J. HARNER. *Mohave Pottery*. Berkeley: University of California Press, 1955. (Anthropology Records vol. 16, no. 1) 30 pp., illus.

998. KRUTCH, JOSEPH W. *The Desert Year*. New York: William Sloane, 1952. 270 pp., illus.
      Perhaps the most distinguished Arizona book of the decade 1950–1960. Reissued in paper by Viking Press, 1960.

999. ———. *Grand Canyon, Today and All Its Yesterdays*. New York: William Sloane, 1958. 276 pp.
      Reissued in paper in 1968.

1000. ———. *The Voice of the Desert, a Naturalist's Interpretation*. New York: William Sloane, 1955. 223 pp., illus.
      Reissued in paper in 1968.

1001. KUHN, PAUL J. *Oil and Gas in the Four Corners*. Amarillo, Texas: National Petroleum Bibliography, 1958. 298 pp., maps, diags.

1002. KURTZ, KENNETH. *Literature of the American Southwest; a Selective Bibliography*. Los Angeles: Occidental College, 1956. 63 pp.

1003. KURTZ, RONALD J. *Role Change and Cultural Change: The Canyoncito Navaho Case*. Ann Arbor: University Microfilms, 1964. 316 pp.
      A University of New Mexico doctoral dissertation.

1004. [Kyrene] *Proposed General Development Plan for the Kyrene Industrial District*. [Phoenix]: Maricopa County Planning and Zoning Department, 1961. 26 pp., maps.

1005. [Labor] *Nature of the Nonagricultural Labor Supply in Arizona*. [Phoenix]: Arizona State Employment Service, 1951. 31 pp., tables.

1006. [Labor] *Post-Season Farm Labor Report for . . . State of Arizona*. [Phoenix]: Arizona State Employment Service, 1952–
      Annual. Title varies.

1007. LADD, JOHN. *The Structure of a Moral Code: A Philosophical Analysis of Ethical Discourse Applied to the Ethics of the Navaho Indians.* Cambridge: Harvard University Press, 1957. 474 pp.

1008. LAIDLEY, RICHARD A. *An X-ray Fluorescent Analysis Study of the Distribution of Selected Elements Within the Hopi Buttes Volcanics, Navajo County, Arizona.* Ann Arbor: University Microfilms, 1966. 136 pp.
A University of Arizona doctoral dissertation.

1009. *Land of Arizona: Twenty-One Years of Progress, 1942–1963.* [Phoenix?]: Arizona Association of Soil Conservation Districts, [1963?]. 39 pp., illus.
Soil conservation in Arizona. Some text, many pictures.

1010. LANDGRAF, JOHN L. *Land-Use in the Ramah Area of New Mexico.* Cambridge, Massachusetts: Peabody Museum, 1954. (Peabody Papers vol. 42, no. 1) 97 pp., maps.

1011. LANDGREN, NORMAN E. AND JAMES S. ST. CLAIR. *The Influence of Some Factors on Prices in the Phoenix Cotton Market.* Tucson: University of Arizona Agricultural Experiment Station, 1956. (Report no. 142) 14 pp., tables.

1012. LANE, ALBERT M. AND E. B. STANLEY. *Cattle Feeding in Arizona.* Tucson: Arizona Agricultural Extension Service, 1959. (Circular 131, revised) 20 pp., illus.

1013. LANE, JAMES A. *A Birdwatcher's Guide to Southeastern Arizona.* Distributed by L & P Photography, Santa Ana, Calif., 1965. 46 pp.
Subtitle: "A travel guide designed especially for the vacationing birdwatcher. Precise mileage and directions are given for finding the best birding spots." No pictures!

1014. LANGLEY, ELIZABETH G. *The Development of a Literacy Program among the Navaho Indians.* Ann Arbor: University Microfilms, 1958. 235 pp.
A New York University doctoral dissertation.

1015. LARSON, EMIL L. *Arizona School Law.* Tucson: University of Arizona Press, 1964. 202 pp.

1016. ———. *Survey of Northern Yuma County High School, 1954.* [Tucson?], 1954. 60 pp., tables, maps.

1017. LAWRENCE, BARBARA. *Mammals Found at the Awatovi Site.* Part I. *Cranial Skeletal Characteristics of Deer, Pronghorn and Sheep-Goat with Notes on Bos and Bison.* Part II. Cambridge, Massachusetts: Peabody Museum, 1951. (Peabody Papers vol. 35, no. 3) 43 pp., illus.

1018. LAYNE, JOSEPH G. *Western Wayfaring: Routes of Exploration and Trade in the American Southwest.* Los Angeles: Automobile Club of Southern California, 1954. 63 pp., maps.
For the traveler.

1019. LEASE, PAUL V. *Pimas, Dead Padres and Gold.* Menlo Park, California: Archivist's Press, 1965. 61 pp., illus., map.
Subtitle: "Intrigue, death and lost riches in the Pima uprising of 1751." Prepared from Lease's journal and notes.

1020. LEE, ARTHUR M. *Engineering and Technology in Arizona.* Flagstaff: Northern Arizona University, 1968. 274 pp., tables, diags.
Subtitle: "A report on the education of engineers, technicians, and skilled craftsmen and the educational needs of industry."

1021. LEE, WESTON AND JEANNE LEE. *Torrent in the Desert.* Flagstaff, Arizona: Northland Press, 1962. [204 pp.], illus., maps.
The Lees did the text as well as the dozens of beautiful color photographs which distinguish this handsome book about the Colorado River.

1022. LEFT HANDED (Navajo Indian). *Son of Old Man Hat: a Navaho Autobiography.* Recorded by Walter Dyk. Lincoln: University of Nebraska Press, 1967. 378 pp.
Originally published in 1938.

1023. LEFT-HANDED MEXICAN CLANSMAN AND OTHERS. *The Trouble at Round Rock.* Introduction by Robert W. Young and William Morgan. [Washington?: U.S. Indian Service], 1952. 88 pp., illus.
"An . . . account of a fight between Agent Shipley and . . . Black Horse has been utilized as a nucleus [for] a fairly detailed . . . account of . . . conditions in the Navajo country a little more than a half century ago."

1024. *Legislation Concerning the Navajo Tribe.* Hearing. 86th Congress, 2nd Session. Joint Committee on Navajo-Hopi Indian Administration. Washington, 1960. 38 pp.

1025. LEHNER, ROBERT E. *Geology of the Clarkdale Quadrangle, Arizona.* Washington: U. S. Geological Survey, 1958. (Bulletin 1021-N) pp. 511–92, maps.

1026. LEIGHTON, ALEXANDER AND DOROTHEA C. LEIGHTON. *The Navaho Door: An Introduction to Navaho Life.* New York: Russell & Russell, 1967. 149 pp., illus., map.
A facsimile of the original of 1944.

1027. LEIGHTON, ELIZABETH ROBY. *The Nature of Cultural Factors Affecting the Success or Failure of Navajo College Students.* Ann Arbor: University Microfilms, 1965. 546 pp.
A University of Arizona doctoral dissertation.

1028. LESURE, THOMAS B. *Adventures in Arizona.* San Antonio: Naylor, 1956. 169 pp., illus.
All about Arizona for the tourist.

1029. ———. *All about Arizona, the Healthful State.* Greenlawn, New York: Harian Publications, 1957. 119 pp.
An *olla podrida* printed on wretched paper. Annual, irregular.

1030. ———. *Sightseeing Arizona from Phoenix and the Valley of the Sun.* Phoenix: Phoenix Chamber of Commerce, [1954?]. 34 pp., maps.
Tour booklet.

1031. LEVINE, ALBERT J., ed. *Snowflake, a Pictorial Review, 1878–1964.* [Snowflake? 1964?]. 128 pp., illus.
Mostly photographs.

1032. LEWIS, BILL. *Fishing in Arizona; a Guide to Available Waters.* Phoenix: Arizona Game and Fish Department, [1959?]. 23 pp., illus.

1033. LEWIS, DOUGLAS D. *Desert Floods: A Report on Southern Arizona Floods of September, 1962.* Tucson: Arizona State Land Department, 1963. (Water Resources Report no. 13) 30 pp., illus., maps.

1034. LEWIS, JERROLD M. *Vocational and Educational Training in Arizona, a Guidance Handbook.* Tempe: Arizona State College, School of Education, 1954. (Bulletin no. 9) 43 pp.
Information about public and private schools.

1035. LEWIS, ROGER AND VIRGIL MEIBERT. *Do You Belong in Amazing Arizona?* [Phoenix]: Published by arrangement with Phoenix Sun Publishing Co., 1960. 95 pp.
Some good information. Poorly printed on cheap paper.

1036. LEYDET, FRANCOIS. *Time and the River Flowing: Grand Canyon.* San Francisco: Sierra Club, 1964. (Sierra Club Exhibit Format Series, no. 8) 176 pp., illus.
A superlatively beautiful book illustrated in full color.

1037. *Libraries in the Southwest: Their Growth, Strengths, Needs.* Edited by Lawrence C. Powell. Los Angeles: University of California Library, 1955. (Occasional Papers no. 3) 70 pp.
Much about Arizona libraries.

1038. *Library Plan for the City of Phoenix: a Long-Range Planning Study.* Phoenix: City Planning Department, 1961. 33 pp., maps, tables.

1039. LIGGETT, WILLAM. *My Seventy-five Years along the Mexican Border.* New York: Exposition Press, 1964, 139 pp.
Bisbee, the Cananea riots, El Paso.

1040. LIGHTHISER, "MARGHERITA." *Tombstone's Helldorado.* Tombstone, Arizona: Tombstone Epitaph, 1969. unpaged, illus.
Photographs of Tombstone's annual celebration.

1041. LIGON, JAMES D. *The Biology of the Elf Owl,* Micrathene Whitneyi. Ann Arbor: University Microfilms, 1967. 158 pp.
A University of Michigan doctoral dissertation.

1042. LINDSAY, ALEXANDER J., JR. AND OTHERS. *Survey and Excavations North and East of Navajo Mountain, Utah, 1959–1962.* Flagstaff: Northern Arizona Society of Science and Art Inc., 1968. (Museum of Northern Arizona Bulletin no. 45, Glen Canyon Series no. 8) 399 pp., illus., tables, diags., 7 maps in pocket.
The area is mostly Utah but the country is Navajo.

1043. LINGENFELTER, RICHARD E. *First through the Grand Canyon.* Los Angeles: Glen Dawson, 1958. (Early California Travel Series 45) 119 pp., illus.
Establishes the claim of James White.

1044. LINK, MARGARET S. *The Pollen Path: A Collection of Navajo Myths Retold.* Psychological comment by Joseph L. Henderson. Stanford: Stanford University Press, 1956. 205 pp., illus.

1045. LINK, MARTIN A., ed. *Navajo: A Century of Progress, 1868–1968.* Window Rock, Arizona: The Navajo Tribe, 1968. 107 pp., illus.

1046. LISITZKY, GENEVIEVE H. *Four Ways of Being Human; an Introduction to Anthropology.* New York: Viking, 1956. 303 pp., illus.
One is the Hopi way.

1047. LISTER, FLORENCE C. AND ROBERT H. LISTER. *Earl Morris & Southwestern Archaeology.* Albuquerque: University of New Mexico Press, 1968. 204 pp., illus., maps.

1048. LISTER, ROBERT H. *The Glen Canyon Survey in 1957.* Salt Lake City: University of Utah Press, 1958. (Department of Anthropology Anthropological Papers no. 30) 57 pp., illus., maps.

1049. LITTLE, ELBERT L., JR. *Southwestern Trees: A Guide to the Native Species of New Mexico and Arizona.* Washington: U.S. Department of Agriculture, 1950. (Agriculture Handbook no. 9) 109 pp., illus., maps.

1050. LIVELY, W. IRVEN. *Ananias of Arizona.* Phoenix: The Author, 1953. 54 pp.
Folklore and tall tales.

1051. ———. *The Mystic Mountains: A History of the Superstition Mountains.* [Phoenix?]: The Author, 1955. 29 pp.

1052. LIVINGSTON, DONALD E. *Geochronology of Older Precambrian Rocks in Gila County, Arizona.* Ann Arbor: University Microfilms, 1969. 277 pp.
A University of Arizona doctoral dissertation.

1053. LOCKETT, H. CLAIBORNE AND LYNDON L. HARGRAVE. *Woodchuck Cave, a Basketmaker II Site in Tsegi Canyon, Arizona.* Flagstaff: Northern Arizona Society of Science and Art, 1953. (Museum of Northern Arizona Bulletin no. 26) 33 pp., illus.

1054. LOCKWOOD, FRANK C. *Pioneer Portraits: Selected Vignettes.* Tucson: University of Arizona Press, 1968. 240 pp., ports.

1055. LOMBARDI, THOMAS P. *Psycholinguistic Abilities of Papago Indian Children.* Ann Arbor: University Microfilms, 1969. 80 pp.
A University of Arizona doctoral dissertation.

1056. LONG, AUSTIN. *Late Pleistocene and Recent Chronologies of Playa Lakes in Arizona and New Mexico.* Ann Arbor: University Microfilms, 1966. 161 pp.
A University of Arizona doctoral dissertation.

1057. LONG, KATHERINE W. AND SAMUEL A. SICILIANO. *Yuma from Hell-Hole to Haven.* Yuma, Arizona: Yuma County Chamber of Commerce, 1950. 63 pp., illus.

1058. LONG, PAUL V., JR. *Archaeological Excavations in Lower Glen Canyon, Utah, 1959–1960.* Flagstaff: Northern Arizona Society of Science and Art Inc., 1966. (Museum of Northern Arizona Bulletin no. 42. Glen Canyon Series no. 7) 80 pp., illus., tables, diags., map.

1059. LONGWELL, CHESTER R. *Reconnaissance Geology Between Lake Mead and Davis Dam, Arizona-Nevada.* Washington: U.S. Geological Survey, 1963. (Professional Paper no. 374-E) 51 pp., illus., tables, maps, diags.

1060. LOOTENS, DOUGLAS J. *Structure and Petrography of the East Side of the Sierrita Mountains, Pima County, Arizona.* Ann Arbor: University Microfilms, 1965. 277 pp.
A University of Arizona doctoral dissertation.

1061. LORENZINI, AUGUST P. *A Study of the Patterns of Communication Used by Fifty Negro and Fifty Spanish-Named Residents of Phoenix, Arizona.* Ann Arbor: University Microfilms, 1963. 442 pp.
A University of Denver doctoral dissertation.

1062. LOVEJOY, EARL M. P. *The Hurricane Fault Zone, and the Cedar Pocket Canyon-Shebit-Gunlock Fault Complex, Southwestern Utah and Northwestern Arizona.* Ann Arbor: University Microfilms, 1964. 260 pp.
A University of Arizona doctoral dissertation.

1063. LOVELACE, LELAND. *Lost Mines and Hidden Treasure.* San Antonio: Naylor, 1956. 252 pp.
Leland Lovelace is the pseudonym of Mrs. J. Lee Lovelace.

1064. LOWE, CHARLES H., ed. *The Vertebrates of Arizona.* Tucson: University of Arizona Press, 1964. 259 pp., illus., maps, tables.
Part 4 is also issued as a separate; see Monson below. Annotated checklists with an extensive illustrated introduction on landscape and habitats.

1065. *Lower Colorado River Basin Project.* Hearings. 89th Congress, 2nd Session. Subcommittee on Irrigation and Reclamation of the House Committee on Interior and Insular Affairs. Washington, 1965, 1966. 2 parts, illus., tables, diags.
Hearings of August and September 1965 and May 1966.

1066. *Lower Colorado River Problems.* Hearings. 85th Congress, 1st Session. Special Subcommittee of the House Committee on Interior and Insular Affairs. Washington, 1958. 131 pp.
Illegal water diversion, squatters, recreation.

1067. LUCCHITTA, IVO. *Cenozoic Geology of the Upper Lake Mead Area Adjacent to the Grand Wash Cliffs, Arizona.* Ann Arbor: University Microfilms, 1967. 274 pp.
A Pennsylvania State University doctoral dissertation.

1068. LUEBBEN, RALPH A. *A Study of Some Off-Reservation Navaho Miners.* Ann Arbor: University Microfilms, 1956. 377 pp.
A Cornell University doctoral dissertation.

1069. LUMMIS, CHARLES F. *Bullying the Moqui.* Edited by Robert Easton and Mackenzie Brown. [Prescott, Arizona]: Prescott College Press, 1968. 132 pp.
Lummis' polemic against the Indian Bureau's attempts to "civilize" the Hopi Indians. Reprinted from *Out West,* April–October 1903, where title was "Bullying the Quaker Indians."

1070. ———. *General Crook and the Apache Wars.* Edited by Turbesé Lummis Fiske, Foreword by Dudley Gordon. Flagstaff, Arizona: Northland Press, 1966. 148 pp., illus.
"Selected dispatches [which] originally appeared in the Los Angeles Times during April and May, 1886."

1071. LUSTER, GERTRUDE. *Well, for the Love of Greg!* San Antonio: Naylor, 1962. 102 pp.
Light-weight account of brief winter sojourn in Phoenix.

1072. LUTRELL, ESTELLE. *Newspapers and Periodicals of Arizona, 1859–1911.* Tucson: University of Arizona, 1950. (General Bulletin no. 15) 123 pp., illus.
Copyright date, 1950; bulletin date 1949! Issued in 1950. History and bibliography.

1073. LYTLE, CLIFFORD M. *The Public Defender in Arizona: A Case Study of State Policy-Making.* Tucson: University of Arizona Press, 1969. (Institute of Government Research, Arizona Government Studies no. 6) 48 pp.

1074. MACALLESTER, DAVID P. *Enemy Way Music; a Study of Social and Esthetic Values as Seen in Navaho Music.* Cambridge: Peabody Museum, 1954. (Papers vol. 41, no. 3) 96 pp., illus.

1075. MACK, LAWRENCE E. *Economic Implications of a Dynamic Land and Water Base for Agriculture in Central Arizona.* Ann Arbor: University Microfilms, 1969. 157 pp.
A University of Arizona doctoral dissertation.

1076. MAGOUN, CREIGHTON F. AND ROBERT J. LETSON. *A Comprehensive Educational Survey of the Sahuarita Public Schools.* [Tucson]: University of Arizona, Bureau of Educational Research and Service, 1969. various paging.

1077. MANJE, JUAN MATEO. *Luz de Tierra Incógnita.* Translated by Harry J. Karns. Tucson: Arizona Silhouettes, 1954. 303 pp., illus., maps.
A translation of part II of Manje's manuscript. At head of title: "Unknown Arizona and Sonora, 1693–1721."

1078. MANLEY, RAY. *Ray Manley's Arizona.* Tucson: Sun Country Publications, 1965. 64 pp., illus.
Color photographs, brief captions.

1079. MANN, DEAN E. *The Politics of Water in Arizona.* Tucson: University of Arizona Press, 1963. 317 pp., illus., maps.
"The policy issues in water development and management and the public machinery through which decisions are made constitute the primary focus of this study." Preface.

1080. MANNING, REGINALD W. *What is Arizona Really Like? A Guide to Arizona's Marvels.* Phoenix: Reganson Cartoon Books, 1968. 117 pp., illus.
Light-hearted guide to places of interest with cartoon illustrations.

1081. *Manpower Directions '75.* [Phoenix?] Employment Security Commission of Arizona, 1967. 42 pp., illus., tables, diags.

1082. *Manpower Outlook '80: Arizona Agriculture.* [Phoenix?]: Employment Security Commission of Arizona, 1968. 40 pp., illus., tables, diags.

1083. *Manpower Requirements and Training Needs Study; Manufacturing and All Industry Summary.* [Phoenix]: Arizona State Employment Service, [1957]. 40 pp., tables.

1084. *Manpower Requirements and Training Needs Study; Phoenix Labor Market Area.* [Phoenix]: Arizona State Employment Service, 1957. 52 pp., tables.

1085. *Manpower Requirements and Training Needs Study; Tucson Labor Market Area.* [Phoenix]: Arizona State Employment Service, 1957. 48 pp., tables.

1086. MANSFIELD-JONES, DOROTHY. *Structure of Desert Vegetation in Two Widely Separated Homoclimatic Areas: Arizona and South Australia.* Ann Arbor: University Microfilms, 1968. 148 pp.
A Duke University doctoral dissertation.

1087. [Maps] *Folio of Geologic and Mineral Maps of Arizona.* Tucson: University of Arizona Press, 1962.
The maps prepared by the Arizona Bureau of Mines and issued between 1957 and 1962 have been gathered in 22 plastic envelopes in a limp leatherette cover. Included are Bulletins 170 and 171 by J. D. Forrester and by Eldred D. Wilson, listed separately.

1088. *Maricopa County Migratory Housing Study.* Phoenix: Arizona State Employment Service, [1958?]. 61 pp., illus., tables.

1089. [Maricopa County] *Atlas of Maricopa County.* [Phoenix]: Arizona State Highway Department, 1960. 42 sheets.
Detailed road and street maps in a spiral binding.

1090. [Maricopa County] *Atlas of Maricopa County.* 1969 edition. [Phoenix]: Arizona Highway Department, [1969]. 61 sheets.
Detailed road and street maps in a spiral binding.

1091. [Maricopa County] *Comprehensive Flood Control Program Report.* [Phoenix?]: Maricopa County Flood Control District, 1963. 80 pp., maps, tables.

1092. [Maricopa County] *Comprehensive Plan for Maricopa County.* [Phoenix]: Maricopa County Planning and Zoning Department, 1963–1967. 3 parts.
Part 1, History, economics, physical features. Part 2, Population, community growth, existing land use. Part 3, Future general land use.

1093. [Maricopa County] *Economic Survey of Eastern Maricopa County.* Tempe: Arizona State College Bureau of Business Services, 1955. (Arizona Counties Economic Survey Series 3) 181 pp., maps, tables, diags.

1094. [Maricopa County] *The Economy of Maricopa County, 1965 to 1980.* Phoenix: Western Management Consultants, Inc., 1965. 337 pp., tables, maps, diags.

1095. [Maricopa County] *Maricopa County Regional Park System Plan.* [Phoenix? 1965?]. 2 vols., illus. tables, maps.
Plan prepared by Sam L. Huddleston & Associates, Denver.

1096. [Maricopa County] *A Report Upon a Proposed General Land Use Plan for Eastern Maricopa County, Arizona.* [Phoenix]: Maricopa County Planning and Zoning Department, 1968. 75 pp., tables, maps.

1097. [Maricopa County] *A Report Upon Mobile Home Parks and Subdivisions.* [Phoenix]: Maricopa County Planning and Zoning Department, 1963. 51 pp., tables, maps, diags.

1098. [Maricopa County] *A Report Upon 1960 Census of Population, Maricopa County.* [Phoenix]: Maricopa County Planning and Zoning Department, 1962. 77 pp., tables, maps, diags.

1099. [Maricopa County] *A Report upon the Land Area Required for Future Urban Uses in Maricopa County, Arizona.* [Phoenix]: Maricopa County Planning and Zoning Department, 1968. 25 pp., tables.

1100. [Maricopa County] *U. S. Census Bureau Tracts for Maricopa County with 1965 Population Counts.* Phoenix: Maricopa Planning and Zoning Department, 1966. 48 pp., tables, maps.

1101. [Maricopa County] *White Tank Mountains Regional Park: Master Development Plan.* [Scottsdale, Arizona: Van Cleve Associates, 1964]. 51 pp., illus., maps.

1102. MARION, JOHN H. *Notes of Travel Through the Territory of Arizona: Being an Account of a Trip Made by General George Stoneman and Others in the Autumn of 1870.* Edited by Donald M. Powell, Tucson: University of Arizona Press, 1965. 62 pp., illus.

1103. MARLATT, ROBERT B. *Races of* Fusarium Oxysporum *F. Lini in Arizona.* Ann Arbor: University Microfilms, 1952. 141 pp.
A University of Arizona doctoral dissertation.

1104. MARLOWE, JAMES I. *Late Cenozoic Geology of the Lower Safford Basin on the San Carlos Indian Reservation, Arizona.* Ann Arbor: University Microfilms, 1961. 247 pp.
A University of Arizona doctoral dissertation.

1105. MARLOWE, TRAVIS. *Superstition Treasures.* Phoenix: Tyler Printing Co., 1965. 64 pp., illus.
The Lost Dutchman and other Superstition mines.

1106. MARSHALL, JOE T., JR. *Birds of the Pine-Oak Woodland in Southern Arizona and Adjacent Mexico.* Berkeley, California: Cooper Ornithological Society, 1957. (Pacific Coast Avifauna no. 32) 125 pp., illus., maps.

1107. MARSHALL, OTTO M. *The Wham Paymaster Robbery.* [Pima, Arizona?], 1967. 79 pp., illus.

1108. MARSHALL, ROBERT H. *Commercial Banking in Arizona: Structure and Performance Since World War II.* Tucson: University of Arizona, College of Business and Public Administration, 1966. 41 pp.

1109. MARSHALL, WILLIAM T. *Arizona's Cactuses.* [Tempe?]: Desert Botanical Garden of Arizona, 1950. (Science Bulletin no. 1) 111 pp., illus.

1110. ———. *Introduction to Desert Plants.* Phoenix: Desert Botanical Garden of Arizona, [1956]. 49 pp., illus.

1111. MARTIN, DOUGLAS D. *An Arizona Chronology: the Territorial Years, 1846–1912.* Tucson: University of Arizona Press, 1963. unpaged.

1112. ———. *An Arizona Chronology: Statehood, 1913–1936.* Edited by Patricia Paylore. Tucson: University of Arizona Press, 1966. unpaged.

1113. ———. *The Earps of Tombstone.* Tombstone: The Tombstone Epitaph, 1959. 65 pp.
   Subtitle: "The truth about the OK Corral gun fight and other events . . . compiled from the files of the Tombstone Epitaph."

1114. ———. *The Lamp in the Desert; the Story of the University of Arizona.* Tucson: University of Arizona Press, 1960. 304 pp., illus.

1115. ———. *Silver, Sex and Six Guns; Tombstone Saga of the Life of Buckskin Frank Leslie.* Tombstone, Arizona: Tombstone Epitaph, 1962. 62 pp., illus.
   Compiled from the files of the *Epitaph.*

1116. ———. *Tombstone's Epitaph.* Albuquerque: University of New Mexico Press, 1951. 272 pp., illus.
   News stories from the *Epitaph* correlated by Douglas Martin.

1117. ———. *Yuma Crossing.* Albuquerque: University of New Mexico Press, 1954. 243 pp.
   History of the Yuma crossing of the Colorado to the time of the railroad.

1118. MARTIN, F. ELLEN. *Bibliography: The Navajo Indians.* Tempe: Arizona State University Indian Education Center, 1968. 40 pp.
   Issued in Ditto form; no statement of scope or purpose given.

1119. MARTIN, HOLLIS K. *School Bonding in Arizona.* Tucson: University of Arizona Bureau of Business and Public Research, 1961. (Special Studies no. 18) 60, 153 pp., tables, maps.
   ". . . intended chiefly as a reference hand book for the . . . public school administrators, in Arizona's 305 school districts . . ."

1120. MARTIN, JOHN H. *The Function and Responsibilities of a State Music Supervisor for the State of Arizona.* Ann Arbor: University Microfilms, 1960. 102 pp.
   A University of Arizona doctoral dissertation.

1121. MARTIN, PAUL SCHULTZ. *The Last 10,000 Years: A Fossil Pollen Record of the American Southwest.* Tucson: University of Arizona Press, 1963. 87 pp., illus., tables, diags., maps.
   The areas studied were the Sulphur Spring Valley and the White Mountains. A revision of the following entry.

1122. —— AND OTHERS. *Southwestern Palynology and Prehistory, the Last 10,000 Years.* [Tucson]: University of Arizona Geochronology Laboratories, 1961. 119 pp. illus., tables.
See preceding entry.

1123. MARTIN, PAUL SIDNEY AND JOHN B. RINALDO. *Excavations in the Upper Little Colorado Drainage, Eastern Arizona.* Chicago: Chicago Natural History Museum, 1960. (Fieldiana: Anthropology, vol. 51, no. 1) 127 pp., illus. diags.

1124. —— AND ——. *Table Rock Pueblo, Arizona.* Chicago: Chicago Natural History Museum, 1960. (Fieldiana: Anthropology, vol. 51, no. 2) pp. 131–298, illus., tables, maps.

1125. —— AND OTHERS. *Chapters in the Prehistory of Eastern Arizona.* Chicago: Chicago Natural History Museum, 1962–67. (Fieldiana: Anthropology, vol. 53, 55, 57) 3 vols., illus., tables, diags.
Archeological reports on sites in the Springerville-Little Colorado area.

1126. —— AND ——. *Documentation for Some Late Mogollon Sites in the Upper Little Colorado Drainage, Eastern Arizona.* Madison: Society for American Archaeology and University of Wisconsin Press, 1960. (Archives of Archaeology, no. 6) 65 pp. on 3 microcards.
Published only on microcards.

1127. —— AND ——. *Mineral Creek Site and Hooper Ranch Pueblo, Eastern Arizona.* Chicago: Chicago Natural History Museum, 1961. (Fieldiana: Anthropology vol. 52) 181 pp., illus.

1128. MARTIN, SAMUEL C. *The Santa Rita Experimental Range.* Fort Collins, Colorado: Rocky Mountain Forest and Range Experiment Station, 1966. (U.S. Forest Service Research Paper RM-22) 24 pp., illus., diags.

1129. ——. *Some Factors Affecting Vegetation Changes on a Semidesert Grass-Shrub Cattle Range in Arizona.* Ann Arbor: University Microfilms, 1964. 136 pp.
A University of Arizona doctoral dissertation.

1130. MARTIN, THOMAS L., JR. *The Effects of Nuclear Weapons on Tucson.* Tucson: University of Arizona Press, 1961. (Engineering Experiment Station Bulletin no. 15, Nuclear Engineering Series no. 1) 30 pp., tables, maps.

1131. MARTIN, WILLIAM E. AND WILLIAM K. GOSS. *Cost-Size Relationships for Southwestern Arizona Cattle Ranches.* Tucson: University of Arizona Agricultural Experiment Station, 1963. (Technical Bulletin no. 155) 38 pp., tables, diags.

1132. MARTIN, WILLIAM E. AND JAMES S. HALL. *Cost-Size Relationships for Central Arizona Dairies.* Tucson: University of Arizona Agricultural Experiment Station, 1962. (Technical Bulletin no. 149) 40 pp., tables.

1133. MASON, BRUCE B. *Arizona General Election Results, 1911–1960.* [Tempe]: Arizona State University Bureau of Government Research, 1961. (Research Study no. 3) 140 pp., tables.
Statistical tables of elections for President, Congressmen, and state officials.

1134. ————. *Congressional Redistricting in Arizona.* Tempe: Arizona State University Bureau of Government Research, [1961]. (Research Study no. 2) 28 pp., tables, maps.
Reissued 1963.

1135. ———— AND HEINZ R. HINK. *Constitutional Government in Arizona.* [Tempe]: Arizona State University, Bureau of Government Research, 1963. 162 pp., tables, diags.

1136. ———— AND ————. *Constitutional Government in Arizona.* Second edition. [Tempe]: Arizona State University, Bureau of Government Research, 1965. 223 pp., tables, diags.
A thorough revision.

1137. ———— AND ————. *Constitutional Government in Arizona.* Third revised edition. [Tempe]: Arizona State University, 1968. 247 pp., illus., tables, diags.

1138. ———— AND ————. *Revision of the Arizona Constitution, a Commentary.* Tempe: Arizona State University Bureau of Government Research, 1961. (Research Study no. 4) 96 pp.

1139. MASON, JOHN A. *The Language of the Papago of Arizona.* Philadelphia: University Museum, University of Pennsylvania, 1950. (Museum Monographs no. 3) 84 pp.

1140. MATLOCK, WILLIAM G. AND OTHERS. *Progress Report on Study of Water in the Santa Cruz Valley, Arizona.* Tucson: University of Arizona Agricultural Experiment Station, 1965. (Report no. 233) 55 pp., tables, diags., maps.
Supplements Schwalen and Shaw, items 1592 and 1593.

1141. MATTHEWS, DAVID S. *The Story of Scottsdale.* Scottsdale, Arizona: The Author, 1965. 60 pp., illus.

1142. MATTHEWS, JOHN I. *The Role of the Department Chairman in Arizona Community Colleges.* Ann Arbor: University Microfilms, 1969. 190 pp.
An Arizona State University doctoral dissertation.

1143. MATTHEWS, WASHINGTON. *Navajo Weavers, Navajo Silversmiths.* Palm Lake, Colorado: Filter Press, 1968. (Wild and Woolly West Books no. 7) 37 pp., illus.
Extracted from the second and third annual reports of the U. S. Bureau of American Ethnology, 1880–1882. Facsimile.

1144. MAUGER, RICHARD L. *A Petrographic and Geochemical Study of Silver Bell and Pima Mining Districts, Pima County, Arizona.* Ann Arbor: University Microfilms, 1966. 156 pp.
A University of Arizona doctoral dissertation.

1145. MAUGHAM, W. DON AND OTHERS. *Salinity Problems in the Lower Colorado River Area.* [Los Angeles?]: Colorado River Board of California, 1962. 27 pp., illus., maps.

1146. MAUGHAN, SCOTT J. *Francisco Garcés and New Spain's Northwestern Frontier, 1763–1781.* Ann Arbor: University Microfilms, 1969. 322 pp.
A University of Utah doctoral dissertation.

1147. MAXSON, JOHN H. *Grand Canyon, Origin and Scenery.* Grand Canyon: Grand Canyon Natural History Association, 1961. (Bulletin no. 13) 31 pp., maps., illus.
Designed for the interested visitor who has no technical background.

1148. MAXWELL, GILBERT S. *Navajo Rugs, Past, Present & Future.* In collaboration with Eugene L. Conrotto. Palm Desert, California: Desert-Southwest Publications, 1963. 72 pp., illus.

1149. MAY, BRUCE T. *Magnetic Properties of Rocks Associated With the New Cornelia Porphyry Copper Deposit, Pima County, Arizona.* Ann Arbor: University Microfilms, 1968. 185 pp.
A University of Arizona doctoral dissertation.

1150. MCALLESTER, DAVID P. *Enemy Way Music: A Study of Social and Esthetic Values as Seen in Navaho Music.* Cambridge, Massachusetts: Peabody Museum, 1954. (Peabody Papers vol. 41, no. 3) 96 pp., illus.
This is also Reports of the Rimrock Project, Values Series no. 3.

1151. MCCLEARY, JAMES ALBERT. *Some Factors Affecting the Distribution of Mosses in Arizona.* Ann Arbor: University Microfilms, 1952. 156 pp.
A University of Michigan doctoral dissertation.

1152. MCCLENEGHAN, THOMAS J. AND CHARLES R. GILDERSLEEVE. *Land Use Contrasts in a Border Economy.* Tucson: University of Arizona Bureau of Business and Public Research, 1964. (Special Study no. 23) 12 pp., illus., table, maps.
A study of Nogales, Arizona and Nogales, Sonora.

1153. McCleneghan, Thomas J. and Philip G. Olson. *Douglas, Arizona, an Economic Report.* Tucson: University of Arizona Bureau of Business Research, 1957. (Special Studies no. 13) 11 pp., illus., tables, diags.

1154. ——— and ———. *Flagstaff, Arizona: Planning for the Future.* Tucson: University of Arizona Bureau of Business and Public Research, 1959. (Special Studies no. 15) 8 pp., illus., maps.

1155. McCombe, Leonard. *Navaho Means People.* Photographs by McCombe; text by Evon Vogt and Clyde Kluckhohn. Cambridge: Harvard University Press, 1951. 159 pp., illus.
  A picture essay on Navajo life with explanatory text.

1156. McCool, Grace. *So Said the Coroner: How They Died in Old Cochise.* [Tombstone, Arizona]: Tombstone Epitaph, 1968. 93 pp.

1157. McCormick, Richard C. *Arizona: Its Resources and Prospects.* Introduction by Sidney B. Brinckerhoff. Tucson: Territorial Press, 1968. 22 pp., map.
  A facsimile of the original of 1865.

1158. McCracken, Robert D. *Urban Migration and the Changing Structure of Navajo Social Relations.* Ann Arbor: University Microfilms, 1968. 406 pp.
  A University of Colorado doctoral dissertation.

1159. McCullough, Edgar J., Jr. *A Structural Study of the Pusch Ridge-Romero Canyon Area, Santa Catalina Mountains, Arizona.* Ann Arbor: University Microfilms, 1963. 107 pp.
  A University of Arizona doctoral dissertation.

1160. McDonald, Charles C. and Gilbert H. Hughes. *Studies of Consumptive Use of Water by Phreatophytes and Hydrophytes Near Yuma, Arizona.* Washington: U.S. Geological Survey, 1968. (Professional Paper no. 486-F) 24 pp., illus., tables, diags., maps.

1161. McDonald, James E. *Cloudiness Over the Southwestern United States and Its Relation to Astronomical Observing.* Tucson: University of Arizona Institute of Atmospheric Physics, 1958. (Scientific Report no. 7) 68 pp., tables, maps.

1162. ———. *Variability of Precipitation in an Arid Region; a Survey of Characteristics for Arizona.* Tucson: University of Arizona Institute of Atmospheric Physics, 1956. (Technical Reports on the Meteorology and Climatology of Arid Regions no. 1) 88 pp., tables, diags.

1163. McDougall, Walter B. *Grand Canyon Wild Flowers.* Flagstaff: Museum of Northern Arizona and The Grand Canyon Natural History Association, 1964. (Museum of Northern Arizona Bulletin no. 43) 259 pp., illus.
  A manual for the identification of more than nine hundred species.

1164. ———. *Seed Plants of Wupatki and Sunset Crater National Monuments.* Flagstaff: Northern Arizona Society of Science and Art, 1962. (Museum of Northern Arizona Bulletin no. 37) 67 pp., illus.
Technical botany.

1165. ——— AND H. S. HASKELL. *Seed Plants of Montezuma Castle National Monument, with Keys for the Identification of Species.* Flagstaff: Northern Arizona Society of Science and Art, 1960. (Museum of Northern Arizona Bulletin, no. 35) 80 pp., illus.

1166. ——— AND ———. *Typical Seed Plants of the Ponderosa Pine Zone.* Flagstaff: Northern Arizona Society of Science and Art, 1959. (Museum of Northern Arizona Bulletin no. 32) 63 pp., illus.

1167. McDOWELL, EDWIN. *Barry Goldwater, Portrait of an Arizonan.* Chicago. Henry Regnery, 1964. 269 pp., illus.
Biographical.

1168. McFARLANE, MARY. *Motorist Guide to the Navajo Indian Reservation.* Gallup, New Mexico: Reservation Publications, 1960. 44 pp., illus., map.

1169. McGAVOCK, E. H. *Basic Ground-Water Data for Southern Coconino County, Arizona.* Phoenix: Arizona State Land Department, 1968. (Water-Resources Report no. 33) 48 pp., maps, tables.

1170. McGEORGE, WILLIAM T. *Fertilization of Field Crops in Arizona.* Tucson: University of Arizona Agricultural Experiment Station, 1953. (Bulletin no. 247) 31 pp., tables, diags.

1171. ———. *Nutrient Status of Grapefruit Orchards as Related to Fruit Quality.* Tucson: University of Arizona Agricultural Experiment Station, 1955. (Report no. 120) 19 pp., tables, diags.

1172. McGLOTHLIN, ROBERT S. *Marketing Hay in Arizona.* Tucson: University of Arizona Agricultural Experiment Station, 1957. (Report no. 162) 16 pp., diags.

1173. ——— AND RAY BARLOW. *Marketing Barley and Grain Sorghum in Arizona.* Tucson: University of Arizona Agricultural Experiment Station, 1958. (Report no. 177) 15 pp., tables, diags.

1174. McGOWAN, JOSEPH C. *History of Extra-Long Staple Cottons.* [El Paso, Texas]: SuPima Association of America and Arizona Cotton Growers Association, 1961. 169 pp., illus., tables.
M. A. thesis, University of Arizona, 1960. Relates in part to Arizona.

1175. McGRATH, G. D. AND OTHERS. *Higher Education of Southwestern Indians with Reference to Success and Failure.* Tempe: Arizona State University, 1962. 275 pp. and 24 unnumbered pp., tables.
A cooperative research project of the U. S. Office of Education.

1176. MCGRATH, G. D. AND OTHERS. *Report of the Survey of Scottsdale Public Schools, November, 1956.* [Tempe: Arizona State University?], 1956. 321 pp., tables, maps.

1177. MCGRATH, JOHN T. *A Handbook for Arizona School Board Members.* Tempe: Arizona State University Bureau of Educational Research 1959. (Research and Service Bulletin no. 4) 79 pp.
For a second edition see item 108.

1178. MCGREGOR, JOHN C. *The Cohonina Culture of Mount Floyd, Arizona.* Lexington: University of Kentucky Press, 1967. (Studies in Anthropology no. 5) 145 pp., illus., diags.

1179. ———. *The Cohonina Culture of Northwestern Arizona.* Urbana: University of Illinois Press, 1951. 158 pp., illus.

1180. ———. *Southwestern Archaeology.* Second edition. Urbana: University of Illinois Press, 1965. 511 pp., illus., maps, diags.
Extensively revised and rewritten. Like the first edition of 1941 it is very largely concerned with Arizona.

1181. MCINTIRE, ELLIOT G. *The Impact of Cultural Change on the Land Use Patterns of the Hopi Indians.* Ann Arbor: University Microfilms, 1969. 278 pp.
A University of Oregon doctoral dissertation.

1182. MCKEE, EDWIN D. *Stratigraphy and History of the Moenkopi Formation of Triassic Age.* New York: Geological Society of America, 1954. (Memoir no. 61) 133 pp., illus., tables, maps.

1183. ——— AND OTHERS, eds. *Evolution of the Colorado River in Arizona.* Flagstaff: Museum of Northern Arizona, 1967. (Museum of Northern Arizona Bulletin no. 44) 67 pp., maps, diags.
Subtitle: "An hypothesis developed at the Symposium on Cenozoic Geology of the Colorado Plateau in Arizona, August 1964."

1184. MCKINNEY, MARION W. *Ned White — Arizona's "Bard of Brewery Gulch."* Denver: Golden Bell Press, 1965. 152 pp., illus.
Fictionalized biography of the author's father with selections from his verse.

1185. MCKINNEY, W. A. AND CARL RAMPACEK. *Acid Curing and Countercurrent Decantation Washing of an Oxidized Copper Ore from Pinal County, Arizona.* [Washington]: U. S. Bureau of Mines, 1960. (Report of Investigations no. 5685) 10 pp., illus., tables.

1186. MCKNIGHT, TOM. *Manufacturing in Arizona.* Berkeley: University of California Press, 1962. (University of California Publications in Geography, vol. 8, no. 4) pp. 289–344, tables, maps, diags.
Survey of structure, attractions, distribution.

1187. MCLOUGHLIN, EMMETT. *People's Padre.* Boston: Beacon Press, 1954. 288 pp., illus.
Autobiography of a former Phoenix priest.

1188. McNARY, JAMES G. *This is My Life.* Albuquerque: University of
New Mexico Press, 1956. 271 pp., illus.
Autobiography of the lumberman for whom McNary is named.

1189. McNITT, FRANK. *The Indian Traders.* Norman: University of
Oklahoma Press, 1962. 393 pp., illus.
The Southwest with emphasis on Arizona and the Navajo traders.

1190. MEADOR, BRUCE AND ROBERT A. ROESSEL, JR. *Havasupai School
Survey.* Tempe: Arizona State University Indian Education
Center, 1962. 80 pp., tables.
Reprinted by the Arizona Commission of Indian Affairs.

1191. ——— AND OTHERS. *Navajo Education Today after Nearly a
Century, 1869–1961.* [Tempe?: Arizona State University?], 1961.
40 pp., tables.
A brief outline prepared for the Fourth Annual Conference on
Navajo Education.

1192. MEANS, FLORENCE C. *Sagebrush Surgeon.* New York: Friendship
Press, 1955. 166 pp.
Clarence Salsbury and the mission hospital at Ganado.

1193. ———. *Sunlight on the Hopi Mesas.* Philadelphia: Judson Press,
1960. 171 pp., illus.
The story of Abigail E. Johnson, Baptist missionary. Pious.

1194. MEARS, BRAINERD, JR. *Cenozoic Faults, Gravels and Volcanics of
Oak Creek Canyon, Arizona.* Ann Arbor: University Microfilms,
1951. 128 pp.
A Columbia University doctoral dissertation.

1195. MEES, QUENTIN M. *Tucson Air Pollution, 1959–1964.* Tucson:
University of Arizona, College of Engineering, [1965]. (Engineering Experiment Station Report no. 7) 41, 8 pp., illus., tables, diags.

1196. ——— AND ROBERT L. WORTMAN. *Preliminary Report, Air Pollution Surveillance Study, Tucson, Arizona.* Tucson: University
of Arizona Engineering Experiment Station, 1960. (Bulletin no.
13, Civil Engineering Series, no. 6) 26 pp. and appendices, tables,
charts.

1197. MELVILLE, ROBERT S. *What are the Factors Which Enhance or
Retard Educational Achievement of Navajo Indian Students in the
Sevier School District?* Ann Arbor: University Microfilms, 1968.
149 pp.
A Utah State University doctoral dissertation.

1198. *Memorial and Affidavits Showing Outrages Perpetrated by the
Apache Indians, in the Territory of Arizona, during the Years
1869 and 1870.* Tucson: Territorial Press, 1964. 32 pp.
A facsimile of the original of 1871; 500 copies printed.

1199. MENAGH, HARRY B. *An Investigation of Navaho Mimicry.* Ann Arbor: University Microfilms, 1963. 378 pp.
A Denver University doctoral dissertation.

1200. *Mental Health and Emotional Stability.* Research report prepared by Northern Arizona University. Phoenix: Arizona Academy, [1968]. 144 pp.
Twelfth Arizona Town Hall, April 1968.

1201. *Mental Health in Arizona.* Phoenix: Arizona Governor's Mental Health Research Committee, 1957. 128 pp., tables, diags.

1202. MERA, HARRY P. *Indian Silverwork of the Southwest, Illustrated.* Globe, Arizona: Dale Stuart King, 1959. 122 pp., illus.

1203. MERRY, EDWARD S. *So You Want To Buy a Navajo Rug?* Gallup, New Mexico: Inter-Tribal Indian Ceremonial Association, [1962?]. 15 pp., illus.
Attractive little pamphlet telling the prospective buyer what to look for.

1204. [Mesa] *A Comprehensive Plan for Mesa, Arizona.* [Phoenix?]: Maricopa County and City of Mesa Planning and Zoning Departments, 1961. 90 pp.

1205. [Mesa] *The Industrial Advantages of Mesa, Arizona.* Phoenix: Western Management Consultants, Inc., 1961. 53 pp., illus., tables, maps.
Subtitle: "A survey of the locational features of Arizona's third largest city."

1206. [Mesa] *An Inventory of Educational Improvement Projects.* Mesa, Arizona: Mesa Public Schools, 1968. 78 pp.

1207. [Mesa] *Report of the Survey, Mesa Public Schools July 1955.* 519 pp., tables, maps.
Irving R. Melbo, editor.

1208. [Mesa] *Report of the Survey of the Mesa Public Schools, September 1961.* Tempe: Arizona State University Bureau of Educational Research and Services, 1961. 646 pp., tables, maps.

1209. *Metropolitan Air Pollution in Arizona.* Prepared jointly by the University of Arizona, Arizona State University, and U.S. Department of Commerce, Weather Bureau. [Tucson?], 1961. 109 pp., tables, diags.

1210. METZGER, DONALD G. *Geology in Relation to Availability of Water Along the South Rim, Grand Canyon National Park, Arizona.* Washington: U.S. Geological Survey, 1961. (Water-Supply Paper no. 1475-C) pp. 105–38, illus., map.

1211. MEYER, LOUIS S. *Federal Aid to Education: Its Impact on Arizona.* Tempe: Arizona State University Bureau of Government Research, 1962. (Research Study no. 5) 36 pp., tables.

1212. ———. *Federal Grants-in-Aid and States' Rights in Arizona.* Ann Arbor: University Microfilms, 1965. 262 pp.
A University of Arizona doctoral dissertation.

1213. MILES, CHARLES H. *Metamorphism and Hydrothermal Alteration in the Lecheguilla Peak Area of the Rincon Mountains, Cochise County, Arizona.* Ann Arbor: University Microfilms, 1966. 104 pp.
A University of Arizona doctoral dissertation.

1214. *Milestones: A History of Seventy-five Years of Progress at the Arizona State Hospital, Phoenix, Arizona, 1887–1962.* [Phoenix, 1962?]. 150 pp., illus.

1215. MILLER, FRED K. *Structure and Petrology of the Southern Half of the Plomosa Mountains, Yuma County, Arizona.* Ann Arbor: University Microfilms, 1966. 173 pp.
A Stanford University doctoral dissertation.

1216. MILLER, JOSEPH. *Monument Valley and the Navajo Country, Arizona-Utah.* New York: Hastings House, 1951. 96 pp.
Photographs and brief text.

1217. ———, ed. *Arizona Cavalcade: The Turbulent Times.* New York: Hastings House, 1962. 300 pp., illus.
Spicy bits from territorial newspaper files. Appropriate illustrations by Ross Santee.

1218. ———. *The Arizona Story.* New York: Hastings House, 1952. 345 pp., illus.
Stories of Arizona's past compiled and edited from original newspaper stories. Illustrated by Ross Santee.

1219. ———. *Arizona: The Last Frontier.* New York: Hastings House, 1956. 350 pp., illus.
Sequel to item 1218 which skimmed the cream. Illustrated by Ross Santee.

1220. MILLER, PETER S. *Secular Change Among the Western Apache, 1940 to 1967.* Ann Arbor: University Microfilms, 1969.
A University of Arizona doctoral dissertation.

1221. MILLER, SHERMAN R. *Tropic of Tucson.* Tucson: Rutz Press, 1964. 142 pp., illus.
About the city and why the author, and a good many other people, like to live there.

1222. MILLIRON, JAMES S. *The Influence of School Business Management Practices on Curriculum in Selected School Districts in Arizona and California.* Ann Arbor: University Microfilms, 1965. 148 pp.
An Arizona State University doctoral dissertation.

1223. MILLS, GEORGE T. *Navaho Art and Culture.* Colorado Springs: Taylor Museum, Fine Arts Center, 1959. 221 pp., illus.
Anthropological study of Navajo drawings.

1224. *Mineral and Water Resources of Arizona.* Tucson: University of Arizona, 1969. (Arizona Bureau of Mines Bulletin no. 180) 638 pp., tables, maps, diags.

1225. *The Mineral Industries of Arizona: a Brief History of the Development of Arizona's Mineral Resources.* Tucson: University of Arizona Press, 1962. (Arizona Bureau of Mines Bulletin no. 169) 20 pp.
Contains a useful chronological record of events related to mining in Arizona.

1226. *Mingus Union High School, Cottonwood-Oak Creek District 6, Verde Elementary District 3 Survey.* [Flagstaff: Northern Arizona University, 1966]. 132 pp., tables, diags.

1227. *Mining in Arizona: Its Past, Its Present, Its Future.* Phoenix: Arizona Department of Mineral Resources, 1953. 22 pp., illus.
Reissued with some revisions in 1958, 1961, and 1964.

1228. MITCHELL, EMERSON BLACKHORSE AND T. D. ALLEN. *Miracle Hill: The Story of a Navaho Boy.* Norman: University of Oklahoma Press, 1967. 230 pp.
A Navajo boy's own written account of his childhood and school years astride two cultures. Revealing and touching.

1229. MITCHELL, JOHN D. *Lost Mines and Buried Treasures along the Old Frontier.* Palm Desert, California: Desert Magazine, 1953. 240 pp., illus.

1230. MITCHELL, OLIVE KIMBALL B. *Life Is a Fulfilling.* Provo, Utah: Brigham Young University Press, 1967. 267 pp., illus.
Subtitle: "The story of a Mormon pioneer woman — Sarah Diantha Gardner Curtis and her part in the colonization of the San Pedro Valley in southern Arizona, the homeland of the powerful and antagonistic Apache."

1231. MITCHELL, WILLIAM H. *Looking at Alhambra through Fifty Years.* [Phoenix?], 1964. 60 pp., illus.
History of the Alhambra School District.

1232. MOELLER, BEVERLEY B. *Phil Swing in Washington: The Boulder Canyon Project Legislation.* Ann Arbor: University Microfilms, 1969. 320 pp.
A University of California at Los Angeles doctoral dissertation.

1233. *The Mojave of the Colorado.* Sausalito, California: Pages of History, 1960. 23 pp., illus.
Subtitle: "The story of the Mojave Indians of the Colorado River and their meetings with the explorers of the Southwest."

1234. MONSON, GALE AND ALLAN R. PHILLIPS. *A Checklist of the Birds of Arizona.* Tucson: University of Arizona Press, 1964. 74 pp.
This is also part 4 of Lowe's *Vertebrates . . .* above.

1235. MOODY, RALPH. *Shaking the Nickel Bush.* New York: W. W. Norton, 1962. 234 pp., illus.
Autobiographical, somewhat fictionalized, amusing account of a cowhand's adventures in Arizona after World War I.

1236. MOORE, DANIEL G. *Enter Without Knocking.* Tucson: University of Arizona Press, 1969. 261 pp., illus.
The author's experiences as a guard at the Arizona State Prison.

1237. ———. *Log of a Twentieth Century Cowboy.* Tucson: University of Arizona Press, 1965. 217 pp., illus.
Cowboy life in Arizona at the end of its golden age.

1238. MOORE, RICHARD T. *Mineral Deposits of the Fort Apache Indian Reservation, Arizona.* Tucson: University of Arizona, 1968. (Arizona Bureau of Mines Bulletin no. 177) 84 pp., tables, maps.

1239. ———. *One Hundred Arizona Minerals.* Tucson: University of Arizona, 1955. (Arizona Bureau of Mines Bulletin no. 165) 31 pp.

1240. ———. *A Structural Study of the Virgin and Beaverdam Mountains, Arizona.* Ann Arbor: University Microfilms, 1967. 137 pp.
A Stanford University doctoral dissertation.

1241. ——— AND ELDRED D. WILSON. *Bibliography of the Geology and Mineral Resources of Arizona, 1848–1964.* Tucson: University of Arizona Press, 1965. (Arizona Bureau of Mines Bulletin no. 173) 321 pp.

1242. MOORHEAD, MAX L. *The Apache Frontier: Jacobo Ugarte and the Spanish-Indian Relations in Northern New Spain, 1769–1791.* Norman: University of Oklahoma Press, 1968. 309 pp.
Ugarte's policy for containment of the Apaches on New Spain's northern frontier, its partial success and ultimate failure.

1243. MOORTEN, PATRICIA AND REX NEVINS. *Desert Plants for Desert Gardens.* Palm Desert, California: Best-West Publications, 1969. 112 pp.
Good manual for those who want relatively carefree gardening.

1244. MORAN, LEO J. *Nonfeed Costs of Arizona Cattle Feeding.* Tucson: Arizona Agricultural Experiment Station, 1959. (Technical Bulletin, no. 138) 20 pp., tables.

1245. ——— AND WALLACE R. GREENE. *Arizona Milk Production Costs.* Tucson: University of Arizona Agricultural Experiment Station, 1960. (Technical Bulletin no. 141) 16 pp., tables.

1246. MOREY, ROY D. *The Governor as Chief Legislator in Arizona.* Ann Arbor: University Microfilms, 1964. 282 pp.
A University of Arizona doctoral dissertation.

1247. MOREY, ROY D. *Politics and Legislation: The Office of Governor in Arizona.* Tucson: University of Arizona Press, 1965. (Institute of Government Research, Arizona Government Studies no. 3) 135 pp.
Published form of the preceding item.

1248. MORRIS, ELIZABETH A. *Basketmaker Caves in the Prayer Rock District, Northeastern Arizona.* Ann Arbor: University Microfilms, 1959. 808 pp.
A University of Arizona doctoral dissertation.

1249. MORROW, ROBERT E. *Mohave County Lawmakers: A Biographical Summary.* Kingman, Arizona: Mohave County Miner, 1968. 35 pp., ports.

1250. MORSS, NOEL. *Archaeological Explorations on the Middle Chinlee, 1925.* New York: Kraus Reprint Corporation, 1964. (Memoirs of the American Anthropological Association, no. 34) 41 pp., illus.
Originally published in 1927.

1251. MOSER, DON AND JERRY COHEN. *The Pied Piper of Tucson.* New York: New American Library, 1967. 211 pp., illus.
The notorious Charles Schmid murder case.

1252. *Mountain Men, 1804–1954.* Williams, Arizona: Bill Williams Mountain Men, 1954. 32 pp., illus.
Another edition with title *Mountain Men, 1804–1955* is numbered vol. 2. There is some variation in text. No more published?

1253. MOWRY, SYLVESTER. *Memoir of the Proposed Territory of Arizona.* Tucson: Territorial Press, 1964. 30 pp., map.
A facsimile of the original of 1857.

1254. MUENCH, JOYCE R. AND JOSEF MUENCH. *Grand Canyon, a Pictorial Interpretation.* New York: Hastings House, 1950. 101 pp., illus.
Black and white photographs.

1255. MULCH, ERNEST E. AND WILLIAM C. GAMBLE. *Game Fishes of Arizona.* [Phoenix]: Arizona Game and Fish Department, [1953]. 19 pp., illus.
Popular pamphlet with some color illustrations.

1256. MULLANE, WILLIAM H., ed. *Apache Raids: News About Indian Activity in the Southwest as Reported in the Silver City* Enterprise, *November, 1882 Through August, 1886.* [Silver City, New Mexico?], 1968. 95 pp., illus.
Stories from the *Enterprise* and dispatches from other papers in Arizona and New Mexico.

1257. *Municipal Election Manual.* Phoenix: League of Arizona Cities and Towns, 1966. 47 pp.

1258. MUNSELL, MARVIN R. *Land and Labor at Salt River: Household Organization in a Changing Economy.* Ann Arbor: University Microfilms, 1967. 386 pp.
A University of Oregon doctoral dissertation. A study of the Pima Indians of the Salt River Indian Reservation.

1259. MURBARGER, NELL. *Ghosts of the Adobe Walls.* Los Angeles: Westternlore Press, 1964. 398 pp., illus.
Subtitle: "Human interest and historical highlights from 400 ghost haunts of old Arizona."

1260. MURPHY, JAMES M. *The Spanish Legal Heritage in Arizona.* Tucson: Arizona Pioneers' Historical Society, 1966. 46 pp. (Arizona History Series no. 1)
Specifically water and marital rights.

1261. MYERS, JOHN MYERS. *Doc Holliday.* Boston: Little, Brown, 1955. 287 pp.

1262. ———. *I, Jack Swilling, Founder of Phoenix, Arizona.* New York: Hastings House, 1961. 308 pp.
Written as if by Swilling while he was in the penitentiary at Yuma. Fictionalized biography.

1263. MYRICK, DAVID F. *Pioneer Arizona Railroads.* Golden, Colorado: Colorado Railroad Museum, 1968. 29 pp.

1264. *The Myth and Prayers of the Great Star Chant and the Myth of the Coyote Chant.* Recorded by Mary C. Wheelwright and edited by David P. McAllester. Santa Fe: Museum of Navajo Ceremonial Art, 1956. (Navajo Religion Series vol. 4) 190 pp., illus.

1265. *National Forest Facts, Southwestern Region.* Albuquerque: U. S. Forest Service, 1954–?
Annual. 1954? to 1957; no more published.

1266. *Native Plants and Animals as Resources in Arid Lands of the Southwestern United States.* Edited by J. Linton Gardner. Flagstaff, Arizona, 1966. (Committee on Desert and Arid Zones Research, Southwestern and Rocky Mountains Division, American Association for the Advancement of Science, Contribution no. 8) 80 pp.
Symposium held at Flagstaff, May 1965. Much material on Arizona.

1267. *The Natural History of the Southwest.* Edited by William A. Burns. New York: Franklin Watts, Inc., 1960. 141 pp., illus.
Contributors are William H. Woodin, Merwin W. Larson, Lewis W. Walker, and Peggy P. Larson of the Arizona-Sonora Desert Museum.

1268. *The Natural Resources of Arizona.* Washington: U. S. Department of Interior, 1963. 52 pp., illus.

1269. *Navajo County, Arizona, Industrial and Commercial Summary.* [Phoenix?]: Yavapai County Chambers of Commerce and Arizona Development Board, [1962?]. 20 pp., tables.

1270. *Navaho Ethnographic Notes.* Flagstaff: Northern Arizona Society of Science and Art, 1954. (Museum of Northern Arizona Reprint Series no. 6) 105 pp., illus.
    Articles reprinted from *Museum Notes* and *Plateau.* Cover title: "Navaho Customs: A Booklet of the History, Beliefs and Knowledge of Navaho Indians."

1271. . . . *Navajo-Hopi Indian Administration.* 85th Congress, 1st Session, Joint Committee on Navajo-Hopi Administration. Committee Print. Washington, 1958. 68 pp., map.
    At head of title, "Memorandum from the chairman." Hearings held at Gallup on road development on the reservations.

1272. [Navajo Indians] *Record of the Special Advisory Committee of the Navajo Tribal Council, February 27, 1960.* [Window Rock, Arizona? 1960?]. 50 pp.
    Verbatim record of a meeting with a group of state legislators. Mimeographed.

1273. [Navajo Indians] *Treaty Between the United States of America and the Navajo Tribe of Indians: With a Record of the Discussions That Led To Its Signing.* Flagstaff, Arizona: KC Publications, 1968. 26 pp.
    The treaty of 1868 which ended the captivity at Bosque Redondo.

1274. *Navajo Tribal Code.* Orford, New Hampshire: Equity Publishing Corp. 1962. 2 vols.

1275. *Navajo Tribal Council Resolutions, 1922–1951.* [Washington: Bureau of Indian Affairs, 1952]. 701 pp.

1276. *Navaho Urban Relocation Research.* [Boulder: University of Colorado Institute of Behavioral Science], 1964–
    A series of mimeographed publications chiefly concerned with the sociological and psychological implications of Navajo relocation in Colorado. The reports are not listed separately in this bibliography.

1277. *The Navajo Yearbook.* Window Rock, Arizona: Navajo Agency, 1952–1961.
    Title varies. Originally titled *Planning in Action.* Valuable compilation of information on all phases of tribal life today. Eight volumes issued between 1952 and 1961. No more published.

1278. *Navajoland USA: First Hundred Years, 1868–1968.* Edited by Perry Allen. Window Rock, Arizona: The Navajo Tribe, 1968. 60 pp., illus.
    History, government, and other matters.

1279. [Navajo Indians] *You Asked about the Navajo: Education, Health and Economic Problems of the Navajo.* Washington: Bureau of Indian Affairs, [1957]. 42 pp.
Revision of a pamphlet published in 1949. Reprinted with minor changes in 1958.

1280. NEFF, DON J. *The Effects of Clipping on the Vigor of Big Game Browse Plants and Related Studies in the Arizona Chaparral.* Ann Arbor: University Microfilms, 1964. 128 pp.
An Oregon State University doctoral dissertation.

1281. NELSON, AARON G. *Costs and Returns for Major Field Crops in Central Arizona by Size of Farm.* Tucson: University of Arizona Agricultural Experiment Station, 1965. (Technical Bulletin no. 174) 71 pp., tables.

1282. ———— AND P. THOMAS COX. *Water Priority Rights and Their Effect on Farm Planning in the San Carlos Irrigation and Drainage District in Central Arizona.* Tucson: University of Arizona Agricultural Experiment Station, 1968. (Technical Bulletin no. 184) 48 pp., tables, maps, diags.

1283. ———— AND CHARLES D. BUSCH. *Cost of Pumping Irrigation Water in Central Arizona.* Tucson: University of Arizona Agricultural Experiment Station, 1967. (Technical Bulletin no. 182) 44 pp., tables.

1284. NELSON, RONALD A. *Analogs of Yuma Climate in North America.* Natick, Massachusetts: U. S. Army Quartermaster Research and Development Command, 1957. (Environmental Protection Research Division RER-12) 21 pp., maps.

1285. ————. *Comparison of Yuma Test Station and Yuma Weather Bureau Meteorological Records, 1952 through 1956.* Natick, Massachusetts: U. S. Army Quartermaster Research and Engineering Command, 1957. (Research Study Report RER-16) 23 pp., diags.

1286. [NENTUIG, JUAN BAUTISTA.] *Rudo Ensayo by an Unknown Jesuit Padre, 1763.* Translated by Eusebio Guiteras. Tucson: Arizona Silhouettes, 1951. 151 pp., illus.
A description of conditions in Sonora and southern Arizona. Edition limited to 500 copies.

1287. NEWBURN, H. K. AND M. M. CHAMBERS. *Higher Education in Arizona.* Tempe: Arizona State University Bureau of Educational Research and Services, 1967. (Educational Services Bulletin no. 20) 28 pp.

1288. NEWCOMB, FRANC J. *Hosteen Klah, Navaho Medicine Man and Sand Painter.* Norman: University of Oklahoma Press, 1964. 227 pp., illus.
History of a family of Navajo Indians through four generations based on interviews and first-hand knowledge.

1289. ———. *Navaho Folk Tales.* Santa Fe: Museum of Navaho Ceremonial Art, 1967. 203 pp., illus.

1290. ———. *Navaho Neighbors.* Norman: University of Oklahoma Press, 1966. 236 pp., illus.
Recollections of friends and neighbors during twenty-five years at the Blue Mesa trading post.

1291. ——— AND OTHERS. *A Study of Navajo Symbolism.* Cambridge, Massachusetts: Peabody Museum, 1956. (Peabody Papers vol. 32, no. 3) 100 pp., illus.

1292. NEWHALL, NANCY. *Mission San Xavier del Bac.* Photographs by Ansel Adams, drawings by Edith Hamlin. San Francisco: 5 Associates, 1954. 71 pp., illus.
Expanded from an article in *Arizona Highways,* April, 1954.

1293. NEWMAN, WILLIAM L. *Distribution of Elements in Sedimentary Rocks of the Colorado Plateau — a Preliminary Report.* Washington: U. S. Geological Survey, 1962. (Bulletin no. 1107-F) pp. 337–445, maps.

1294. NEWTON, C. T. *Report on Survey for Flood Control, Gila River Camelsback Reservoir Site to Salt River, Ariz. Gila River Basin, Ariz. and N. Mex.* Los Angeles: U. S. Army Corps of Engineers, 1957. Various paging, illus., tables, maps, aerial photographs.

1295. NEWTON, CHARLES H. *The Reason Why Place Names in Arizona Are So Named!* Phoenix: Charles H. Newton Publishing Company, 1954. 47 pp.

1296. NICHOL, ANDREW A. *The Natural Vegetation of Arizona.* Tucson: University of Arizona Agricultural Experiment Station, 1952. (Technical Bulletin no. 127) pp. 189–230, illus., map.
Revision of Technical Bulletin no. 68, 1937.

1297. NICHOLS, DALE. *The Story of Carlos Jácome.* Tucson: The Pioneer Press, 1955. unpaged, illus.
Illustrations by the author. Issued to commemorate the opening of the new Jácome store.

1298. NIMS, FRANKLIN A. *The Photographer and the River, 1889–1890: The Colorado Cañon Diary of Franklin A. Nims with the Brown-Stanton Railroad Survey Expedition.* Edited by Dwight L. Smith. Santa Fe: Stagecoach Press, 1967. 75 pp., illus.
First printing limited to 600 copies.

1299. *1950 Arizona Cotton Harvest; a Study of Hand and Machine Picking* . . . . [Phoenix]: Arizona State Employment Service, [1951?]. 40 pp., tables.

1300. NININGER, HARVEY H. *Arizona's Meteorite Crater, Past, Present, Future.* Sedona, Arizona: American Meteorite Museum, 1956. 232 pp., illus.

1301. NIX, LONNIE E. *Promotion of Higher Education Within Arizona Indian Groups.* Ann Arbor: University Microfilms, 1964. 217 pp. An Arizona State University doctoral dissertation.

1302. [NOGALES] *Comprehensive Plan . . . Nogales, Santa Cruz County, Arizona.* [Phoenix?]: Gonzales Associates, [196–?]. 3 vols., illus., tables, maps.
Vol. 1, Population, housing and the economy.
Vol. 2, Existing land use and historical summary.
Vol. 3, Proposed zoning ordinances.

1303. *Norman's Who's Who for Arizona, 1951–1952; Combined with Arizona Today.* Portland, Oregon: R. O. Norman, 1952. 288 pp., illus.
No more published?

1304. NÚÑEZ CABEZA DE VACA, ALVAR. *The Journey of Alvar Nuñez Cabeza de Vaca.* Translated from his own narrative by Fanny Bandelier. Chicago: Rio Grande Press, 1964. 231 pp.
A facsimile? of the original published in 1905.

1305. NYE, THOMAS S. *The Relationship of Structure and Alteration to Some Ore Bodies in the Bisbee (Warren) District, Cochise County, Arizona.* Ann Arbor: University Microfilms, 1968. 244 pp.
A University of Arizona doctoral dissertation.

1306. *Oak Creek Canyon, Its Geology, Plant and Animal Life.* Flagstaff: Northern Arizona Society of Science and Art, 1962. Unpaged, illus.
A useful pamphlet containing a log of the canyon for the interested traveler.

1307. OAKS, GEORGE W. *Man of the West; Reminiscences of George Washington Oaks, 1840–1917.* Recorded by Ben Jaasted; edited and annotated by Arthur Woodward. Tucson: Arizona Pioneers' Historical Society, 1956. (Pamphlet Series no. 1) 65 pp.
Limited edition of 400 copies designed and printed by Lawton Kennedy.

1308. O'BRYAN, AILEEN. *The Dîné; Origin Myths of the Navaho Indians.* Washington: U. S. Bureau of American Ethnology, 1956. (Bulletin no. 163) 187 pp., illus.

1309. OCH, JOSEPH. *Missionary in Sonora: The Travel Reports of Joseph Och, S. J., 1755–1767.* Translated and annotated by Theodore E. Treutlein. San Francisco: California Historical Society, 1965. 196 pp., maps.
Not about, but sheds much light on Spanish southern Arizona.

1310. O'CONNOR, JACK. *Horse and Buggy West: A Boyhood on the Last Frontier.* New York: Alfred A. Knopf, 1969. 302 pp., illus.
Tempe in the years before World War I, clearly recollected in tranquility and without sentimentality.

1311. ODENS, PETER. *Fire over Yuma: Tales from the Lower Colorado.* Yuma, Arizona: Southwest Printers, 1966. 59 pp., illus.
Historical sketches from the Yuma area.

1312. OFFICER, JAMES E. *Indians in School: A Study of the Development of Educational Facilities for Arizona Indians.* Tucson: University of Arizona Bureau of Ethnic Research, 1956. (American Indian Series no. 1) 148 pp., illus.

1313. ————. *Sodalities and Systematic Linkage: the Joining Habits of Urban Mexican-Americans.* Ann Arbor: University Microfilms, 1964. 470 pp.
The study was made in Tucson. A University of Arizona doctoral dissertation.

1314. *Oil, Gas and Helium in Arizona; Its Occurrence and Potential.* [Phoenix?]: Arizona Development Board for the Arizona Oil and Gas Conservation Commission, [1962?]. 108 pp., illus., maps, tables, diags.

1315. O'KANE, WALTER C. *The Hopis: Portrait of a Desert People.* Norman: University of Oklahoma Press, 1953. 267 pp., illus.
Handsome photographic portraits in full color.

1316. ————. *The Intimate Desert.* Tucson: University of Arizona Press, 1969. 143 pp., illus.
Sketches of desert life.

1317. ————. *Sun in the Sky.* Norman: University of Oklahoma Press, 1950. 261 pp., illus.
A book about the Hopi.

1318. *Older Citizens in Our Town: A Report of a Fact-Finding Survey with Recommendations by the Committee on the Aged.* Tucson: Tucson Community Council, [1960]. 20 pp.

1319. OLIN, GEORGE. *Animals of the Southwest Deserts.* Globe, Arizona: Southwestern Monuments Association, 1954. (Popular Series no. 8) 112 pp., illus., maps.

1320. ————. *Mammals of the Southwest Deserts.* Globe, Arizona: Southwestern Monuments Association, 1959. (Popular Series no. 8) 112 pp., illus., maps.
A second edition of item 1319 with slight revisions. A third edition was issued in 1965.

1321. ————. *Mammals of the Southwest Mountains and Mesas.* Globe, Arizona: Southwestern Monuments Association, 1961. (Popular Series no. 9) 126 pp., illus., maps.

1322. OLSON, ALAN P. *An Evaluation of the Phase Concept in Southwestern Archaeology As Applied to the Eleventh and Twelfth Century Occupations at Point of Pines, East Central Arizona.* Ann Arbor: University Microfilms, 1959. 641 pp.
A University of Arizona doctoral dissertation.

1323. OLSON, GEORGE C. AND JOHN T. LONG, JR. *Arizona's Natural Resources.* Prepared by Arizona Research Consultants. Phoenix: Arizona Development Board, [1958?]. 47 pp.
Mineral resources.

1324. *The Oncoming Tide.* Report of the Arizona White House Conference on Education, 1955. [Phoenix, 1956?]. 23 pp., tables, diags.

1325. OPLER, MORRIS. *An Apache Life-Way: The Economic, Social, and Religious Institutions of the Chiricahua Indians.* New York: Cooper Square Publishers, 1965. 500 pp., illus.
A reprint of the original of 1941.

1326. *Origin and Destination Traffic Survey, 1951, of Mesa, Arizona.* [Phoenix]: Arizona Highway Department, [1953?]. 77 pp., maps, diags.

1327. *The Other Side of the Mountain.* Tucson: Southern Arizona Bank and Trust Company, 1954. 80 pp., illus.
Subtitle: "A guide to the highways and byways of the Grand Canyon State."

1328. *Our Cultural Heritage and Arizona Highways.* [Tucson: Arizona State Museum, 1966]. unpaged, illus.
Highway salvage archaeology.

1329. *Our Friends the Navahos.* By members of the Young People's Fellowship, Church of the Holy Faith. Santa Fe, 1957. 32 pp., illus.

1330. PACK, ARTHUR N. *We Called it Ghost Ranch.* Abiquiu, New Mexico: Ghost Ranch Conference Center, 1965. 148 pp.
Arizona and New Mexico, dude ranching and hotel keeping, civic work and conservation.

1331. PADFIELD, HARLAND I. *Technological and Social Change in Farm Industries of Arizona.* Ann Arbor: University Microfilms, 1965. 544 pp.
A University of Arizona doctoral dissertation. Formed the basis of the book *Farmers, Workers and Machines.* See following entry.

1332. ———— AND WILLIAM E. MARTIN. *Farmers, Workers and Machines: Technological and Social Change in Farm Industries of Arizona.* Tucson: University of Arizona Press, 1965. 325 pp., tables, diags.

1333. *Padre Kino: Memorable Events in the Life and Times of the Immortal Priest-Colonizer Depicted in Drawings by DeGrazia.* Los Angeles: Southwest Museum, 1962. 54 pp., illus., maps.
Subtitle: "With commentaries on the artist and his work by noted authorities on Southwestern history and art." More about De Grazia than about Kino.

1334. PAGE, HARRY G. *Water Regimen of the Inner Valley of the San Pedro River Near Mammoth, Arizona (a Pilot Study).* Washington: U. S. Geological Survey, 1963. (Water-Supply Paper no. 1669-I) 22 pp., tables.

1335. PAINE, LAURAN. *Tom Horn: Man of the West.* London: John Lang, 1962. 190 pp.
Somewhat fictionalized, no bibliography, no index.

1336. ———. *Tom Horn, Man of the West.* Barre, Massachusetts: Barre Publishing Co., 1963. 186 pp.

1337. PAINTER, MURIEL T. *Easter at Pascua Village.* Tucson: University of Arizona Press, 1960. 35 pp., illus.
A revision of the next item.

1338. ———. *The Yaqui Easter Ceremony at Pascua.* Tucson: Tucson Chamber of Commerce, [1950]. 40 pp., maps.

1339. ——— AND EDWIN B. SAYLES. *Faith, Flowers and Fiestas: The Yaqui Indian Year,* a *Narrative of Ceremonial Events.* Tucson: University of Arizona Press for the Arizona State Museum, 1962. unpaged, illus.
Pleasing pamphlet about the ceremonies at Pascua Village in Tucson, lavishly set forth with color photographs and reproductions of drawings by Yaqui children.

1340. ——— AND OTHERS. *A Yaqui Easter Sermon.* Tucson: University of Arizona Press, 1955. (Social Science Bulletin no. 26) 89 pp., illus.
Sermon recorded at Pascua Village, Tucson, in 1941, with translation and notes.

1341. PALMER, K. T. *The Carefree Story.* [Carefree, Arizona: The Author?], 1967. 23 pp., illus.

1342. *Pan America in Microcosm: A History of the Arizona-Sonora Project.* Tucson: University of Arizona, 1960. 64 pp., illus.
Cooperative program between the universities of the two states.

1343. [PAPAGO INDIANS] *The Off-Reservation Papagos.* [Phoenix?]: Arizona Commission of Indian Affairs, [1957?]. 71 pp., tables, maps.
Minutes of a meeting held at Sells, December 1957.

1344. [PAPAGO INDIANS] *Rehabilitation of Papago Tribe of Indians, Arizona.* Hearings, 82nd Congress, 1st Session. Senate Interior and Insular Affairs Committee, Washington, 1952. 25 pp.

1345. PARACHEK, RALPH E. *Desert Architecture.* Phoenix: Parr of Arizona, 1967. 93 pp., illus.
Most of the examples are from Arizona.

1346. [PARADISE VALLEY] *A Land Use Plan for the Town of Paradise Valley.* [Paradise Valley? 1965?]. 45 pp., maps.
Based on material prepared by the Maricopa County Planning and Zoning Department.

1347. [PARADISE VALLEY] *A Report upon a Future General Land Use Plan for Northern Paradise Valley, Arizona.* [Phoenix]: Maricopa County Planning and Zoning Department, 1969. 32 pp., tables, maps.

1348. PARÉ, MADELINE F. *Arizona Pageant: a Short History of the 48th State.* By Madeline Ferrin Paré with the collaboration of Bert M. Fireman. Phoenix: Arizona Historical Foundation, 1965. 336 pp., illus., maps.
Written as a text for high schools. There was also a teacher's edition.

1349. PARKER, KENNETH W. AND S. CLARK MARTIN. *The Mesquite Problem on Southern Arizona Ranges.* Washington: U. S. Department of Agriculture, 1952. (Circular no. 908) 70 pp., illus., tables.

1350. PARKER, KITTIE F. *Arizona Ranch, Farm and Garden Weeds.* Tucson: University of Arizona Agricultural Extension Service, 1958. (Circular no. 265) 288 pp., illus.

1351. PARKMAN, I. H. *History of Buckeye Canal.* [Buckeye, Arizona, 1957?]. 37 pp., illus.

1352. PARMEE, EDWARD A. *Formal Education and Culture Change: A Modern Apache Indian Community and Government Education Programs.* Tucson: University of Arizona Press, 1968. 132 pp.
A study of the San Carlos Apaches.

1353. PARMEE, LEILA K. *Perception of Personal-Social Problems by Students of Different Ethnic Backgrounds.* Ann Arbor: University Microfilms, 1966. 202 pp.
A University of Arizona doctoral dissertation. A study of eighty Mexican-Americans, eighty Anglo-Americans, and eighty Negroes from Pueblo High School in Tucson.

1354. PARSONS, ARTHUR B. *The Porphyry Coppers in 1956.* New York: American Institute of Mining, Metallurgical and Petroleum Engineers, 1957. 270 pp., illus., maps.
A sequel to the author's *The Porphyry Coppers* of 1933; deals mostly with the period 1932 to 1955.

1355. PASHLEY, EMIL F., JR. *Structure and Stratigraphy of the Central, Northern and Eastern Parts of the Tucson Basin, Arizona.* Ann Arbor: University Microfilms, 1966. 366 pp.
A University of Arizona doctoral dissertation.

1356. PATCH, JOSEPH D. *Reminiscences of Fort Huachuca, Arizona.* [Washington, D.C., 1962?]. 21 pp., illus., maps.

1357. PATRAW, PAULINE M. *Flowers of the Southwest Mesas.* Santa Fe: Southwestern Monuments Association, 1951. (Popular Series no. 5) 112 pp., illus.

1358. PATTIE, JAMES OHIO. *The Personal Narrative of James O. Pattie.* Philadelphia: J. B. Lippincott, 1962. 269 pp.
The 1831 edition unabridged with introduction by William H. Goetzmann. This wildly romantic narrative of early Southwest exploration was reissued by A. H. Clark in 1905 and by R. R. Donnelley in 1930.

1359. PAWSON, WALTER W. AND AARON G. NELSON. *Economics of Skip-Row Cotton Production.* Tucson: University of Arizona Agricultural Experiment Station, 1966. (Report no. 231) 19 pp., tables.

1360. PAYLORE, PATRICIA. *Seventy-five Years of Arid-lands Research at the University of Arizona: a Selective Bibliography, 1891–1965.* [Tucson]: University of Arizona, Office of Arid Lands Research, 1966. 95 pp.

1361. ———— AND GLENDORA HALL. *Checklist of Official University of Arizona Publications, 1888–1950.* Tucson: University of Arizona Library, 1951. 78 pp.

1362. PAYNE, ANTHONY L. *Geology and Uranium Deposits of the Colorado Plateau.* Ann Arbor: University Microfilms, 1962. 287 pp.
A Stanford University doctoral dissertation.

1363. PEARSON, KEITH L. *Process of Political Development in a Navajo Community.* Ann Arbor: University Microfilms, 1969. 294 pp.
A University of Arizona doctoral dissertation.

1364. PECK, ANNE M. *The March of Arizona History.* Tucson: Arizona Silhouettes, 1962. 373 pp., illus., maps.
Written as a high school text.

1365. PECORA, ALDO. *Ricerche di Geografia Agraria nell'Arizona Centro-Meridionale.* Napoli: Institute di Geografia dell'Universita, 1964. (Memorie di Geografia Economica e Antropica, Nuova serie, vol. II) 223 pp., illus., maps, tables, diags.
The natural setting, human setting, utilization of water, agricultural economy.

1366. PEIRCE, FREDERICK L. *Structure and Petrography of Part of the Santa Catalina Mountains.* Ann Arbor: University Microfilms, 1958. 192 pp.
A University of Arizona doctoral dissertation.

1367. PEIRCE, H. WESLEY. *Geologic Guidebook 2 — Highways of Arizona: Arizona Highways 77 and 177.* Tucson: University of Arizona, 1967. (Arizona Bureau of Mines Bulletin no. 176) 73 pp., tables, illus., diags., maps.
Oracle Junction, Globe, Show Low, Holbrook, Keams Canyon.

1368. ————. *Stratigraphy of the DeChelly Sandstone of Arizona and Utah.* Ann Arbor: University Microfilms, 1963. 291 pp.
A University of Arizona doctoral dissertation.

1369. PENFIELD, THOMAS. *Dig Here!* San Antonio: Naylor, 1962. 196 pp., illus.
Lost mines, mostly in Arizona. Good bibliography.
— Revised edition, 1966. 240 pp.

1370. PEPLOW, EDWARD H., JR. *History of Arizona.* New York: Lewis Historical Publishing Company, 1958. 3 vols., illus.
Volume 3 is biography.

1371. PEPLOW, ELIZABETH W. AND EDWARD H. PEPLOW, JR. *Holiday on Oak Creek.* Clarkdale, Arizona, 1952. 88 pp., illus.

1372. ———— AND ————. *When the Cow Jumped over the Moon: The Story of Cattle Growing in Yavapai County, Arizona.* [Prescott: Yavapai Cattle Growers Incorporated?], 1952. unpaged, illus.

1373. PERCEVAL, DON. *Maynard Dixon Sketch Book.* Introduction and descriptive text by Don Perceval. Foreword by Lawrence Clark Powell. Flagstaff, Arizona: Northland Press, 1967. unpaged, illus.

1374. ————. *A Navajo Sketch Book.* By Don Perceval, with a descriptive text by Clay Lockett. Flagstaff, Arizona: Northland Press, 1962. 98 pp., illus.
The text is subordinate to the pictures in this handsomely produced book. A "Trailfinders Edition" of 55 copies, each with an original watercolor, was issued by Muir and Glen Dawson of Los Angeles.

1375. PERRIL, LESTER S. *Ackerman of Arizona.* Scottsdale, Arizona: Educational Publications, 1960. 54 pp., illus.
Campaign biography of Lee Ackerman. Poorly written.

1376. PERRY, DAVID V. *Genesis of the Contact Rocks at the Christmas Mine, Gila County, Arizona.* Ann Arbor: University Microfilms, 1968. 253 pp.
A University of Arizona doctoral dissertation.

1377. PETERS, WILLIAM S. *Manufacturing Plants in Arizona.* [Tempe]: Arizona State University, Bureau of Business Research and Services, 1962. (Arizona Industry Reports no. 2) 17 pp., tables.
Other editions in 1963, 1964, and 1965. Title and author varies.

1378. PETERS, WILLIAM S. *Patterns of Success for Selected Small Businesses in Arizona.* [Tempe?]: Bureau of Publications, Arizona State University, 1962. 214 pp., tables.
Contains surveys of Arizona small business operations such as groceries, service stations, gift shops, etc.

1379. PETERSON, CHARLES S. *Settlement on the Little Colorado, 1873–1900: A Study in the Processes and Institutions of Mormon Expansion.* Ann Arbor: University Microfilms, 1967. 534 pp.
A University of Utah doctoral dissertation.

1380. PETERSON, DONALD W. *Dacitic Ash-Flow Sheet near Superior and Globe, Arizona.* Ann Arbor: University Microfilms, 1961. 178 pp.
A Stanford University doctoral dissertation. Volcanic ash.

1381. PETERSON, NELS P. *Geology and Ore Deposits of the Globe-Miami District, Arizona.* Washington: U. S. Geological Survey, 1962. (Professional Paper no. 342) 151 pp., diags., tables, maps.

1382. ————. *Geology of the Pinal Ranch Quadrangle, Arizona.* Washington: U. S. Geological Survey, 1963. (Bulletin no. 1141-H) 18 pp., maps.

1383. ———— AND ROGER W. SWANSON. *Geology of the Christmas Copper Mine, Gila County, Arizona.* Washington: U. S. Geological Survey, 1956. (Bulletin no. 1027-H) pp. 351–73, illus., maps.

1384. ———— AND OTHERS. *Geology and Ore Deposits of the Castle Dome Area, Gila County, Arizona.* Washington: U. S. Geological Survey, 1951. (Bulletin no. 971) 134 pp., illus., maps.

1385. PETERSON, RICHARD C. *A Structural Study of the East End of the Catalina Forerange, Pima County, Arizona.* Ann Arbor: University Microfilms, 1968.
A University of Arizona doctoral dissertation.

1386. [PETRIFIED FOREST] *Golden Anniversary of the Establishment of Petrified Forest National Monument, 1906–1956.* [Holbrook]: Northern Arizona Printers and Publishers, [1956]. unpaged, illus.

1387. PEW, WEYMOUTH D. *Growing Cole Crops in Arizona.* Tucson: Cooperative Extension Service and Agricultural Experiment Station, 1960. (Bulletin A-5) 32 pp., illus.

1388. PÉWÉ, TROY L. *Colorado River Guidebook: A Geologic and Geographic Guide from Lees Ferry to Phantom Ranch, Arizona.* [Tempe, Arizona: the Author?], 1969. 78 pp., illus., maps.
This is a second edition; the first, 1968, I have not seen.

1389. PHILLIPS, ALLAN AND OTHERS. *The Birds of Arizona.* Tucson: University of Arizona Press, 1964. 212 pp., illus., maps.

1390. PHIPPEN, GEORGE. *The Life of a Cowboy.* Tucson: University of
Arizona Press, 1969. 104 pp., illus.
Told through the drawings, paintings, and bronzes of the artist as
selected by his widow, Louise Phippen.

1391. PHOENIX, DAVID A. *Geology of the Lees Ferry Area, Coconino
County, Arizona.* Washington: U. S. Geological Survey, 1963.
(Bulletin no. 1137) 86 pp. illus., tables, maps, diags.

1392. *Phoenix Downtown Study.* [Tempe?]: Arizona State University
Bureau of Business Research and Services, 1966. various paging,
illus., map, diags.

1393. [PHOENIX] *Business Locations in Greater Phoenix.* Tempe: Arizona
State College Bureau of Business Services, 1952. (Miscellaneous
Papers no. 1) 27 unnumbered maps.

1394. [PHOENIX] *Creighton School District, No. 14: Report of Survey,
May 1966.* [Tempe]: Arizona State University Bureau of Educational Research and Services, 1966. 2 vols., tables, maps.

1395. [PHOENIX] *Economic Analysis and Projection for Phoenix and
Maricopa County.* Phoenix: Western Business Consultants, Inc.,
1959. 169 pp., tables, diags., maps.

1396. [PHOENIX] *Findings and Recommendations of the Community
Health Survey.* Phoenix: Community Council, 1962. 2 vols.,
tables.

1397. [PHOENIX] *Land Use of the Phoenix Urban Area: A Study Basic to
Long Range Planning.* [Phoenix?]: Advance Planning Task Force,
City of Phoenix and Maricopa County, Arizona, 1959. 49 pp.,
maps.

1398. [PHOENIX] *A Major Street and Highway Plan, Phoenix Urban Area,
Maricopa County.* [San Francisco]: Wilbur Smith and Associates,
1960. 126 pp., tables, maps.

1399. [PHOENIX] *The Papago Freeway: A Report Prepared for the Arizona Highway Department.* Phoenix: Johannessen & Girand,
Consulting Engineers, 1968. 164 pp., illus., tables, diags., maps.

1400. [PHOENIX] *Population Growth of the Phoenix Urban Area: A Study
Basic to Long Range Planning.* [Phoenix?]: Advance Planning
Task Force, City of Phoenix and Maricopa County, Arizona,
1959. 29 pp.

1401. [PHOENIX] *Redevelopment Plan for East Jefferson Urban Renewal
Area.* Phoenix: Urban Renewal Commission, 1960. 19 pp., maps.

1402. [PHOENIX] *Redevelopment Plan for Southwest Urban Renewal Area.*
Phoenix: Urban Renewal Commission, 1960. 28 pp., maps.

1403. [PHOENIX] *Report of the Survey, Phoenix Union High Schools and Phoenix College System.* [Los Angeles? 1954]. 2 vols., tables, maps.
Irving R. Melbo, editor.

1404. [PHOENIX] *Report on the Water Works Survey of the Phoenix Metropolitan Area.* Phoenix: John A. Carollo, Consulting Engineers, 1960. 80 pp., tables, maps.

1405. [PHOENIX] *75th Anniversary, 1881–1956.* Phoenix, [1956?]. unpaged, illus.
Report of the mayor on the anniversary of incorporation.

1406. [PHOENIX] *A Street Arterial Plan for Phoenix, Arizona.* State Highway Department, 1950. 72 pp., illus., maps, diags.

1407. [PHOENIX] *A Transportation Plan for Downtown.* Phoenix: Transportation Planning Team, 1963. 31 pp., maps.

1408. PICKERING, ROBERT L. *Some Significant Events in the History of Arizona Education.* Phoenix: [State Department of Public Instruction], 1966. 31 pp., tables.

1409. PILKINGTON, HAROLD D. *Structure and Petrology of a Part of the East Flank of the Santa Catalina Mountains, Pima County, Arizona.* Ann Arbor: University Microfilms, 1962. 155 pp.
A University of Arizona doctoral dissertation.

1410. *Pima County.* Tucson: League of Women Voters of Tucson, 1956. 32 pp.
A description of the county government.

1411. [PIMA COUNTY] *Atlas of Pima County.* [Phoenix]: Arizona State Highway Department, 1963. 28 sheets.
Detailed road and street maps in a spiral binding.

1412. *Pinal County Agricultural Employment Study, September 1956– August 1957.* [Phoenix]: Arizona State Employment Service, [1958]. 36 pp., tables, diags.

1413. *Pinal County, Arizona, an Industrial and Commercial Survey.* [Florence, Arizona?]: Pinal County Development Board in cooperation with Arizona Development Board, [1957?]. unpaged.
Mimeographed. Later printed editions of 1961 and 1964 bring information up to date.

1414. *Pinal County 1985 Development Plan, Part 1, Eastern Pinal County.* Phoenix and Denver: Holland & Rabin Associates and the Ken R. White Company, 1966. various paging, illus., tables, maps, diags.

1415. *Pinal County 1985 Development Plan.* Phoenix and Denver: Ken R. White Co., and Holland & Rabin, 1967. 3 parts, tables, maps.
Three unnumbered parts include the Development Plan, Zoning Ordinance, and Subdivision Regulations.

1416. [PINAL COUNTY] *Atlas of Pinal County.* [Phoenix]: Arizona State Highway Department, 1964. 20 sheets.
Detailed road and street maps in a spiral binding.

1417. [PINAL COUNTY] *Directory of Social and Economic Resources, Pinal County, Arizona, 1969.* Prepared by Central Arizona College. Coolidge, Arizona: The College, [1969]. 78 pp.

1418. [PINAL COUNTY] *Economic Survey of Pinal County.* Tempe: Arizona State College Bureau of Business Services, 1955. (Arizona Counties Economic Survey no. 4) 175 pp., illus., maps, tables, diags.

1419. [PINAL COUNTY] *The General Plan for Western Pinal County, Arizona, 1964.* Scottsdale, Arizona: Van Cleve Associates, [1964?]. 56 pp., illus., tables, maps, diags.
Prepared for the Pinal County Board of Supervisors.

1420. *Pinal Creek and Tributaries, Arizona.* 87th Congress, 2nd Session, House Document no. 512. Washington, 1962. 89 pp., tables, maps.

1421. *Pinal Profiles: Data for Planning Report, Western Pinal County, Arizona.* [Scottsdale, Arizona]: Van Cleve Associates, 1963–64. 5 parts.
No. 1, History, physiography, natural resources.
No. 2, Physical characteristics, existing land use.
No. 3, Population, residential environment, economics.
No. 4, Community facilities.
No. 5, Street and thoroughfares, public utilities.

1422. PINART, ALPHONSE. *Journey to Arizona in 1876.* Translated by George H. Whitney. Biography and bibliography by Henry R. Wagner. Introduction and notes by Carl S. Dentzel. Los Angeles: The Zamorano Club, 1962. 47 pp., illus.
Five hundred copies, designed and composed at the Plantain Press. Translated from the extract from the *Bulletin de la Société de Géographie,* Paris, March, 1877.

1423. PINE, GORDON L. *Devonian Stratigraphy and Paleogeography in Gila, Graham, Greenlee, and Pinal Counties, Arizona.* Ann Arbor, University Microfilms, 1968. 361 pp.
A University of Arizona doctoral dissertation.

1424. *Pinetop-Lakeside Schools: Report of a Survey.* [Tempe]: Arizona State University Bureau of Educational Research and Services, n.d. 103 pp., tables.

1425. *Pioneer Stories of Arizona's Verde Valley.* Edited by Edward H. Peplow, Jr. [Camp Verde, Arizona]: Verde Valley Pioneers Association, 1954. 219 pp., illus.
Section 1, pp. 1–106, originally published in 1953.

1426. *Pipeline Archaeology; Reports of Salvage Operations in the South-west on El Paso Natural Gas Company Projects, 1950–1953.* Santa Fe and Flagstaff: The Laboratory of Anthropology and The Museum of Northern Arizona, 1956. 410 pp., illus., maps, diags.

1427. PIPKIN, BERNARD W. *Clay Mineralogy of the Willcox Playa and Its Drainage Basin, Cochise County, Arizona.* Ann Arbor: University Microfilms, 1965. 178 pp.
    A University of Arizona doctoral dissertation.

1428. *The Place of the Navajo People and Their Reservation in the Future of Northeastern Arizona.* [Phoenix?]: Arizona Commission of Indian Affairs, [1957?]. 80 pp.
    Minutes of a meeting held on the Navajo Reservation, September 1957.

1429. *Planning Health and Hospital Services for Greater Tucson.* Prepared for the Hospital Planning Council for Greater Tucson, Inc. New York City: John G. Steinle and Associates, 1968. various paging.

1430. *Plants of Northern Arizona.* Flagstaff: Northern Arizona Society of Science and Art, 1951. (Museum of Northern Arizona Reprint Series no. 1) 52 pp., illus.
    Articles reprinted from *Museum Notes* and *Plateau.*

1431. PLASKOW, ELI P. *The Training Resources of the Luke & Williams Gunnery Complex.* Luke Air Force Base, [Arizona] 1957. 31 pp., illus., diags.

1432. POE, CHARLSIE. *Angel to the Papagos.* San Antonio: Naylor, 1964. 159 pp., illus.
    The story of Goldie Richmond and a trading post on the Papago reservation.

1433. POE, STANLEY. *Equalization Legislation for Arizona.* Ann Arbor: University Microfilms, 1961. 421 pp.
    An Arizona State University doctoral dissertation.

1434. POLK, LEONARD W. *The Role and Functions of the Intermediate School District in Arizona.* Ann Arbor: University Microfilms, 1969. 223 pp.
    An Arizona State University doctoral dissertation.

1435. POLLOCK, PAUL W. *Arizona.* Centennial edition. Phoenix: The Author, 1962. 176 pp., illus.
    History, present conditions, and some fine color photographs marred by advertising where the captions should be.

1436. POLZER, CHARLES. *A Kino Guide.* Tucson: Southwestern Mission Research Center, 1968. 42 pp., illus., maps.
    Subtitle: "A Life of Eusebio Francisco Kino, Arizona's First Pioneer and a Guide to His Missions and Monuments."
    Two hundred copies clothbound and signed. Also issued in wrappers. Includes an account of the discovery of Kino's grave in Magdalena, Sonora, in 1966.

1437. *Population Growth of the Phoenix Urban Area.* Prepared by Advance Planning Task Force, Phoenix and Maricopa County [Phoenix], 1959. 29 pp., tables, maps.

1438. PORTER, CHARLES. *Charles Porter's Account of the Confederate Attempt to Seize Arizona and New Mexico.* Austin, Texas: Pemberton Press, 1964. 33 pp.

1439. PORTER, ELIOT. *The Place No One Knew: Glen Canyon of the Colorado.* San Francisco: Sierra Club, 1963. 170 pp., illus.
   Though most of the canyon is in Utah it qualifies for admission because it is a beautiful Colorado River book with stunning color plates. Reissued in 1966 as no. 5 in the Exhibit Format Series with 8 additional plates.

1440. POSTON, CHARLES D. *Building a State in Apache Land: The Story of Arizona's Founding by Arizona's Founder.* Preface and notes by John Myers Myers. Tempe: Aztec Press, 1963. 174 pp., illus.

1441. POTTER, ALVINA. *The Many Lives of the Lynx.* Prescott, 1964. 167 pp., illus.
   The Lynx Creek mining district near Prescott. Privately printed in an edition of 350 copies by the Northland Press, Flagstaff.

1442. POULSON, EDWIN N. AND L. K. STROMBERG. *Soil Survey of the Duncan Area, Arizona-New Mexico.* Washington: U. S. Department of Agriculture, 1950. (Series 1941, no. 1) 48 pp., maps.

1443. ———— AND OTHERS. *Soil Survey of the Sulphur Spring Valley Area, Arizona.* Washington: U. S. Department of Agriculture, 1954. (Series 1940, no. 14) 79 pp., illus., maps.

1444. POWELL, DONALD M. *Arizona Fifty: A List of Fifty Books About Arizona, Published Since Statehood.* Tucson, 1962. unpaged.
   Bibliography with annotations issued as a commemorative booklet for the 1962 Arizona Historical Convention. Designed and printed by the Northland Press, Flagstaff.

1445. ————. *An Arizona Gathering: A Bibliography of Arizoniana 1950–1959.* Tucson: Arizona Pioneers' Historical Society, 1960. (Pamphlet Series no. 2) 77 pp., illus.
   Designed and printed by Lawton Kennedy; 400 copies issued in the pamphlet series; 200 copies bound in cloth, numbered and signed.

1446. ————. *The Peralta Grant: James Addison Reavis and the Barony of Arizona.* Norman: University of Oklahoma Press, 1960. 186 pp., illus.

1447. POWELL, JOHN WESLEY. *Canyons of the Colorado.* New York: Argosy-Antiquarian Ltd., 1964. 400 pp., illus.
   A facsimile of the original of 1895; 750 copies printed.

1448. ————. *Down the Colorado: Diary of the First Trip through the Grand Canyon, 1869.* Photographs and epilogue by Eliot Porter. New York: E. P. Dutton, 1969. 168 pp., illus.

1449. POWELL, JOHN WESLEY. *The Exploration of the Colorado River.* Introduction by Wallace Stegner. Chicago: University of Chicago Press, 1957. 137 pp., illus.
    Abridged from the first edition of 1875.

1450. ———. *The Exploration of the Colorado River and Its Canyons.* New York: Dover Publications, 1961. 400 pp., illus.
    An unabridged and unaltered reproduction, in paper covers, of the work first published in 1895 with the title *Canyons of the Colorado.*

1451. POWELL, LAWRENCE C. *Heart of the Southwest.* Los Angeles: Dawson's Book Shop, 1955. 42 pp.
    Personal selection of novels about Arizona and New Mexico.

1452. ———. *Southwestern Book Trails: A Reader's Guide to the Heartland of New Mexico & Arizona.* Albuquerque: Horn & Wallace, 1963. 91 pp.
    First publication by Horn & Wallace of a work based on an original manuscript.

1453. ———. *A Southwestern Century.* Van Nuys, California: J. E. Reynolds, 1958. 29 pp.
    Subtitle: "A bibliography of one hundred books of non-fiction about the Southwest." Edition limited to 500 copies. The list first appeared in the March, 1958, issue of *Arizona Highways.*

1454. POWERS, BRUCE AND K. C. HAMILTON. *Revegetation of a Cleared Section of a Floodway.* Tucson: University of Arizona Agricultural Experiment Station, 1961. (Report no. 198) 23 pp., illus.
    The Snyder floodway in the Gila Valley near Wellton.

1455. *Practical Gardening in the Salt River Valley.* [Phoenix?]: Valley Garden Center, [1950?]. 70 pp.

1456. PRATT, JEROME J. *White Flags of Apacheland.* New York: Vantage Press, 1966. 114 pp., illus.
    About the Coues white-tailed deer in the Chiricahua and Huachuca mountains.

1457. *Preliminary Survey and Recommendations Relating to the Establishment of a State Parks and Recreation Board.* [Phoenix?]: Arizona Development Board, [1956?]. 40 pp.

1458. PRESSON, WILLIAM O., JR. *The Professional Preparation of Physical Education Teachers for the High Schools of Arizona.* Ann Arbor: University Microfilms, 1965. 156 pp.
    A University of Southern California doctoral dissertation.

1459. PRINCE, JOHN F. *A Biography of E. W. Montgomery During His Superintendency of the Phoenix Union High School and Phoenix College District, 1925–1953.* Ann Arbor: University Microfilms, 1960. 210 pp.
    A University of Arizona doctoral dissertation.

1460. *Problems of Bilingualism in Arizona: Selected Writings by Educators.* Phoenix: State Department of Public Instruction, [1965]. unpaged.

1461. PROCTER, GIL. *People of the Moonlight.* Pasadena: Publication Press for the Pete Kitchen Museum, 1958. 116 pp., illus.
    Stories of events in the Santa Cruz Valley. Limited edition of 1000 copies.

1462. ———. *Tucson, Tubac, Tumacacori, Tohell.* Tucson: Arizona Silhouettes, 1956. 110 pp., illus.
    More stories from the past in the Santa Cruz Valley. Edition limited to 1000 signed copies.

1463. *Public Land Use, Transfer and Ownership in Arizona.* Research report prepared by University of Arizona. Phoenix: Arizona Academy, [1965]. 160 pp., tables, map, diag.
    Seventh Arizona Town Hall, October 1965.

1464. *Public Lands and the Public Schools of Arizona.* Phoenix: Arizona Education Association, [1960]. unpaged.

1465. *Public Welfare Services in Pima County, Success or Failure?* Tucson: Tucson Community Council, 1960. 18 pp., appendix, tables.
    Nearer failure than success.

1466. PUMPELLY, RAPHAEL. *Pumpelly's Arizona: An Excerpt from Across America and Asia by Raphael Pumpelly, Comprising those Chapters which Concern the Southwest.* Tucson: Palo Verde Press, 1965. 141 pp., maps, illus.

1467. PUTNAM, GEORGE W. *A Study of the Distribution of Trace Elements in Some Igneous Rocks of Northwestern and Central Arizona.* Ann Arbor: University Microfilms, 1961. 142 pp.
    A Pennsylvania State University doctoral dissertation.

1468. QOYAWAYMA, POLINGAYSI (Elizabeth Q. White). *No Turning Back.* As told to Vada F. Carlson. Albuquerque: University of New Mexico Press, 1964. 180 pp., illus.
    Subtitle: "A true account of a Hopi Indian girl's struggle to bridge the gap between the world of her people and the world of the White Man."

1469. QUEBBEMAN, FRANCES E. *Medicine in Territorial Arizona.* Phoenix: Arizona Historical Foundation, 1966. 424 pp., illus.

1470. *Queen Creek Watershed, Arizona.* 82nd Congress, 2d Session, House Document no. 397. Washington, 1952. 22 pp., tables, map.

1471. QUINN, CHARLES R. *Christmas Journey into the Desert.* Downey, California: Elena Quinn, 1959. 61 pp., illus., map.
    The Anza colonizing expedition from Tubac to California, 1775.

1472. QUINN, CHARLES R. *The Story of St. Thomas Indian Mission and the Forgotten Colorado River Missions at the Historic Yuma Crossing.* Downey, California: Elena Quinn, [1968]. 36 pp., illus.

1473. RAHN, PERRY H. *The Inselbergs of Southwestern Arizona.* Ann Arbor: University Microfilms, 1966. 158 pp.
A Pennsylvania State University doctoral dissertation.

1474. *Railroad Relocation and Track Depression of the Southern Pacific Railroad, Tucson, Arizona; the O'Dowd Plan.* Prepared by City-County Planning Department, Tucson, 1955. 28 pp., illus., maps.

1475. RAMEY, JAMES E. AND OTHERS. *A Statistical Handbook for the Desert Citrus Industry.* Tucson: University of Arizona Agricultural Experiment Station, 1967. (Report no. 244) 68 pp., tables, diags.

1476. RAMOS, JUAN. *Spanish-Speaking Leadership in Two Southwestern Cities: A Descriptive Study.* Ann Arbor: University Microfilms, 1969. 218 pp.
Phoenix and San Antonio are the cities. A Brandeis University doctoral dissertation.

1477. RAND, PATRICIA J. *Factors Related to the Distribution of Ponderosa and Pinyon Pines at Grand Canyon, Arizona.* Ann Arbor: University Microfilms, 1966. 325 pp.
A Duke University doctoral dissertation.

1478. RANSOM, JAY E. *Arizona Gem Trails and the Colorado Desert of California.* Portland, Oregon: Mineralogist Publishing Company, 1955. 96 pp., illus.
Guide for the gem hunter and mineral collector.

1479. RAPOPORT, ROBERT N. *Changing Navaho Religious Values: A Study of Christian Missions to the Rimrock Navahos.* Cambridge: Peabody Museum, 1954. (Peabody Papers vol. 41, no. 2) 152 pp., illus., map.

1480. RASCOE, JESSE. *Old Arizona Treasures.* Fort Davis, Texas: Frontier Book Co., 1968. 119 pp.
Lost mines and buried treasure.

1481. RATTÉ, JAMES C. AND OTHERS. *Mineral Resources of the Blue Range Primitive Area, Greenlee County, Arizona, and Catron County, New Mexico.* Washington: U.S. Geological Survey, 1969. (Bulletin no. 1261-E) 91 pp., illus., tables, maps.

1482. RAY, HOWARD E. AND J. R. CARTER. *Growing Short Staple Cotton in Maricopa County.* Tucson: University of Arizona Agricultural Extension Service, 1959. (Circular no. 268) 24 pp., illus.

1483. READ, CHARLES B. AND A. A. WANEK. *Stratigraphy of Outcropping Permian Rocks in Parts of Northeastern Arizona and Adjacent Areas.* Washington: U. S. Geological Survey, 1961. (Professional Paper no. 374-H) 10 pp., tables, maps.

1484. *Recovering Rainfall: More Water for Irrigation*. [Tucson?: Arizona Watershed Program], 1956. 2 parts, illus., tables.
Part I is the summary report; part II consists of reports by consultants. Only a limited number of copies of part II were issued. George W. Barr was in charge of the study.

1485. [Recreation] *A Plan for Outdoor Recreation in Arizona*. [Phoenix: Arizona Outdoor Recreation Commission?], 1967. various paging.

1486. REED, HAINES W. *Arizona Cowman*. Tucson: Reed Publications, [1951]. 200 pp., illus.
Contemporary ranching, the ranchman's problems, tales of the range, and some verse.

1487. *Re-evaluation and Projections; a Study of Arizona's Financial Experience during the Initial Planning Period with Estimates for the 1958–1965 Period*. Phoenix: Employment Security Commission, 1957. 49 pp., tables, diags.
Unemployment insurance.

1488. REHNBERG, REX D. *The Cost of Pumping Irrigation Water, Pinal County — 1951*. Tucson: University of Arizona Agricultural Experiment Station, 1953. (Bulletin no. 246) 27 pp., tables, diags.

1489. ———. *Irrigation Ditch Management on Arizona Irrigated Farms*. Tucson: University of Arizona Agricultural Experiment Station, 1951. (Bulletin no. 237) 25 pp., illus., diags.

1490. REICHARD, GLADYS A. *Navaho Grammar*. New York: J. J. Augustin, [1951]. (Publications of the American Ethnological Society vol. 21) 393 pp.

1491. ———. *Navaho Religion; a Study of Symbolism*. New York: Pantheon Books, 1950. (Bollingen Series no. 18) 2 vols., illus.

1492. ———. *Navaho Religion: A Study of Symbolism*. One-volume edition. New York: Pantheon Books, 1963. (Bollingen Series no. 18) 804 pp., illus.

1493. ———. *Navajo Shepherd and Weaver*. Glorieta, New Mexico: Rio Grande Press, 1968. 222 pp., illus.
A facsimile of the original edition of 1936. The techniques of Navajo weaving and design.

1494. ———. *Spider Woman: A Story of Navajo Weavers and Chanters*. Glorieta, New Mexico: Rio Grande Press, 1968. 287 pp., illus.
A facsimile of the original edition of 1934. The author's experiences during several summers on the reservation learning to weave in Navajo fashion.

1495. REID, ALASTAIR M., II. *Biostratigraphy of the Naco Formation (Pennsylvanian) in South-Central Arizona*. Ann Arbor: University Microfilms, 1968. 322 pp.
A University of Arizona doctoral dissertation.

1496. REITAN, CLAYTON H. *The Role of Precipitable Water Vapor in Arizona's Summer Rains.* Tucson: University of Arizona Institute of Atmospheric Physics, 1957. (Technical Reports on the Meteorology and Climatology of Arid Regions no. 2) 18 pp., tables, diags.

1497. REPENNING, C. A. AND OTHERS. *Stratigraphy of the Chinle and Moenkopi Formations, Navajo and Hopi Indian Reservations, Arizona, New Mexico, and Utah.* Washington: U. S. Geological Survey, 1969. (Professional Paper 521-B) 34 pp., maps.

1498. *Report on Congestion Caused by Trucks on Uphill Mountain Grades.* [Phoenix]: Arizona Highway Department, 1953. 37 pp., illus., tables, diags., maps.

1499. *Report on Congressional Redistricting in Arizona.* [Phoenix?]: Arizona Legislative Council, 1964. 98 pp., maps.

1500. *Report on Industrial Zoning in Arizona.* Tempe: Arizona State College Bureau of Business Services, 1955. 72 pp., maps.

1501. *Report on Study of Public Assistance Grants . . . for Arizona and Selected States.* [Phoenix?]: Community Councils of Phoenix and Tucson, 1964. 94 pp., tables.
Charities in Arizona.

1502. *Revision of Arizona's Constitution.* Research report prepared by Arizona State University, Tempe. Phoenix: Arizona Academy, [1965?]. 199 pp., tables, diag.
Fifth Arizona Town Hall, October 1964.

1503. REYNOLDS, HUDSON G. *Managing Grass-Shrub Cattle Ranges in the Southwest.* Washington: U. S. Department of Agriculture, 1959. (Handbook, no. 162) 40 pp., illus. diags.
Describes the Santa Rita Experimental Range south of Tucson.

1504. RICE, INEZ. *Valley over the Hill.* San Antonio: Naylor, 1959. 266 pp.
Homesteading near Flagstaff in the early 1900s.

1505. RICHARDS, JOSEPH M. *The Hopi Snake Dance.* Winslow, 1953. 28 pp., illus.

1506. RICHARDSON, GLADWELL. *Two Guns, Arizona.* Santa Fe: The Press of the Territorian, 1968. (Number 15 of a Series of Western Americana) 28 pp., illus.

1507. RICHARDSON, HAROLD D. *Arizona State University: Dynamic Educational Leadership in the Great Southwest.* New York.: Newcomen Society, 1964. 28 pp., illus.
Traces the history of the university.

1508. RICKARDS, COLIN. *"Buckskin Frank" Leslie, Gunman of Tombstone.* El Paso: Texas Western College Press, 1964. (Southwestern Studies, vol. 2, no. 2) 39 pp., illus.

1509. ———. *Buckskin Frank Leslie, Gunman of Tombstone.* El Paso: Texas Western Press, 1964. 45 pp., illus.
Originally issued as vol. 2, no. 2, of Southwestern Studies. This special edition of 450 clothbound copies has a reset title page and additional drawings by Russell Waterhouse.

1510. RIECKER, FRED A. *Horatio Algebra and Chief One and One.* Tucson: Pima Printing Co., 1960. 67 pp.
Reminiscences of Tucson and elsewhere.

1511. RIGBY, DOUGLAS. *Desert Happy.* Philadelphia: J. B. Lippincott, 1957. 313 pp., illus.
A book about the desert of the Tucson area.

1512. RIGGS, ROBERT E. *Arizona State Personnel Policies.* Tucson: University of Arizona Bureau of Business and Public Research, 1962. (Special Studies no. 20) 187 pp., tables.

1513. ———. *The Movement for Administrative Reorganization in Arizona.* Tucson: University of Arizona Bureau of Business and Public Research, 1961. (Special Studies no. 17) 88 pp., charts.
"This study deals with problems of personnel administration in Arizona state government as revealed through a survey of 24 state agencies."

1514. ———. *The Movement for Administrative Reorganization in Arizona.* Tucson: University of Arizona Press, 1964. (Institute of Government Research, Arizona Government Studies no. 4) 88 pp.
Reissue without revision of the above item. Blank pages 16 and 40 have been omitted in this reprint.

1515. ———. *Vox Populi: The Battle of 103.* Tucson: University of Arizona Press, 1964. (Institute of Government Research, Arizona Government Studies no. 2) 42 pp.
The battle of the real estate agents for legal authorization to prepare legal documents incident to the conveyance of property.

1516. RINALDO, JOHN B. *Foote Canyon Pueblo, Eastern Arizona.* Chicago: Natural History Museum, 1959. (Fieldiana, Anthropology, vol. 49, no. 2) pp. 149–298, illus., tables, maps.

1517. ——— AND OTHERS. *Documentation for Prehistoric Investigations in the Upper Little Colorado Drainage, Eastern Arizona.* Madison: Society for American Archaeology and University of Wisconsin Press, 1961. (Archives of Archaeology, no. 13) 53 pp. on 3 microcards.
Published only on microcards.

1518. RINGGOLD, JENNIE P. *Frontier Days in the Southwest.* San Antonio: Naylor, 1952. 197 pp., illus.
Eastern Arizona in the 80s and 90s. The Morenci strike of 1903.

1519. RINGSTROM, NORMAN H. *Arizona Drug Store Operations, 1951.* Tucson: University of Arizona Bureau of Business Research, 1953. (Special Studies no. 6) 10 pp.

1520. RITTENHOUSE, JACK D. *Disturnell's Treaty Map: The Map That Was Part of the Guadalupe Hidalgo Treaty on Southwestern Boundaries, 1848.* Santa Fe: Stagecoach Press, 1965. 20 pp., map.
A limited edition with hard covers and a folded facsimile of the map bound in, or in pamphlet binding with a rolled map in a case.

1521. ROADIFER, JACK E. *Stratigraphy of the Petrified Forest National Park, Arizona.* Ann Arbor: University Microfilms, 1966. 182 pp.
A University of Arizona doctoral dissertation.

1522. ROAT, EVELYN C. *The Museum of Northern Arizona.* Flagstaff, Arizona: KC Publications, 1968. 64 pp., illus.

1523. ROBERTS, JOHN M. *Three Navaho Households: A Comparative Study in Small Group Culture.* Cambridge, Massachusetts: Peabody Museum, 1951. (Peabody Papers vol. 40, no. 3) 87 pp., illus., tables.

1524. ROBERTS, PAUL H. *Them Were the Days.* San Antonio: Naylor, 1965. 134 pp., illus.
Reminiscences of the author's early career in the Forest Service in Arizona.

1525. ROBINSON, ALAMBERT E. *The Basket Weavers of Arizona.* Albuquerque: University of New Mexico Press, 1954. 164 pp., illus.
The basketry of contemporary tribes. Illustrated partly in color.

1526. ROBINSON, HARRY E. *Some Economic Implications of the Tourist Industry for Northern Arizona.* Phoenix: Stanford Research Institute, Mountain States Division, 1954. 87 pp. tables, diags.

1527. ROCA, PAUL M. *The Life Insurance Law of Arizona.* Phoenix? 1958? pp. 69–164.
Subtitle: "Paper read before The Association of Life Insurance Counsel, Monday, May 5, 1958, at the Greenbrier, White Sulphur Springs, West Virginia, by Paul M. Roca, Scoville, Beauchamp & Linton, General Counsel, Commercial Life Insurance Company, Phoenix, Arizona." Reprinted from *Proceedings of the Association of Life Insurance Counsel* vol. 14, 1958/59.

1528. ROCKFELLOW, JOHN A. *Log of an Arizona Trail Blazer.* Tucson: Arizona Silhouettes, 1955. 183 pp., illus.
Originally published in 1933. Limited edition of 1000 copies. Reminiscences of early days in southern Arizona.

1529. ROESSEL, ROBERT A., JR. *An Analysis of Select Navaho Needs with Implications for Navaho Education.* Ann Arbor: University Microfilms, 1961. 265 pp.
A 1960 Arizona State University doctoral dissertation.

1530. ———. *Indian Communities in Action.* Tempe: Arizona State University Bureau of Publications, 1967. 223 pp., illus.
Community action in several locations on the Navajo Reservation with a chapter on action at San Carlos.

1531. ———. *San Carlos Apache Indian Education.* Tempe: Arizona State University Indian Education Center, 1963. 186 pp.
Includes material prepared by other educators.

1532. ROGERS, MALCOLM J. AND OTHERS. *Ancient Hunters of the Far West.* Edited by Richard F. Pourade. San Diego: Union Tribune Publishing Co., 1966. 208 pp., illus.
A summary of what has been revealed about the San Dieguitoans, prehistoric desert dwellers whose culture extended into southwestern Arizona.

1533. ROMSLO, THOMAS M. *Investigations of the Lake Shore Copper Deposits, Pinal County, Arizona.* [Pittsburgh]: U. S. Bureau of Mines, 1950. (Report of Investigations no. 4760) 24 pp., maps.

1534. ——— AND CHARLES S. ROBINSON. *Copper Giant Deposits, Pima County, Arizona.* [Pittsburgh]: U. S. Bureau of Mines, 1952. (Report of Investigations no. 4850) 9 pp., maps.

1535. ROOT, VIRGINIA V. *Following the Pot of Gold at the Rainbow's End in the Days of 1850.* Edited by Leonore Rowland. Downey, California, 1960. 31 pp., illus.
Overland reminiscences — Tucson, Oatman massacre.

1536. ROSS, STANLEY H. *The Prehistoric Use of Copper in Arizona.* Ann Arbor: University Microfilms, 1964. 170 pp.
A University of California, Los Angeles, doctoral dissertation.

1537. ROTH, LAWRENCE J. *An Analysis of Public Interest in the Operation of Arizona Elementary School Districts.* Ann Arbor: University Microfilms, 1966. 249 pp.
An Arizona State University doctoral dissertation.

1538. ROWE, ERNEST R. *A Study of Formal Educational Provisions for Emotionally Handicapped Children in the Public Elementary Schools of Arizona.* Ann Arbor: University Microfilms, 1965. 145 pp.
An Arizona State University doctoral dissertation.

1539. RUND, NADINE H. AND OTHERS. *Demographic and Socio-Cultural Characteristics, Papago Indian Reservations, Arizona.* Tucson: U. S. Department of Health, Education and Welfare, Health Program Systems Center, 1968. 115 pp., tables.

1540. *Rural Poverty.* Hearings before the National Advisory Commission on Rural Poverty, Tucson, Arizona. Washington, 1967. 403 pp.
Hearings held in January 1967. Many of those who testified or submitted material for the record were from Arizona and describe conditions there.

1541. RUSCO, ELMER R. *Voting Behavior in Arizona.* Reno: University of Nevada Bureau of Governmental Research, 1967. 27 pp.

1542. RUSSEL, J. C. AND T. F. BUEHRER. *The Iraq College of Agriculture, Its History and Development, 1952–1959.* Tucson: University of Arizona, 1960. 160 pp., illus.
Final report on the University of Arizona's work in Iraq under an International Cooperation Administration contract.

1543. RUSSO, JOHN P. *The Desert Bighorn Sheep in Arizona.* Phoenix: Arizona Game and Fish Department, 1956. (Wildlife Bulletin no. 1) 153 pp., illus., tables, maps.

1544. ————. *The Kaibab North Deer Herd — Its History, Problems and Management.* Phoenix: Arizona Game and Fish Department, 1964. (Wildlife Bulletin no. 7) 195 pp., illus., tables, maps, diags.

1545. RYAN, J. CLYDE. *A Skeptic Dude in Arizona.* San Antonio: Naylor, 1952. 176 pp., illus.
Ranching near Elgin with imaginative reconstruction of part of the area's history.

1546. SABELS, BRUNO E. *Late Cenozoic Volcanism in the San Francisco Volcanic Field and Adjacent Areas in North Central Arizona.* Ann Arbor: University Microfilms, 1960. 345 pp.
A University of Arizona doctoral dissertation.

1547. SACKS, B[ENJAMIN]. *Be It Enacted: The Creation of the Territory of Arizona.* Phoenix: Arizona Historical Foundation, 1964. 200 pp., illus., maps.

1548. *The Sacred Mountains of the Navajo in Four Paintings by Harrison Begay.* Explanatory text by Leland C. Wyman. Flagstaff: Museum of Northern Arizona, 1967. unpaged, illus.

1549. [SAFFORD] *A Report on the Organization and Administration of Safford, Arizona.* Chicago: Public Administration Service, [1959]. 39 pp., diags.

1550. ST. CLAIR, JAMES S. *Some Quality Aspects of Marketing Arizona Cotton with Special Reference to Grading Standards and Practices.* Ann Arbor: University Microfilms, 1956. 222 pp.
A University of Illinois doctoral dissertation.

1551. ———— AND ARTHUR L. ROBERTS. *Quality and Cost of Ginning Upland Cotton in Arizona.* Tucson: University of Arizona Agricultural Experiment Station, 1956. (Bulletin no. 277) 63 pp., tables.

1552. *Salado Red Ware Conference: Ninth Southwestern Ceramic Seminar, October 13–14, 1967.* Recorded and Compiled by Alexander J. Lindsay, Jr., and Calvin H. Jennings. Flagstaff: Northern Arizona Society of Science and Art, 1968. (Museum of Northern Arizona Ceramic Series no. 4) 18 pp.

1553. SALMON, VINCENT M. *The Retention or Abandonment of Educational Innovations in Selected Arizona High Schools.* Ann Arbor: University Microfilms, 1969. 148 pp.
A University of Arizona doctoral dissertation.

1554. SALPOINTE, JEAN BAPTISTE. *Soldiers of the Cross: Notes on the Ecclesiastical History of New-Mexico, Arizona and Colorado.* Albuquerque: Calvin Horn, 1967. 299 pp., illus.
A facsimile of the 1898 edition with the unpaged Appendix VII added by the publisher in 1900.

1555. ————. *John Baptist Salpointe, Soldier of the Cross.* Edited by Odie Faulk. Tucson: Diocese of Tucson, 1966. 181 pp., illus.
A reprint of the last third of Salpointe's book *Soldiers of the Cross.* Banning, California, 1898.

1556. SALSBURY, CLARENCE G., WITH PAUL HUGHES. *The Salsbury Story: A Medical Missionary's Lifetime of Public Service.* Tucson: University of Arizona Press, 1969. 277 pp., illus.

1557. [SALT RIVER] *Rio Salado III.* [Tempe]: Arizona State University College of Architecture, 1969. unpaged, maps.
Plan for flood control and recreational development of the channel.

1558. [SALT RIVER INDIAN RESERVATION] *Background for Planning and Policy Recommendations . . . Salt River Pima-Maricopa Indian Community, Arizona, 1969.* Pasadena, California: Simon Eisner and Associates, 1969. 94 pp., maps.
Cover title.

1559. SALTER, RICHARD H. AND OTHERS. *Arizona Lettuce Production Survey, Fall-Spring Harvest, 1961–1962.* [Phoenix?]: Employment Security Commission of Arizona, [1962?]. 30 pp., tables.

1560. *The San Carlos Apache Indian Reservation; A Resources Development Study.* Prepared for the San Carlos Apache Tribal Council by Stanford Research Institute, [Phoenix? 1955]. 343 pp., illus., maps, tables.
A summary report of 41 pp. was issued at the same time.

1561. *San Juan-Chama Reclamation Project and Navajo Indian Irrigation Project.* Hearing. 86th Congress, 2nd Session. House Committee on Interior and Insular Affairs, Subcommittee on Irrigation and Reclamation. Washington, 1960. 212 pp.

1562. *Santa Cruz County, Arizona, Industrial and Commercial Survey.* [Nogales, Arizona?]: Nogales Chamber of Commerce in cooperation with Arizona Development Board, [1964?]. 29 pp., illus., tables.

1563. [SANTA CRUZ COUNTY] *Atlas of Santa Cruz County.* [Phoenix]: Arizona State Highway Department, 1961. 3 sheets.
Detailed road and street maps in a spiral binding.

1564. SANTEE, ROSS. *Lost Pony Tracks.* New York: Scribner's, 1953. 303 pp., illus.
    Autobiography. Reminiscences of cowboy life in the area south of Globe at the turn of the century.

1565. SAPIR, EDWARD AND HARRY HOIJER. *The Phonology and Morphology of the Navaho Language.* Berkeley and Los Angeles: University of California Press, 1967. (University of California Publications in Linguistics vol. 50) 124 pp.

1566. SASAKI, TOM T. *Fruitland, New Mexico: A Navaho Community in Transition.* Ithaca, New York: Cornell University Press, 1960. 217 pp., illus.

1567. SAVAGE, PAT. *One Last Frontier: A Story of Indians, Early Settlers and Old Ranches of Northern Arizona.* New York: Exposition Press, 1964. 236 pp., illus.
    Early days in the Prescott area.

1568. SAVARD, ROBERT J. *Cultural Stress and Alcoholism; A Study of Their Relationship among Navaho Alcoholic Men.* Ann Arbor: University Microfilms, 1969. 222 pp.
    A University of Minnesota doctoral dissertation.

1569. SAXTON, DEAN AND LUCILLE SAXTON. *Dictionary: Papago & Pima to English; English to Papago & Pima.* Tucson: University of Arizona Press, 1969. 191 pp., illus.

1570. SAYLES, EDWIN B. *Fantasies of Gold: Legends of Treasures and How They Grew.* Tucson: University of Arizona Press, 1968. 135 pp., illus.
    Some recent stories of lost treasures and a few hoaxes.

1571. *A Scenic Interest Acquisition Program for the Arizona Highway Department.* Tempe, Arizona: James C. Wells, 1966–67. 2 vols., illus., maps.
    Report prepared by Western Landscape Associates, Phoenix. Vol. 1, Study of land acquisition for preservation and enhancement of highway beauty. Vol. 2, Highway log of sites.

1572. SCHAAFSMA, POLLY. *Early Navaho Rock Paintings and Carvings.* [Santa Fe]: Museum of Navaho Ceremonial Art, [1966]. 32 pp.

1573. SCHAFROTH, DON W. *Structure and Stratigraphy of the Cretaceous Rocks South of the Empire Mountains, Pima and Santa Cruz Counties, Arizona.* Ann Arbor: University Microfilms, 1966. 194 pp.
    A University of Arizona doctoral dissertation.

1574. SCHALDACH, WILLIAM J. *Path to Enchantment: An Artist in the Sonoran Desert.* New York: Macmillan, 1963. 225 pp., illus.
    The desert and its inhabitants, copiously illustrated with the author's excellent sketches and drawings.

1575. SCHAPPS, JOHN. *Good People in Bad Trouble: A Report and a Plan for Apache Action.* [New York]: National Probation and Parole Association, 1953. 54 pp., tables.

1576. SCHARFF, ROBERT. *Exploring Grand Canyon National Park.* New York: World Publishing, 1969. 47 pp., illus., map.

1577. ———. *Grand Canyon National Park.* New York: David McKay, 1967. 198 pp., illus.
   All about the park, compiled for the visitor.

1578. SCHELLIE, DON. *Vast Domain of Blood: The Story of the Camp Grant Massacre.* Los Angeles: Westernlore Press, 1968. 268 pp., illus.

1579. SCHMEDDING, JOSEPH. *Cowboy and Indian Trader.* Caldwell, Idaho: Caxton Printers, 1951. 364 pp., illus.
   Cowpunching in the Four Corners area and trading at Keams Canyon.

1580. SCHMIDLI, R. J. AND OTHERS. *Climate of Phoenix, Arizona.* Salt Lake City: [U. S. Weather Bureau, Western Region], 1969. 51 pp., tables.

1581. SCHMUTZ, ERVIN M. AND OTHERS. *Livestock-Poisoning Plants of Arizona.* Tucson: University of Arizona Press, 1968. 176 pp., illus.

1582. *School Costs; the Per Pupil Cost of Operating Public Schools in Arizona . . . .* Phoenix: Arizona Tax Research Association, 1953–
   Annual, beginning with the year 1952–53.

1583. SCHROEDER, ALBERT H. *The Archeological Excavations at Willow Beach, Arizona, 1950.* Salt Lake City: University of Utah Press, 1961. (University of Utah, Department of Anthropology, Anthropological Papers no. 50) 163 pp., illus., maps, tables.
   A site on the Colorado River south of Hoover Dam.

1584. ———. *A Brief Survey of the Lower Colorado River from Davis Dam to the International Border.* Boulder City, Nevada: U. S. Bureau of Reclamation, [1953]. 77 pp., illus.
   An archaeological survey.

1585. ———. *The Hohokam, Sinagua and the Hakataya.* Madison Society for American Archaeology and University of Wisconsin Press, 1960. (Archives of Archaeology, no. 5) 209 pp., on 4 microcards.
   Published only on microcards.

1586. ———. *A Study of Yavapai History.* Santa Fe: 1959. 3 pts.
   Cover title. Mimeographed; prepared for the Department of Justice.

1587. ——— AND HOMER F. HASTINGS. *Montezuma Castle National Monument, Arizona.* Washington: National Park Service, 1958. (Historical Handbook Series no. 27) 40 pp., illus., maps.

1588. SCHULMAN, EDMUND. *Dendroclimatic Changes in Semiarid America.* Tucson: University of Arizona Press, 1956. 142 pp., tables, diags.

1589. SCHULTZ, VERNON B. *Southwestern Town: The Story of Willcox, Arizona.* Tucson: University of Arizona Press, 1964. 140 pp., illus.

1590. SCHWALEN, HAROLD C. *Little Chino Valley Artesian Area & Groundwater Basin.* Tucson: University of Arizona Agricultural Experiment Station, 1967. (Technical Bulletin no. 178) 63 pp., illus., tables, maps, diags.

1591. ———. *Suspended Sediment and Chemical Analysis of San Pedro River at Charleston, Arizona.* Tucson: University of Arizona Agricultural Experiment Station, 1961. (Report no. 202) 21 pp., tables, diags.

1592. ——— AND RICHARD J. SHAW. *Ground Water Supplies of Santa Cruz Valley of Southern Arizona between Rillito Station and the International Boundary.* Tucson: University of Arizona Agricultural Experiment Station, 1957. (Bulletin no. 288) 119 pp., illus., tables, maps.

1593. ——— AND ———. *Progress Report on Study of Water in the Santa Cruz Valley, Arizona.* Tucson: University of Arizona Agricultural Experiment Station, 1961. (Report no. 205) various paging, tables, diags., maps.
    Supplements and brings to date Schwalen and Shaw above.

1594. SCHWARTZ, DOUGLAS W. *Havasupai Prehistory: Thirteen Centuries of Cultural Development.* Ann Arbor: University Microfilms, 1967. 313 pp.
    A Yale University doctoral dissertation.

1595. SCHWARTZ, GEORGE M. *Geology of the San Manuel Copper Deposit, Arizona.* Washington: U. S. Geological Survey, 1953. (Professional Paper no. 256) 65 pp., maps, diags.

1596. SCHWEINSBURG, RAYMOND E. *Social Behavior of the Collared Peccary* (Pecari tajacu) *in the Tucson Mountains.* Ann Arbor: University Microfilms, 1969. 129 pp.
    A University of Arizona doctoral dissertation.

1597. SCOTT, GERALD L. *Permian Sedimentary Framework of the Four Corners Region.* Ann Arbor: University Microfilms, 1960. 137 pp.
    A University of Wisconsin doctoral dissertation.

1598. [SCOTTSDALE] *A Comprehensive Plan for Scottsdale, Arizona.* [Phoenix]: Maricopa County Planning and Zoning Department, 1960–62. 2 vols.
Vol. 1, Scope and objectives, economic analysis, population and land use.
Vol. 2, Major streets and highways.

1599. [SCOTTSDALE] *Economic Base Study, City of Scottsdale, Arizona.* Prepared by Real Estate Research Corporation. [South Pasadena, California?]: Eisner-Stewart and Associates, [1966]. 162 pp., tables, maps.

1600. [SCOTTSDALE] *Introduction to Scottsdale and the Valley.* [Scottsdale, Arizona]: League of Women Voters of Scottsdale, 1961. (Publication no. 1) 32 pp., diags.

1601. [SCOTTSDALE] *Land Use Analysis, City of Scottsdale, Arizona.* [South Pasadena, California?]: Eisner-Stewart and Associates, [1966]. 31 pp., charts.

1602. [SCOTTSDALE] *Report of the Survey of Scottsdale Public Schools, November 1956.* [Tempe]: Arizona State University Bureau of Educational Research and Services, 1956. 321 pp., tables.

1603. SEAGER, WILLIAM R. *Geology of the Bunkerville Section of the Virgin Mountains, Nevada and Arizona.* Ann Arbor: University Microfilms, 1966. 188 pp.
A University of Arizona doctoral dissertation.

1604. SEARGEANT, HELEN H. *House by the Buckeye Road.* San Antonio: Naylor, 1960. 210 pp., illus.
Farming in the Salt River Valley, c1915–1925.

1605. SEDELMAYR, JACOBO. *Jacobo Sedelmayr, Missionary, Frontiersman, Explorer in Arizona and Sonora; Four Original Manuscript Narratives, 1744–1751.* Translated and annotated by Peter M. Dunne. [Tucson]: Arizona Pioneers' Historical Society, 1955. 82 pp., map.
Printed by Lawton Kennedy and limited to 600 copies.

1606. SEFF, PHILIP. *Stratigraphic Geology and Depositional Environments of the 111 Ranch Area, Graham County, Arizona.* Ann Arbor: University Microfilms, 1962. 216 pp.
A University of Arizona doctoral dissertation.

1607. SEKAQUAPTEWA, HELEN. *Me and Mine: The Life Story of Helen Sekaquaptewa As Told to Louise Udall.* Tucson: University of Arizona Press, 1969. 262 pp., illus.
Autobiography of a Hopi woman.

1608. ... *Selected Natural Resources*. Prepared by Arizona Research Consultants. Phoenix: Arizona Development Board, [1954?]. 85 pp.
Nonmetallic resources.

1609. SELLERS, WILLIAM D. *The Annual and Diurnal Variations of Cloud Amounts and Cloud Types at Six Arizona Cities*. Tucson: University of Arizona Institute of Atmospheric Physics, 1958. (Scientific Report no. 8) 104 pp., illus., diags.

1610. ———, ED. *Arizona Climate*. Prepared by the staff of the Institute of Atmospheric Physics ... with ... the United States Weather Bureau. Tucson: University of Arizona Press, 1960. 60 pp., voluminous appendices, tables, maps.
Detailed summaries for 91 locations and abbreviated summaries for 19 more.

1611. SELTZER, RAYMOND E. *Seasonal Variations in Prices and Shipments of Arizona Beef Cattle*. Tucson: University of Arizona Agricultural Experiment Station, 1953. (Bulletin no. 251) 32 pp., illus.

1612. ——— AND E. E. PFUEHLER. *Prices and Production of Arizona Farm and Ranch Products*. Tucson: Arizona Agricultural Experiment Station, 1959. (Special Report, no. 1) 41 pp., tables.
Statistical tables.

1613. SENIOR, WILLOUGHBY F. *Smoke upon the Winds*. Denver: Sage Books, 1961. 144 pp., illus.
About the traditional Hopi way.

1614. SHADEGG, STEPHEN C. *Barry Goldwater: Freedom Is His Flight Plan*. New York: Fleet Publishing, 1962. 304 pp., illus.
Biography.

1615. ———. *Century One, 1869–1969: One Hundred Years of Water Development in the Salt River Valley*. Phoenix: W. A. Krueger, 1969. 48 pp., illus., maps.

1616. ———. *The Phoenix Story, an Adventure in Reclamation*. Phoenix, 1958. 39 pp., illus., maps.
Issued as a separate but also bound in with the 1957 annual report of the Salt River Project.

1617. SHAEFFER, JAMES B. *The Mogollon Complex; Its Cultural Role and Historical Development in the American Southwest*. Ann Arbor: University Microfilms, 1954. 234 pp.
A Columbia University doctoral dissertation.

1618. SHAW, ANNA M. *Pima Indian Legends*. Tempe: Arizona State University Indian Education Center, 1963. 116 pp., illus.
Mimeographed. Mrs. Shaw is a Pima.

1619. ———. *Pima Indian Legends*. Tucson: University of Arizona Press, 1968. 111 pp., illus.
A revision of the item above.

1620. SHELTON, CHARLES E., COMP. *Photo Album of Yesterday's Southwest.* Palm Desert, California: Desert Magazine, 1961. unpaged.
One hundred ninety-one fascinating photographs mostly taken in the last three decades of the nineteenth century and mostly of Arizona scenes.

1621. SHEPARDSON, MARY. *Navajo Ways in Government.* Menasha, Wisconsin: American Anthropological Association, 1963. (Memoir no. 96) 132 pp.

1622. SHERER, LORRAINE M. *The Clan System of the Fort Mojave Indians.* Los Angeles: Historical Society of Southern California, 1965. 85 pp., illus.
Originally printed in the March 1965 issue of the *Southern California Quarterly.* This edition limited to 300 copies.

1623. SHERMAN, JAMES E. AND BARBARA SHERMAN. *Ghost Towns of Arizona.* Norman: University of Oklahoma Press, 1969. 208 pp., illus., maps.

1624. SHIRER, JOHN. *Postwar Chart Book of Business Indicators, Arizona and the United States.* Tucson: University of Arizona Bureau of Business Research, 1955. (Special Studies no. 10) 11 pp., diags.

1625. SHOEMAKER, EUGENE M. *Impact Mechanics at Meteor Crater, Arizona.* Ann Arbor: University Microfilms, 1960. 55 pp.
A Princeton University doctoral dissertation.

1626. SHREVE, FORREST. *Vegetation of the Sonoran Desert.* Washington, D. C.: Carnegie Institution of Washington, 1951. (Publication no. 591) 192 pp., illus., maps.
See item 1627 below.

1627. ———— AND IRA L. WIGGINS. *Vegetation and Flora of the Sonoran Desert.* Stanford, California: Stanford University Press, 1964. 2 vols.
The first part reprints Shreve's *Vegetation of the Sonoran Desert,* above, the index of which has been moved to the end of the second volume. The rest is a technical flora.

1628. SHRIDE, ANDREW F. *Some Aspects of Younger Precambrian Geology in Southern Arizona.* Ann Arbor: University Microfilms, 1962. 294 pp.
A University of Arizona doctoral dissertation.

1629. ————. *Younger Precambrian Geology in Southern Arizona.* Washington: U. S. Geological Survey, 1967. (Professional Paper no. 566) 89 pp., illus., maps, diags.
"Stratigraphic, lithologic, and structural features of younger Precambrian rocks of southern Arizona as a basis for understanding their paleogeography and establishing their correlation."

1630. SHUKRY, LAILA S. *The Role of Women in a Changing Navaho Society.* Ann Arbor: University Microfilms, 1954. 337 pp.
A Cornell University doctoral dissertation.

1631. Shutler, Mary E. *Persistence and Change in the Health Beliefs and Practices of an Arizona Yaqui Community.* Ann Arbor: University Microfilms, 1967. 238 pp.
A University of Arizona doctoral dissertation.

1632. Sides, Dorothy S. *Decorative Art of the Southwestern Indians.* With annotations by Clarice Martin Smith. New York: Dover Publications, Inc., 1961. xviii pp. and 50 numbered plates, illus.
Fifty black-and-white plates of designs with accompanying identification and brief description. An "unabridged and corrected republication of the work first published in portfolio format by the Fine Arts Press, Santa Ana, California in 1936."

1633. *Sierra Vista, Arizona, Planning Report.* [Phoenix?]: Van Cleve Associates, 1963–65. 6 parts, tables, maps.
Part 1, Regional location, history and resources, existing land use.
Part 2, Population, economics.
Part 3, Community facilities.
Part 4, Streets and thoroughfares, public utilities.
Part 5, Housing.
Part 6, Carrying out the plan.

1634. *Sierra Vista General Plan: A Guide for Growth, Sierra Vista Urban Area, Cochise County, Arizona.* Scottsdale, Arizona: Van Cleve Associates, 1961. 1 folded sheet, maps.

1635. Sikorski, Kathryn A. *Modern Hopi Pottery.* Logan: Utah State University Press, 1968. (Utah State University Monograph Series, vol. 15, no. 2) 92 pp., illus.

1636. Simkins, Paul D. *Regionalisms in the Recent Migration to Arizona.* Ann Arbor: University Microfilms, 1961. 202 pp.
A University of Wisconsin doctoral dissertation.

1637. Simmons, George C. and David L. Gaskill. *River Runners' Guide to the Canyons of the Green and Colorado Rivers, with Emphasis on Geologic Features.* Vol. III. Marble Gorge and Grand Canyon. Flagstaff, Arizona: Northland Press in Cooperation with Powell Society Ltd., 750 Vine St., Denver, Colorado, [1969]. 132 pp., illus., diags., maps.
Volumes I and II described the upper river.

1638. Simmons, Hilah L. *The Geology of the Cabeza Prieta Game Range.* Ajo, Arizona: The Author, 1965. 55 pp., illus., maps, tables.

1639. Simmons, Lansing G. *Survey of the Boundary between Arizona and California.* Washington: U. S. Coast and Geodetic Survey, 1965. (Technical Bulletin no. 27) 94 pp., illus., maps, tables, diags.

1640. SIMONS, FRANK S. *Geology of the Klondyke Quadrangle, Graham and Pinal Counties, Arizona.* Washington: U. S. Geological Survey, 1964. (Professional Paper no. 461) 173 pp., illus., tables, maps, diags.
"Includes a part of the Basin and Range province and several small base-metal mining areas."

1641. SIMPSON, BESSIE W. *Gem Trails of Arizona: A Field Guide for Collectors.* Granbury, Texas: Gem Trails Publishing Co., 1964. 88 pp., illus., maps.

1642. SIMPSON, JAMES H. *Navaho Expedition: Journal of a Military Reconnaissance from Santa Fe, New Mexico, to the Navaho Country Made in 1849.* Edited and annotated by Frank McNitt. Norman: University of Oklahoma Press, 1964. 296 pp., illus.
The journal was originally published in 1850 as part of Senate Executive Document 64, 31st Congress, 1st Session.

1643. SIMPSON, RUTH DEE. *The Hopi Indians.* Los Angeles: Southwest Museum, 1953. (Leaflet no. 25) 91 pp., illus.
Originally published as a series of articles in *Masterkey.*

1644. SIRRINE, GEORGE K. *Geology of the Springerville-St. Johns Area, Apache County, Arizona.* Ann Arbor: University Microfilms, 1959. 273 pp.
A University of Texas doctoral dissertation.

1645. *The Sisters of the Precious Blood in Arizona, 1903–1953.* [Phoenix? 1953?]. 32 pp., illus.

1646. SITGREAVES, LORENZO. *Report of an Expedition down the Zuni and the Colorado Rivers in 1851.* Chicago: Rio Grande Press, 1962. 198 pp., plates variously numbered, map.
A facsimile reissue of the original published in 1853 as Senate Executive Document 59, 32nd Congress, 2nd Session.

1647. SKAU, CLARENCE M. *Some Hydrologic Characteristics in the Utah Juniper Type of Northern Arizona.* Ann Arbor: University Microfilms, 1962. 170 pp.
A Michigan State University doctoral dissertation.

1648. SKINNER, CARL H. *Good Indians.* New York: Comet Press Books, 1958. 150 pp.
A chronicle of the Phoenix Indian School by a former superintendent.

1649. SLOTER, JAMES F. *Eloy.* [Indio, California? 1950?]. 64 pp., illus.
Crime in a contemporary Tombstone.

1650. SMALLEY, GEORGE H. *My Adventures in Arizona: Leaves from a Reporter's Notebook.* Edited by Yndia Smalley Moore. Tucson: Arizona Pioneers' Historical Society, 1966. 154 pp., illus.

1651. SMILEY, TERAH L., ED. *Four Late Prehistoric Kivas at Point of Pines, Arizona.* Tucson: University of Arizona, 1952. (Social Science Bulletin no. 21) 72 pp., illus.

1652. ———. *A Summary of Tree-Ring Dates from Some Southwestern Archaeological Sites.* Tucson: University of Arizona, 1951. (Laboratory of Tree-Ring Research Bulletin no. 5) 32 pp., tables.

1653. SMITH, CORNELIUS C., JR. *William Sanders Oury, History-Maker of the Southwest.* Tucson: University of Arizona Press, 1967. 298 pp., illus., maps.

1654. SMITH, COURTLAND L. *The Salt River Project of Arizona: Its Organization and Integration with the Community.* Ann Arbor: University Microfilms, 1968. 339 pp.
     A University of Arizona doctoral dissertation.

1655. SMITH, DEAN E. *Men to Match Our Buildings: A History of Arizona State University Told in the Biographies of Its Builders.* Tempe: Arizona State University, 1967. 36 pp., illus.

1656. SMITH, DOUGLAS. *Mineralogy and Petrology of an Olivine Diabase Sill Complex and Associated Unusually Potassic Granophyres, Sierra Ancha, Central Arizona.* Ann Arbor: University Microfilms, 1969. 345 pp.
     A California Institute of Technology doctoral dissertation.

1657. SMITH, FAY J. AND OTHERS. *Father Kino in Arizona.* Phoenix: Arizona Historical Foundation, 1966. 142 pp. illus., maps.
     Kino's "Relación Diaria" of his 1698 trip to the Gila and the Pinacate region, and Lieutenant Martin Bernal's diary of 1698 by Fay Smith; "Peaceful Conquest in Southern Arizona," by John Kessell, and a bibliography by Francis J. Fox, S.J.

1658. SMITH, GEORGE E. P. *Arizona Loses a Water Supply.* Tucson: The Author, 1956. 28 pp.
     Supplement, 1958. 28 pp.

1659. SMITH, GEORGE H. *High School Dropouts and Graduates among Pima Indians in Three Arizona High Schools.* Ann Arbor: University Microfilms, 1967. 170 pp.
     An Arizona State University doctoral dissertation.

1660. SMITH, GERALD A. *The Mohaves.* [San Bernardino, California]: San Bernardino County Museum Association, 1966. (San Bernardino County Museum Association Quarterly, vol. XIV, no. 1) 66 pp., illus.

1661. SMITH, GUSSE T. *Birds of the Southwestern Desert.* Scottsdale: Doubleshoe Publishers, 1955. 68 pp., illus.
     Slightly enlarged edition of the author's *Birds of the Arizona Desert,* originally published in 1941.

1662. ———. *Birds of the Southwestern Desert.* Illustrations by Harriet Morton Holmes. Scottsdale, Arizona: Doubleshoe Publishers, 1962.
Originally issued in 1941 with the title *Birds of the Arizona Desert.* Reprinted in 1955 and 1958 under the present title. Here reprinted with the black-and-white drawings crudely colored.

1663. SMITH, HOWARD V. *The Climate of Arizona.* Tucson: University of Arizona Agricultural Experiment Station, 1956. (Bulletin no. 279) 99 pp., tables.
Second revision of Bulletin no. 130 published in 1930.

1664. ——— AND OTHERS. *The Quality of Arizona Irrigation Water.* Tucson: University of Arizona Agricultural Experiment Station, 1964. (Report no. 233) 96 pp., tables, maps.

1665. ——— AND ———. *The Quality of Arizona's Domestic Waters.* Tucson: University of Arizona Agricultural Experiment Station, 1963. (Report no. 217) 77 pp., tables, maps.
Detailed tables of wells.

1666. SMITH, OLGA W. *Gold on the Desert.* Albuquerque: University of New Mexico Press, 1956. 249 pp., illus.
The Lechuguilla Desert southeast of Yuma.

1667. SMITH, RICHARD K. AND J. MELVIN NELSON. *Datelines and By-Lines: A Sketchbook of Presbyterian Beginnings and Growth in Arizona.* [Phoenix: Synod of Arizona, United Presbyterian Church in the U. S. A.], 1969. 90 pp., illus.

1668. SMITH, RILEY S. *A Study of the Chinle-Shinarump Beds in the Leupp-Holbrook Area, Arizona.* Ann Arbor: University Microfilms, 1957. 170 pp.
A University of Arizona doctoral dissertation.

1669. SMITH, WATSON. *Excavations in Big Hawk Valley, Wupatki National Monument, Arizona.* Appendix by George Ennis. Flagstaff: Northern Arizona Society of Science and Art, 1952. (Museum of Northern Arizona Bulletin no. 24) 203 pp., illus., tables, maps.

1670. ———. *Kiva Mural Decorations at Awatovi and Kawaika-a with a Survey of Other Wall Paintings in the Pueblo Southwest.* Cambridge, Massachusetts: Peabody Museum, 1952. (Peabody Papers vol. 37) 363 pp., illus.

1671. ———. *The Story of the Museum of Northern Arizona.* [Flagstaff]: Museum of Northern Arizona, 1969. 38 pp., illus.
Text of an address before the Newcomen Society.

1672. SMITH, WILLIAM O. AND OTHERS. *Comprehensive Survey of Sedimentation in Lake Mead, 1948–49.* Washington: U. S. Geological Survey, 1960. (Professional Paper, no. 295) 254 pp., illus., tables, maps, diags.

1673. ———— AND ————. *Lake Mead Comprehensive Survey of 1948–49.* [Washington]: U. S. Geological Survey, 1954. 3 vols., illus., maps, diags.
      Detailed reservoir survey for operational purposes — water quality, sedimentation, etc.

1674. SMITHSON, CARMA L. *The Havasupai Woman.* Salt Lake City: University of Utah Press, 1959. (University of Utah Department of Anthropology, Anthropological Papers no. 38) 170 pp., illus., maps.

1675. ———— AND ROBERT C. EULER. *Havasupai Religion and Mythology.* Salt Lake City: University of Utah Press, 1964. (University of Utah Department of Anthropology, Anthropological Papers no. 68) 112 pp.

1676. SNODGRASS, RICHARD AND LORINE GARRETT. *Prescott, Arizona: A Pictorial History.* Phoenix: Toney Publishing, 1964. unpaged, illus.

1677. [SNOWFLAKE] *Union High School District No. 60: Report of Survey, May 1966.* Tempe: Arizona State University Bureau of Educational Research and Services, [1966]. 81 pp., tables.

1678. SNYDER, ERNEST E. *Central Arizona Field Guide.* Tempe, Arizona: Lamont Company, 1968. 43 pp., illus., maps.
      Biology of central Arizona.

1679. SNYDER, RICHARD G. *The Dental Morphology of the Point of Pines Indians.* Ann Arbor: University Microfilms, 1959. 349 pp.
      A University of Arizona doctoral dissertation.

1680. SORAUF, JAMES E. *Structural Geology and Stratigraphy of the Whitmore Area, Mohave County, Arizona.* Ann Arbor: University Microfilms, 1963. 398 pp.
      A University of Kansas doctoral dissertation.

1681. SOULE, OSCAR H. *Osmotic Concentration of Tissue Fluids in the Sahuaro Giant Cactus.* Ann Arbor: University Microfilms, 1969. 275 pp.
      A University of Arizona doctoral dissertation.

1682. SOUTH, ZARY. *Southwest Hunting and Fishing.* Tucson: Tucson Chamber of Commerce, [1950?]. 24 pp., maps.

1683. *Southwest Indian Art.* Tucson: University of Arizona, 1960. 37 pp., illus.
      "A report to the Rockefeller Foundation covering the activities of the first exploratory workshop in art for talented younger Indians held at The University of Arizona the summer of 1960."

1684. *The Southwestern Research Station of the American Museum of Natural History.* New York: American Museum of Natural History, 1957. 30 pp., illus.
The station is located in the Chiricahua Mountains near Portal.

1685. *Souvenir of Flagstaff and Coconino County, Arizona.* Flagstaff: Northland Press, 1964. unpaged, illus.
Facsimile edition of a promotional pamphlet of 1918.

1686. SOWLS, LYLE K. *Wildlife Conservation through Cooperation.* Tucson: University of Arizona Press, 1956. 32 pp., illus.
Describes the work of the Arizona Cooperative Research Unit.

1687. SPANGLER, DANIEL P. *A Geophysical Study of the Hydrogeology of the Walnut Gulch Experimental Watershed, Tombstone, Arizona.* Ann Arbor: University Microfilms, 1969.
A University of Arizona doctoral dissertation.

1688. SPENCER, JOHN S., JR. *Arizona's Forests.* Ogden, Utah: Intermountain Forest and Range Experiment Station, 1966. (U. S. Forest Service Resource Bulletin INT-6) 57 pp., illus., maps., tables, diags.

1689. SPENCER, KATHERINE. *Mythology and Values, an Analysis of Navaho Chantway Myths.* Philadelphia: American Folklore Society, 1957. (Memoirs vol. 48) 240 pp.

1690. SPICER, EDWARD H. *Cycles of Conquest: The Impact of Spain, Mexico, and the United States on the Indians of the Southwest, 1533–1960.* Tucson: University of Arizona Press, 1962. 609 pp., illus., maps.

1691. ——— AND OTHERS. *Impounded People: Japanese-Americans in the Relocation Centers.* Tucson: University of Arizona Press, 1969. 342 pp., illus.
Reprint of a War Relocation Authority report of 1946. A few corrections have been made.

1692. SPIER, LESLIE. *Mohave Culture Items.* Flagstaff: Northern Arizona Society of Science and Art, 1955. (Museum of Northern Arizona Bulletin no. 28) 35 pp., illus.

1693. SPIRO, EDWARD *see* Cookridge, E. H.

1694. SPOONER, JANE. *Tubac — Town of 9 Lives.* Tucson: Paragon Press, 1962. unpaged, illus.
Attractively printed and illustrated pamphlet.

1695. SPRING, JOHN. *John Spring's Arizona.* Edited by A. M. Gustafson. Tucson: University of Arizona Press, 1966. 326 pp., illus.
Contents: With the Regulars in Arizona in the sixties. Troublous days in Arizona. Originally appeared in the *National Tribune,* Washington, in 1902 and 1903.

1696. STAHNKE, HERBERT L. *Scorpions*. Revised edition. Tempe: Arizona State College, 1956. 36 pp., illus., tables.
Originally published in 1949.

1697. STANTON, ROBERT BREWSTER. *Down the Colorado*. Edited with an introduction by Dwight L. Smith. Norman: University of Oklahoma Press, 1965. 237 pp., illus.

1698. *The Status of Driver Education in Arizona*. [Phoenix]: Arizona Highway Department, [1961]. 39 pp., tables.

1699. STEADMAN, WILLIAM E. *La Tierra Encantada*. Tucson, 1969. 160 pp., illus.
Brief introduction and 139 color reproductions of paintings and sketches by Tucson artist Hurlstone Fairchild.

1700. STEEN, CHARLIE R. *Excavations at Tse-Ta'a, Canyon de Chelly National Monument, Arizona*. Washington: National Park Service, 1966. (Archeological Research Series no. 9) 160 pp., illus., tables, diags.

1701. ——— AND OTHERS. *Archeological Studies at Tonto National Monument, Arizona*. [Globe, Arizona]: Southwestern Monuments Association, 1962. (Technical Series no. 2) 176 pp., illus., tables, maps, diags.

1702. STEPHEN, ALEXANDER M. *Hopi Journal of Alexander M. Stephen*. Edited by Elsie Clews Parsons. New York: AMS Press, 1969. (Columbia University Contributions to Anthropology Vol. xxiii) 2 vols., illus.
Facsimile reprint of the original edition of 1936.

1703. STEVENS, ROBERT C. *A History of Chandler, Arizona, 1912–1953*. Tucson: University of Arizona Press, 1955. (Social Science Bulletin no. 25) 106 pp., illus.

1704. STEVENS, STANFORD. *Plants of Sun and Sand: The Desert Growth of Arizona*. Tucson: The Print Room, 1955. 46 pp., illus.
Illustrations by Gerry Peirce. Originally issued in smaller format bound in wood boards, 1939.

1705. STEVENSON, CHARLES S. *"We Met at Camelback!"* Scottsdale, Arizona: Desert Publishing Co., 1968. 248 pp., illus.

1706. STEVENSON, GRACE T. *Arizona Library Survey: A Comprehensive Study of Library Services in Arizona With a Projection for Future Services*. Tempe: Arizona State University Bureau of Educational Research and Services, 1968. 272 pp., tables.
Intended to serve as a basis for library development in the state. Another printing of 100 pages omits the appendices.

1707. STEWART, JOHN H. *Stratigraphy and Origin of the Chinle Formation (Upper Triassic) on the Colorado Plateau*. Ann Arbor: University Microfilms, 1961. 247 pp.
A Stanford University doctoral dissertation.

1708. STEWART, LINCOLN A. *Chrysotile-Asbestos Deposits in Arizona.* [Pittsburgh]: U. S. Bureau of Mines, 1955. (Information Circular no. 7706) 124 pp., illus., maps.

1709. ————. *Mining Methods and Costs, Regal Asbestos Mine, Jaquays Mining Corp, Gila County, Ariz.* [Washington]: U. S. Bureau of Mines, [1961]. (Information Circular no. 7986) 53 pp., illus., tables, maps.

1710. ———— AND A. J. PFISTER. *Barite Deposits of Arizona.* [Washington]: U. S. Bureau of Mines, 1960. (Report of Investigations no. 5651) 89 pp., illus., maps.

1711. STIRLING, BETTY. *Mission to the Navajo.* Mountain View, California: Pacific Press Publishing Assn., 1961. 147 pp., illus.
Seventh Day Adventist missions on the reservation.

1712. STOCKER, JOSEPH S. *Arizona, a Guide to Easier Living.* New York: Harper, 1955. 216 pp.
Where and how to live, housing, etc. A good description of the state at the time of writing.

1713. ————. *Jewish Roots in Arizona.* Phoenix: Jewish Community Council, 1954. 36 pp.

1714. STOCKERT, JOHN W. *Common Wildflowers of the Grand Canyon.* Salt Lake City: Wheelwright Press, 1967. 50 pp., illus.

1715. STOKES, MARSDEN B. AND OTHERS. *Arizona Junior Colleges: An Investment in Educational Opportunities for Youth and Adults.* [Tucson]: University of Arizona Bureau of Educational Research and Service, 1968. Various paging.

1716. STORM, BARRY. *Thunder God's Gold.* Quincy, Illinois: Storm-Mollet Publishing, 1953. 167 pp., illus.
Lost mines and buried treasure. Revised edition of the title originally issued in 1945; includes the author's *Practical Prospecting,* issued in 1946.

1717. *The Story of Hoover Dam.* Washington: U. S. Department of the Interior, 1966. 79 pp., illus., maps, diags.

1718. STRAAYER, JOHN A. *The Politics of Water Resource Management in the Tucson, Arizona, S. M. S. A.* Ann Arbor: University Microfilms, 1967. 320 pp.
A University of Arizona doctoral dissertation. S.M.S.A. is Standard Metropolitan Statistic Area.

1719. STRATTON, EMERSON O. AND EDITH S. KITT. *Pioneering in Arizona: The Reminiscences of Emerson Oliver Stratton and Edith Stratton Kitt.* Tucson: Arizona Pioneers' Historical Society, 1964. 178 pp., illus.
One thousand copies printed.

1720. STREETS, RUBERT B., SR. *Diseases of the Cultivated Plants of the Southwest.* Tucson: University of Arizona Press, 1969. 390 pp., illus.

1721. STREIB, GORDON F. *Patterns of Communication among the Navaho Indians.* Ann Arbor: University Microfilms, 1955. 342 pp.
A Columbia University doctoral dissertation.

1722. STUBBLEFIELD, THOMAS M. *Economic Survey of Navajo County.* Tucson: University of Arizona Agricultural Extension Service, 1953. 45 pp., tables, maps.

1723. ———. *Market News and Related Information Received and Used by Arizona Beef Cattle Producers.* Tucson: University of Arizona Agricultural Experiment Station, 1956. (Report no. 141) 16 pp., tables.

1724. ———. *Market News Sources for Arizona Cattle Producers.* Tucson: University of Arizona Agricultural Experiment Station, 1955. (Report no. 125) 16 pp.

1725. ——— AND ARTHUR H. SMITH. *A Survey of the Production and Marketing of Cattle Manure in Arizona.* Tucson: University of Arizona Agricultural Experiment Station and Cooperative Extension Service, 1964. (Bulletin no. A-36) 14 pp., tables.

1726. STUBBS, STANLEY A. *Bird's-Eye View of the Pueblos.* Norman: University of Oklahoma Press, 1950. 122 pp., illus., plans.
Aerial views in Arizona and New Mexico with accompanying text.

1727. *Studies in Southwestern Ethnolinguistics: Meaning and History in the Languages of the American Southwest.* Edited by Dell H. Hymes and William E. Bittle. The Hague: Mouton & Co., 1967. (Studies in General Anthropology III) 464 pp., maps.

1728. *Study and Review of the Arizona Department of Public Welfare and Associated Agencies.* Report of the House Welfare Study Committee of the First Regular Session, 25th Arizona Legislature. [Phoenix, 1962]. 87 pp.

1729. STULIK, R. S. *Effects of Ground-Water Withdrawal, 1954–63, in the Lower Harquahala Plains, Maricopa County, Arizona.* Phoenix: Arizona State Land Dept., 1964. (Water Resources Report no. 17) 8 pp., maps.
Prepared by the U.S.G.S.

1730. ——— AND OTTO MOOSBURNER. *Hydrologic Conditions in the Gila Bend Basin, Maricopa County, Arizona.* Phoenix: Arizona State Land Dept., 1969. (Water-Resources Report no. 39) 63 pp., maps, tables, diags.

1731. —— AND F. R. TWENTER. *Geology and Ground Water of the Luke Area, Maricopa County, Arizona.* Washington: U. S. Geological Survey, 1964. (Water-Supply Paper 1779-P) 30 pp., tables, maps.

1732. SUMMERHAYES, MARTHA. *Vanished Arizona: Recollections of the Army Life of a New England Woman.* Introduction, glossary, and bibliographical notes by Ray Brandes. Tucson: Arizona Silhouettes, 1960. 273 pp., illus.
    A reprint of the second edition of 1911 of this classic of Arizona army life in the 1870s.

1733. ——. *Vanished Arizona: Recollections of My Army Life.* The 1908 edition unabridged with an introduction by W. Turrentine Jackson. New York: Lippincott, 1963. 258 pp.
    Facsimile of the text of the first edition. The second edition of 1911 (see item above) contained some additional material.

1734. *Sunset Discovery Trips in Arizona.* Menlo Park, California: Lane Publishing Company, 1956. 101 pp., illus., maps.
    Revised edition with title *Arizona,* 1962. 101 pp.

1735. SUPPLEE, CHARLES AND OTHERS. *Canyon de Chelly National Monument, Arizona.* Ganado, Arizona: Supplee-Anderson, 1965. 28 pp., illus.
    A pleasantly produced pamphlet for the visitor, with good photographic illustrations.

1736. *Surface Water Records of Arizona, 1961.* Tucson: U. S. Geological Survey, 1962. 167 pp., tables.
    First of an annual series replacing the Water-Supply Papers published on a river-basin basis.

1737. [Surprise] *A Planning Report for Surprise, Arizona.* [Phoenix]: Maricopa County Planning and Zoning Department, 1961. 20 pp., maps.

1738. *A Survey for a Proposed Junior College in Yuma County, Arizona.* Tucson: University of Arizona Bureau of School Services, 1961. 58 pp., tables, maps, diags.

1739. *Survey of Arizona Law. . . .* Tucson: University of Arizona Bar Association, 1957–58.
    Two issued covering 1956 and 1957. Superseded by the *Arizona Law Review.*

1740. SUTTON, ANN AND MYRON SUTTON. *The Life of the Desert.* New York: McGraw-Hill in cooperation with World Book Encyclopedia, 1966. 232 pp., illus., diags.
    Written for young people but should provide a good introduction for anyone.

1741. SWANK, WENDELL G. *The Mule Deer in Arizona Chaparral.* Phoenix: Arizona Game and Fish Department, 1958. (Wildlife Bulletin no. 3) 109 pp., illus., tables, diags.

1742. SWEENY, THOMAS W. *Journal of Lt. Thomas W. Sweeny, 1849–1853.* Edited by Arthur Woodward. Los Angeles: Westernlore Press, 1956. 278 pp., illus.
   Journal kept at Fort Yuma. Limited to 350 copies.

1743. [Sycamore Canyon] *Report on the Proposed Sycamore Canyon Wilderness, Coconino, Kaibab, Prescott National Forests.* Albuquerque: U. S. Forest Service, [1967?]. 70 pp., illus., maps.

1744. TALAYESVA, DON C. *Sonnenhäuptling Sitzende Rispe: Ein Indianer erzählt sein Leben.* Translated and annotated by Heino Gehrts. Kassel: Erich Roth Verlag, 1964. 415 pp.
   A translation of *Sun Chief.* See next item.

1745. ————. *Sun Chief: The Autobiography of a Hopi Indian.* Edited by Leo W. Simmons. New Haven: Yale University Press, 1963. 460 pp., illus.
   This is the fifth printing of the work first issued in 1942. This printing has a new foreword by Robert V. Hine.

1746. TANNER, CLARA LEE. *The James T. Bialac Collection of Southwest Indian Paintings.* Tucson: Arizona State Museum, 1968. unpaged.
   An outline of Southwest Indian painting with black-and-white and color illustrations from the collection.

1747. ————. *Southwest Indian Craft Arts.* Tucson: University of Arizona Press, 1968. 206 pp., illus., maps.
   Pottery, textiles, basketry, jewelry, kachinas, minor crafts.

1748. ————. *Southwest Indian Painting.* Tucson: University of Arizona Press and Arizona Silhouettes, 1957. 157 pp., illus.
   Revised edition in preparation Fall, 1971.

1749. TATE, HARVEY F. *Arizona Home Gardening.* Tucson: University of Arizona Agricultural Extension Service, 1953. (Circular no. 130) 42 pp., illus.
   Revisions issued 1956, 1960, and 1964.

1750. ————. *Flowers for Northern Arizona.* Tucson: University of Arizona Agricultural Extension Service, 1956. (Circular no. 242) 24 pp., illus.

1751. ————. *Flowers for Southern Arizona.* Tucson: University of Arizona Agricultural Extension Service, 1956. (Circular no. 243) 24 pp., illus.

1752. ————. *Growing Grapes in Arizona.* Tucson: University of Arizona Cooperative Extension Service and Agricultural Experiment Station, 1964. (Bulletin A-33) 24 pp., illus.
   Revision of Circular 251.

1753. [Taxes] *Report on Arizona State Taxes; a Survey and Program for Improvements.* Prepared by Griffenhagen and Associates. [Chicago], 1951. 137 pp., tables.

1754. TAYLOR, BENJAMIN J. AND DENNIS J. O'CONNOR. *Indian Manpower Resources in the Southwest: A Pilot Study.* Tempe: Arizona State University Bureau of Business and Economic Research, 1969. 374 pp., tables.
    Covers the Fort Apache, San Carlos, and Papago reservations.

1755. TAYLOR, WALTER W. *Two Archaeological Studies in Northern Arizona. The Pueblo Ecology Study; Hail and Farewell. A Brief Survey through the Grand Canyon of the Colorado River.* Flagstaff: Northern Arizona Society of Science and Art, 1958. (Museum of Northern Arizona Bulletin no. 30) 30 pp., illus.

1756. TEICHERT, CURT. *Devonian Rocks and Paleography of Central Arizona.* Washington: U. S. Geological Survey, 1965. (Professional Paper no. 464) 181 pp., 32 plates, illus., diags., tables, maps.
    Subtitle: "Stratigraphic, lithologic and paleoecologic studies of the Devonian rocks of central Arizona, as a basis of reconstructing Devonian paleography."

1757. [Tempe] *The Comprehensive Planning Program, Tempe, Arizona.* [Tempe?]: Tempe Planning Department and Van Cleve Associates, 1965–66. 9 parts, tables, maps.
    Part 1, Population.
    Part 2, Housing and residential environment.
    Part 3, Economics.
    Part 4, Land use.
    Part 5, Community facilities.
    Part 6, Utilities.
    Part 7, Industrial development.
    Part 8, Streets and thoroughfares.
    Part 9, Commercial development.

1758. [Tempe] *General Plan, Tempe, Arizona.* [Tempe?]: Tempe Planning and Zoning Commission and Van Cleve Associates, 1967. 80 pp., illus., maps.

1759. TERRELL, JOHN U. *Estevanico, the Black.* Los Angeles: Westernlore Press, 1968. (Great West and Indian Series no. 36) 155 pp. illus.
    Story of the slave who accompanied Cabeza de Vaca and later preceded Marcos de Niza into northern Arizona.

1760. ———. *War for the Colorado River.* Glendale, California: The Arthur H. Clark Co., 1965. 2 vols, maps.
    Vol. 1: The California-Arizona Controversy.
    Vol. 2: Above Lee's Ferry.

1761. TEVIS, JAMES H. *Arizona in the '50's.* Albuquerque: University of New Mexico Press, 1954. 237 pp., illus.
The 1850s.

1762. *Texts of the Navajo Creation Chants.* [Cambridge, Massachusetts]: Peabody Museum of Harvard University, [1961]. unpaged.

1763. THEOBALD, JOHN AND LILLIAN THEOBALD. *Arizona Territory Post Offices and Postmasters.* Phoenix: The Arizona Historical Foundation, 1961. 178 pp., illus.

1764. THIELE, HEINRICH J. *Present and Future Water Use and Its Effect on Planning in Maricopa County, Arizona.* Scottsdale, Arizona, 1965. 60 pp., tables, diags, maps.
A study for the county Board of Supervisors and the Planning and Zoning Commission.

1765. *This Is Arizona.* Phoenix: The Arizona Republic, 1962. 560 pp., illus.
A special issue of the newspaper's Sunday magazine section "Arizona Days & Ways." A gold mine of current information which will not be easy to preserve in this newsprint form.

1766. *This is Our Story; the Bisbee Area, Bisbee, Arizona.* Bisbee: Chamber of Commerce, 1959. 20 pp.
Survey of community facilities.

1767. THOMAS, HAROLD E. *First Fourteen Years of Lake Mead.* Washington: U. S. Geological Survey, 1954. (Circular no. 346) 27 pp., tables, maps.

1768. ———— AND OTHERS. *Effects of Drought in the Colorado River Basin.* Washington: U. S. Geological Survey, 1963. (Professional Paper no. 372-F) 51 pp., diags.
Study of the prolonged drought in 1942–56 in the lower basin.

1769. THOMAS, VIOLET S. *The Secondary Teacher Education Program as Perceived by Selected Graduates of the University of Arizona.* Ann Arbor: University Microfilms, 1969. 154 pp.
A University of Arizona doctoral dissertation.

1770. THOMPSON, LAURA. *Culture in Crisis: A Study of the Hopi Indians.* New York: Harper, 1950. 221 pp., illus.

1771. ————. *Personality and Government.* Mexico, D. F.: Ediciones del Instituto Indigenista Interamericano, 1951. 229 pp.
Chapters on the Navajo, the Papago, and the Hopi.

1772. THOMPSON, ROBERT W. *Tidal Flat Sedimentation on the Colorado River Delta, Northwestern Gulf of California.* Ann Arbor: University Microfilms, 1965. 282 pp.
A University of California, San Diego, doctoral dissertation.

1773. THOMS, JOHN A. *The Geology and Ore Deposits of the Tascuela Area, Sierrita Mountains, Pima County, Arizona.* Ann Arbor: University Microfilms, 1967. 309 pp.
A University of Michigan doctoral dissertation.

1774. THOMSEN, B. W. AND H. H. SCHUMANN. *Water Resources of the Sycamore Creek Watershed, Maricopa County, Arizona.* Washington: U. S. Geological Survey, 1968. (Water-Supply Paper no. 1861) 53 pp., illus., tables, maps.

1775. THOMSEN, FREDERICK L. *More Efficient Marketing of Arizona Cattle.* Tucson: University of Arizona Agricultural Experiment Station, 1954. (Bulletin no. 354) 39 pp., diags.

1776. THORNBURG, MARTIN L. AND H. A. MARCOUX. *Cooling for the Arizona Home.* Tucson: University of Arizona, 1954. (Mechanical Engineering Series no. 1) 35 pp., illus., tables, diags.

1777. THRAPP, DAN L. *Al Sieber, Chief of Scouts.* Norman: University of Oklahoma Press, 1964. 432 pp., illus.

1778. ———. *The Conquest of Apachería.* Norman: University of Oklahoma Press, 1967. 405 pp., illus., maps.

1779. THURMOND, R. E. AND W. R. STORMS. *Discovery and Development of the Pima Copper Deposit, Pima Mining Company, Pima County, Arizona.* [Pittsburgh]: U. S. Bureau of Mines, 1958. (Information Circular no. 7822) 19 pp., maps.

1780. TIJORIWALA, ANILKUMAR G. AND OTHERS. *Structure of the Arizona Economy: Output Interrelationships and Their Effects on Water and Labor Requirements.* Part I. The Input-output Model and Its Interpretation. Tucson, University of Arizona Agricultural Experiment Station, 1968. (Technical Bulletin no. 180) 32 pp., tables.

1781. TILGHMAN, ZOE A. *Spotlight: Bat Masterson and Wyatt Earp as U. S. Deputy Marshals.* San Antonio: Naylor, 1960. 21 pp.

1782. TINKER, GEORGE H. *Northern Arizona and Flagstaff in 1887: The People and Resources.* Glendale, California: Arthur H. Clark, 1969. 62 pp., illus., map.
Reprint of a pamphlet which was published in 1887 in an edition of only 50 copies.

1783. TITLEY, SPENCER R. AND CAROL L. HICKS, EDS. *Geology of the Porphyry Copper Deposits, Southwestern North America.* Tucson: University of Arizona Press, 1966. 287 pp., illus., maps, tables, diags.

1784. [Tourists] *Report on Winter and Summer Visitors in Arizona.* Prepared by the University of Arizona Bureau of Business Research. [Phoenix]: Arizona Development Board, [1956]. 50 pp., illus., diags.
Also issued as no. 11 in the Bureau's Special Studies series.

1785. *Toward Better Fishing in Arizona.* Phoenix: Arizona Game and Fish Department, 1958. unpaged, illus., maps.
Descriptions, maps, pictures of Arizona lakes.

1786. TOWNSEND, ROLAND C. *Stone in Arizona, an Economic Study.* Phoenix: Arizona Development Board, [1961?]. 50 pp., illus., map.

1787. *Traffic and Highways.* Research report prepared by Arizona State University, Tempe. Phoenix: Arizona Academy, 1968. 173 pp., tables, diags., maps.
Thirteenth Arizona Town Hall, October 1968.

1788. [Transportation] *The Impact of the Motor Transport on the Economy of Arizona.* Phoenix: Plancor Incorporated, 1957. unpaged, illus., tables.

1789. TSCHIRLEY, FRED H. *A Physio-Ecological Study of Jumping Cholla* (Opuntia Fulgida Engelm.). Ann Arbor: University Microfilms, 1963. 113 pp.
A University of Arizona doctoral dissertation.

1790. ———— AND S. CLARK MARTIN. *Burroweed on Southern Arizona Range Lands.* Tucson: University of Arizona Agricultural Experiment Station, 1961. (Technical Bulletin no. 146) 34 pp., illus., tables, diags., maps.

1791. TUAN, I-FU. *Pediments in Southeastern Arizona.* Berkeley: University of California Press, 1959. (Publications in Geography vol. 13) 163 pp., illus.

1792. TUCK, FRANK J. *History of Mining in Arizona.* Phoenix: Arizona Department of Mineral Resources, 1955. 40 pp.

1793. ————. *History of Mining in Arizona.* Second edition, revised. [Phoenix]: Department of Mineral Resources, 1963. 47 pp.

1794. ————. *Mining's Part in Arizona's Economy.* Phoenix: Arizona Department of Mineral Resources, 1952. 16 pp., illus., tables.
Revised edition 1953. 19 pp.

1795. ————. *Stories of Arizona Copper Mines; the Big Low-Grades and the Bonanzas.* Phoenix: Arizona Department of Mineral Resources, [1957]. 77 pp., illus.

1796. *Tucson and Pima County, 1961.* Tucson: League of Women Voters [1961]. 48 pp.
City and county government and services.

1797. *Tucson Area Transportation Planning Agency Planning Series Report.* Tucson, 1966–1970. 7 vols., illus., tables, diags., maps.
    No. 1, Population change in the central city.
    No. 2, Land status in eastern Pima County.
    No. 3, Central Business District Parking & Traffic.
    No. 4, Progress Report: 1960–1968.
    No. 5, Areawide Mass Transit Planning Study.
    Areawide Mass Transit Planning Study, Supplement A — Field Surveys.
    No. 6, Operations plan.
    No. 7, 1969 Annual Report.

1798. *Tucson Area Transportation Study.* [Tucson?: Tucson Area Transportation Planning Agency, 1960–1965]. 2 vols., illus., maps, tables, diags.
    Vol. 1, Inventory and analysis of existing conditions.
    Vol. 2, Forecasts and the plan.

1799. *Tucson, Arizona: Essential Facts.* [Tucson]: Development Authority for Tucson's Expansion, [1969?]. various paging, illus., maps, tables.

1800. *Tucson Community Goals.* Prepared by the Citizens' Committee on Community Goals. Tucson, 1966. 96 pp., illus., diags.

1801. *Tucson Facts.* Tucson: Industrial Department, Tucson Chamber of Commerce, 1964. various paging, illus., tables.

1802. *Tucson Historical Sites.* [Tucson: Historic Areas Committee], 1969. 318 pp., illus., maps.
    Homes and other buildings that merit preservation.

1803. *Tucson, Mecca for 365 Days-of-Year Living.* Tucson: Southern Arizona Bank & Trust Co.; Tucson Gas, Electric Light & Power Co.; Tucson Newspapers, Inc., 1961. 61 pp., illus.

1804. *Tucson-Pima County Base Book.* Tucson: City-County Planning Department and University of Arizona Bureau of Business Research, 1952. 18 pp., tables.
    Basic statistics.

1805. *Tucson Planting.* Tucson: Tucson Nurserymen's Association, 1959. 40 pp., illus.

1806. *Tucson Regional Plan, Inc.: A Forward Look.* Washington, D. C.: Carl Feiss, Planning Consultant, 1959. 42 pp., map.

1807. *Tucson Shopping Center Study; A Survey of Shopping Center Development of Greater Tucson.* [Tucson]: First National Bank of Arizona, Marketing and Research Department, [1968]. 26 pp.

1808. *Tucson Tourist Study: DECA Market Research Project, February 24, 1967.* Tucson: Pueblo High School, 1967. 29 pp., appendices, illus., tables, diags.

1809. *Tucson Visual Environment: Community Renewal Program.* [Tucson: City Planning and Zoning Commission?], 1969. 80 pp., illus., maps.
    Lavishly and fascinatingly illustrated.

1810. *Tucson Youth in Crisis.* Tucson: Tucson Community Council, 1959. 27, 70 pp., tables.
    Report of the Tucson Youth Study Committee.

1811. [Tucson] *An Action Program for Tucson.* [Washington?]: National Association of Real Estate Boards, Build America Better Committee, 1963. 60 pp., illus.

1812. [Tucson] *Atlas of Tucson, Arizona.* Tucson: T. N. Stevens and Associates, 1956. 104 pp., maps.
    Street maps and classified business directory.

1813. [Tucson] *The City of Tucson.* Tucson: League of Women Voters of Tucson, 1954. 20 pp.
    Explains operation of city government.

1814. [Tucson] *A Community-Convention Center for Tucson.* [Tucson]: Civic Center Planning Group, 1960. 79 pp., illus., map.
    One hundred copies issued.

1815. [Tucson] *Economic Base Analysis of the Tucson Metropolitan Area.* Los Angeles: Development Research Associates, 1968. Various paging, tables.

1816. [Tucson] *General Land Use Plan, Tucson and Environs.* Tucson: City-County Planning Department, 1960. 64 pp., illus., tables, maps.

1817. [Tucson] *1980 Tucson Area Plan Freeway-Arterial Network.* [Tucson]: Tucson Area Transportation Planning Agency, 1965. 18 pp., illus., tables, diags., maps.
    At head of title: Summary Report.

1818. [Tucson] *Population Study, January 1, 1964: Tucson Standard Metropolitan Statistical Area.* Tucson: City-County Planning Department, 1964. 53 pp., tables, diags., maps.

1819. [Tucson] *The Story of the Tucson Airport Authority, 1948–1955.* [Tucson, 1955?]. 28 pp., illus.
    Brief history, articles of incorporation, ordinances and other documents. Other editions in 1959 and 1966.

1820. [Tucson] *A Street Arterial Plan for Tucson, Arizona, 1951.* [Phoenix]: Arizona Highway Department, 1952. 96 pp., illus., maps, diags.

1821. [Tucson] *Survey of Industrial Development Potential of Tucson Metropolitan Area.* Prepared by Booz, Allen and Hamilton for the Tucson Industrial Development Committee. [Los Angeles?], 1959. 113 pp., tables.

1822. [Tucson] *Urban Renewal: A Teamwork of Private Enterprise and Government for Slum Clearance and Redevelopment of the Old Pueblo District.* Tucson: Urban Renewal Office, [1961]. 35 pp., illus., maps.

1823. TURNBOW, BILL. *Bill Turnbow's . . . Arizona Political Almanac.* [Phoenix]: Bill Turnbow, 1950?–
Annual list of officials and things political.

1824. TURNER, CHRISTY G. *Petrographs of the Glen Canyon Region.* Flagstaff: Northern Arizona Society of Science and Art, Inc., 1963. (Museum of Northern Arizona Bulletin 38. Glen Canyon Series no. 4) 74 pp., illus., tables, map.
Subtitle: "Styles, chronology, distribution, and relationships from Basketmaker to Navajo."

1825. ———. *A Summary of the Archeological Explorations of Dr. Byron Cummings in the Anasazi Culture Area.* Flagstaff: Northern Arizona Society of Science and Art, 1962. (Museum of Northern Arizona Technical Series no. 5) 8 pp., tables.

1826. TURNER, HENRY S. *The Original Journals of Henry Smith Turner with Stephen Watts Kearny to New Mexico and California, 1846–1847.* Edited with an introduction by Dwight L. Clark. Norman: University of Oklahoma Press, 1966. 173 pp., illus.

1827. TURNER, SAMUEL F. *Available Water for Urban Development in the Phoenix Area.* Phoenix: Western Business Consultants, Inc., [1959?]. 34 pp., 11 graphs.
Subtitle: "A supplement to 'Economic Analysis and Projection for Phoenix and Maricopa County'." See item 1396.

1828. TURNER, THOMPSON M. *Latest from Arizona! The Hesperian Letters, 1859–1861.* Edited by Constance Wynn Altshuler. Tucson: Arizona Pioneers' Historical Society, 1969. 293 pp., map.
Letters about current events in southern Arizona written to St. Louis and San Francisco newspapers.

1829. TUTTLE, DONALD M. AND EDWARD W. BAKER. *The Spider Mites of Arizona* (Acarina Tetranychidae). Tucson: University of Arizona Agricultural Experiment Station, 1964. (Technical Bulletin no. 158) 44 pp., illus.

1830. TWENTER, F. R. *Geology and Promising Areas for Ground-Water Development in the Hualapai Indian Reservation, Arizona.* Washington: U. S. Geological Survey, 1962. (Water-Supply Paper no. 1576-A) 38 pp., illus., maps.

1831. TWENTER, F. R. AND D. G. METZGER. *Geology and Ground Water in Verde Valley — the Mogollon Rim Region, Arizona.* Washington: U. S. Geological Survey, 1963. (Bulletin no. 1177) 132 pp., illus., tables, maps.

1832. TYLER, DANIEL. *A Concise History of the Mormon Battalion in the Mexican War, 1846–1847.* Chicago: Rio Grande Press, 1964. 376 pp.
A facsimile of the edition of 1881.

1833. TYRRELL, WILLIS W., JR. *Geology of the Whetstone Mountain Area, Cochise and Pima Counties, Arizona.* Ann Arbor: University Microfilms, 1964. 330 pp.
A Yale University doctoral dissertation.

1834. UCHENDU, VICTOR. *Seasonal Agricultural Labor Among the Navaho Indians: a Study in Socio-Economic Transition.* Ann Arbor: University Microfilms, 1966. 337 pp.
A Northwestern University doctoral dissertation.

1835. UDALL, DAVID K. *Arizona Pioneer Mormon; David King Udall, His Story and His Family, 1851–1938.* Written in collaboration with Pearl Udall Nelson. Tucson: Arizona Silhouettes, 1959. 304 pp., illus.

1836. UDELL, JOHN. *Journal of John Udell, Kept during a Trip Across the Plains, Containing an Account of the Massacre of a Portion of his Party by the Mohave Indians in 1858.* New Haven: Yale University Library, 1952. (Western Historical Series no. 1) 45 pp., loose title page and preface.
Facsimile of the 1859, Suisun, California edition; 200 copies issued in slip case.

1837. UNDERHILL, RUTH M. *Here Come the Navaho!* [Washington?]: U. S. Indian Service, 1953. (Indian Life and Customs no. 7) 285 pp., illus., maps.
A history, excellently illustrated.

1838. ———. *The Navajos.* Norman: University of Oklahoma Press, 1956. 299 pp., illus.
History and current conditions.

1839. ———. *People of the Crimson Evening.* [Riverside, California]: U. S. Indian Service, [1951]. 127 pp., illus.
About the Papago.

1840. ———. *Singing for Power: The Song Magic of the Papago Indians of Southern Arizona.* Berkeley: University of California Press, 1968. 158 pp., illus.
Reprint of the original edition of 1938.

1841. ———. *Social Organization of the Papago Indians*. New York: AMS Press, 1969. (Columbia University Contributions to Anthropology. Vol. xxx) 280 pp.
Facsimile reprint of the original edition of 1939.

1842. [Unemployment] *A Study of Arizona's Jobless After Unemployment Insurance Benefits Expired*. Phoenix: Employment Security Commission of Arizona, 1952. 35 pp., tables.

1843. [Unemployment Insurance] *Arizona's Agricultural Workers*. Phoenix: Employment Security Commission of Arizona, 1951. 19 pp., tables.
Includes long-range cost estimates for unemployment insurance coverage.

1844. [Unemployment Insurance] *A Report on Unemployment Insurance Costs in Arizona*. Phoenix: Employment Security Commission of Arizona, 1951. 113 pp.

1845. UNDERWOOD, PAUL S. *Analysis for Policy Decisions Regarding Low-Cost Housing in the Four Corners Region*. Prepared for the Four Corners Regional Commission, Western Interstate Commission for Higher Education, 1969. 58 pp.

1846. *The University of Arizona*. Tucson: [University of Arizona, 1963]. unpaged, illus.
A very handsomely produced promotional pamphlet explaining the function of the university today and its needs for tomorrow.

1847. *Valley Area Traffic and Transportation Study*. [Tempe]: Arizona State University Engineering Center, 1966–1969. 9 parts.
No. 1, An Inventory of Retail Sales.
No. 2, An Inventory of Employment, 1964.
No. 3, A Functional Street Classification System.
No. 4, Procedure Manual for Physical Street Inventory.
No. 5, Travel Forecasting Methods: Internal Trip Generation.
No. 6, Travel Forecasting Methods: Internal Trip Distribution.
No. 7, 1966 Travel Time Study.
No. 7A, 1966 Travel Time Study: Street Section Data.
No. 8, Travel Forecasting Methods: External Travel.
No. 9, Operations Plan.

1848. VAN FLEET, L. A. AND ALLEN D. LOOK. *Central Mine Rescue Station, Globe-Miami District Mine Rescue and First-Aid Association, Globe, Arizona*. [Pittsburgh]: U. S. Bureau of Mines, 1950. (Information Circular no. 7577) 20 pp., illus.

1849. VAN PETTEN, DONALD R. *The Constitution and Government of Arizona*. Phoenix: Jahn-Tyler, 1952. 222 pp.
A second edition, Phoenix Sun Country Publishing, 1956. 234 pp.

1850. Van Petten, Donald R. *The Constitution and Government of Arizona.* Third edition. Phoenix: Tyler Printing Co., 1960. 239 pp.
Comparison with the first, 1952, edition reveals considerable rewriting and revision to bring the text up to date. Statistics from as late as 1960 are included.

1851. Van Scism, James. *An Analysis of the Mean Operating Expenditure per A.D.A. between State Equalization Aid Districts and Basic Aid Districts in Arizona.* Ann Arbor: University Microfilms, 1969. 127 pp.
An Arizona State University doctoral dissertation.

1852. Vanvig, Andrew. *Agricultural Credit in Arizona.* Tucson: University of Arizona Agricultural Experiment Station, 1955. (Bulletin no. 262) 47 pp., illus., tables.

1853. ———. *Cattle Feeding Costs in Arizona.* Tucson: University of Arizona Agricultural Experiment Station, 1956. (Report no. 140) 8 pp., tables.

1854. Variakojis, Danguole J. *Concepts of Secular and Sacred among the White Mountain Apache as Illustrated by Musical Practice.* Ann Arbor: University Microfilms, 1969. 217 pp.
An Indiana University doctoral dissertation.

1855. Vestal, Paul A. *Ethnobotany of the Ramah Navaho.* Cambridge, Massachusetts: Peabody Museum, 1952. (Peabody Papers vol. 40, no. 4) 94 pp.

1856. Villaseñor, David. *Tapestries in Sand: The Spirit of Indian Sandpainting.* Healdsburg, California: Naturegraph Co., [1964?]. 112 pp., illus.
General, but mostly Arizona.

1857. *Vital Statistics of the Arizona Business Population, 1952–1962.* Phoenix: Employment Security Commission of Arizona, 1963. 102 pp., tables.
Subtitle: "An analysis of business births and deaths and growth of existing firms, as an indicator of Arizona's economic health."

1858. Vogt, Evon Z. *Navaho Veterans: A Study of Changing Values.* Cambridge, Massachusetts: Peabody Museum, 1951. (Peabody Papers vol. 41, no. 1) 223 pp., diags.

1859. Volker, Joseph F. *The Arizona Medical School Study.* Tucson: University of Arizona Press, 1962. 258 pp., diags., tables.
The study which preceded the founding of the school at the University of Arizona.

1860. Voth, Henry R. *The Henry R. Voth Hopi Indian Collection at Grand Canyon, Arizona.* Phoenix: Byron Harvey, 1967. 40 pp.
A catalog prepared for the Fred Harvey Company in 1912.

1861. WAAG, CHARLES J. *Structural Geology of the Mt. Bigelow-Bear Wallow-Mt. Lemmon Area, Santa Catalina Mountains, Arizona.* Ann Arbor: University Microfilms, 1969. 220 pp.
A University of Arizona doctoral dissertation.

1862. WADDELL, JACK O. *Adaptation of Papago Workers to Off-Reservation Occupations.* Ann Arbor: University Microfilms, 1966. 456 pp.
A University of Arizona doctoral dissertation.

1863. ———. *Papago Indians at Work.* Tucson: University of Arizona Press, 1969. (Anthropological Papers of the University of Arizona, no. 12) 159 pp.
The dissertation above, item 1862, with slight revisions.

1864. WAGGIN, CHUCK. *A Light-Hearted Look at the Desert.* Tucson: University of Arizona Press, 1969. 94 pp., illus.
Cartoon sketches, brief accompanying text, and light verse.

1865. WAGONER, JAY J. *History of the Cattle Industry in Southern Arizona, 1540–1940.* Tucson: University of Arizona, 1952. (Social Science Bulletin no. 20) 132 pp., illus., maps.

1866. WAGONER, PADERIC L. *Perceptions of Teacher Roles in Arizona Secondary Schools and their Relation to the Secondary Teacher Education Program at the University of Arizona.* Ann Arbor: University Microfilms, 1966. 191 pp.
A University of Arizona doctoral dissertation.

1867. WALKER, GEORGE. *Miracle in Moccasins: My 40 Years as a Missionary to the Indians of the Southwest.* Phoenix: Phoenician Books, Inc., [1969]. 138 pp., illus.
Twenty years experiences as a missionary to the Pimas and twenty years as director of the Cook Christian Training School in Phoenix.

1868. WALKER, JOHN G. AND O. L. SHEPHERD. *The Navajo Reconnaissance: A Military Exploration of the Navajo Country in 1859.* Los Angeles: Westernlore Press, 1964. 111 pp., illus.
An account not previously published.

1869. *Walker's Manual of Arizona Securities, Corporations and Directors.* San Francisco: Walker's Manual Incorporated, 1957–
First issued 1957; new edition, 1959. Continued in *Walker's Manual of Pacific Coast Securities.*

1870. WALL, CLAUDE LEON, *see* WALL, LEON.

1871. WALL, LEON. *Problems in Teaching English to Navajo Children.* Ann Arbor: University Microfilms, 1962. 121 pp.
An Oklahoma State University doctoral dissertation.

1872. ——— AND WILLIAM MORGAN. *Navajo-English Dictionary.* Window Rock, Arizona: Navajo Agency, 1958. 65 pp.

1873. WALLACE, ANDREW, ED. *Sources & Readings in Arizona History; A Check-list of Literature Concerning Arizona's Past.* Tucson: Arizona Pioneers' Historical Society, 1965. 181 pp.

1874. WALLACE, ROBERTS M. *Structures at the Northern End of the Santa Catalina Mountains, Arizona.* Ann Arbor: University Microfilms, 1955. 93 pp.
  A University of Arizona doctoral dissertation.

1875. WALLIS, ETHEL E. *God Speaks Navajo.* New York: Harper & Row, 1968. 146 pp.
  The work of Faye Edgerton as a Presbyterian missionary on the reservation.

1876. WALTERS, LORENZO D. *Tombstone's Yesterday.* Glorieta, New Mexico: Rio Grande Press, 1968. 318 pp., illus.
  Facsimile reprint of the original of 1928.

1877. WALTERS, WINIFRED F. *Navajoland: A Journey of Legends.* Window Rock, Arizona: Navajo Tribe Printing Department, 1964. 65 pp., illus.
  Guide to trips on and near the reservation.

1878. WAMPLER, JOSEPH. *Havasu Canyon, Gem of the Grand Canyon.* Berkeley, California: Howell-North Press, 1959. 121 pp., illus., maps.
  Contains a chapter by Harold C. Bryant and one by Weldon F. Heald.

1879. WARD, ELIZABETH L. *No Dudes, Few Women.* Albuquerque: University of New Mexico Press, 1951. 251 pp.
  Subtitle: "Life with a Navaho Range Rider."

1880. WARES, ALAN C. *A Comparative Study of Yuman Consonantism.* The Hague and Paris: Mouton, 1968. (Janua Linguarum, Series Practica no. 57) 100 pp.

1881. WASLEY, WILLIAM W. AND ALFRED E. JOHNSON. *Salvage Archaeology in Painted Rocks Reservoir, Western Arizona.* Tucson: University of Arizona Press, 1965. (Anthropological Papers of the University of Arizona no. 9) 123 pp., illus., diags.

1882. *Water for Arizona: Feasibility Study [of the] State Central Arizona Project.* Los Angeles: Ralph M. Parsons Co., 1968. 9 vols., tables, maps, diags.
  Volumes numbered III to XI. The first two parts were never issued.

1883. [Water] *Annual Report on Ground Water in Arizona.* Phoenix: Arizona State Land Department, 1956–
  Prepared by the U. S. Geological Survey. The first had the title *Pumpage and Ground-Water Levels in Arizona in 1955.*

1884. [Water] *Arizona Grows Where Water Flows.* [Phoenix: Salt River Project, 1961]. 24 pp., illus.
  Prepared for the golden anniversary of the dedication of Roosevelt Dam; contains stories about the dam, the project, and Phoenix.

1885. [Water] *Arizona v. California and Pacific Southwest Water Problems.* Report of the Assembly Interim Committee on Water to the California Legislature. Assembly Interim Committee Reports 1963–1965, vol. 26, no. 13, 1964. 175 pp., tables, diags., maps.

1886. [Water] *The Availability of Water in Arizona with Special Reference to the Arizona Water Company.* [Phoenix: Arizona Water Company], 1967. 25 pp., illus., diags.

1887. [Water] *Report on Cooperative Water Resource Inventory, Arizona.* Boulder City, Nevada: U. S. Bureau of Reclamation, 1965. 2 vols., tables, maps, diags.
   Vol. I, State of Arizona.
   Vol. II, Hydrologic Study Areas, Arizona.

1888. [Water] *Survey Report, Queen Creek Watershed, Arizona: Program for Runoff and Waterflow Retardation and Soil Erosion Prevention.* 82nd Congress, 2nd Session, House Document no. 397. Washington, 1952. 22 pp., map.

1889. [Water] *The Underground Water Resources of Arizona.* A report by the Underground Water Commission, January, 1953. [Phoenix], 1953. 174 pp., maps, diags.

1890. [Water] *Water and Choice in the Colorado Basin: An Example of Alternatives in Water Management.* Washington: National Academy of Sciences, 1968. 107 pp., tables, maps.
   A report by the Committee on Water of the National Research Council.

1891. [Water] *Water-Resources Development by the U. S. Army Corps of Engineers in Arizona.* San Francisco?: U. S. Army Engineer Division, 1961. 24 pp., illus., tables, maps.
   New editions every two years.

1892. WATERS, FRANK. *Book of the Hopi.* New York: Viking Press, 1963. 347 pp., illus.
   "This, then, is their book of talk. Beginning with their Genesis, and carrying through their Old Testament . . . the tenets of this book are as sacred to the Hopi as the Judaic-Christian Bible is to other people." Introduction.

1893. ———. *The Earp Brothers of Tombstone; the Story of Mrs. Virgil Earp.* New York: Clarkson N. Potter, 1960. 247 pp.

1894. ———. *Masked Gods: Navaho and Pueblo Ceremonialism.* Albuquerque: University of New Mexico Press, 1950. 438 pp., illus.

1895. ———. *Mysticism and Witchcraft.* Fort Collins: Colorado State University, 1966. (Third annual writer in residence lecture) 22 pp., illus.
   Illustrated by references to the Hopi experience.

1896. ———. *Pumpkin Seed Point.* Chicago: Sage Books, 1969. 175 pp.
   The writer's experiences while gathering material for *Book of the Hopi,* above.

1897. *Watershed Management Research in Arizona: Progress Report, 1959.* Fort Collins, Colorado: Rocky Mountain Forest and Range Experiment Station (U.S. Forest Service), 1960. 80 pp., illus., tables, diags.

1898. WATKINS, T. H. AND OTHERS. *The Grand Colorado: The Story of a River and its Canyons.* [Palo Alto, California]: American West Publishing Co., 1969. 310 pp., illus., maps.
History, cartography, conservation, and copious illustrations from early engravings to contemporary photographs.

1899. WATSON, BARRY N. *Structure and Petrology of the Eastern Portion of the Silver Bell Mountains, Pima County, Arizona.* Ann Arbor: University Microfilms, 1964. 255 pp.
A University of Arizona doctoral dissertation.

1900. WATSON, EDITHA L. *Navajo Sacred Places.* Window Rock, Arizona: Navajo Tribal Museum, 1964. (Navajoland Publications, series 5) 28 pp.

1901. WATT, GEORGE. *Summary of Snow Survey Measurement for Arizona.* [Portland, Oregon]: U. S. Department of Agriculture Soil Conservation Service, 1958. 44 pp., tables.

1902. WAY, THOMAS E. *Frontier Arizona.* New York: Carlton Press, 1960. 279 pp.
The lawless and the law in the territorial past.

1903. ———. *Sgt. Fred Platten's Ten Years on the Trail of the Redskins.* Williams, Arizona: Williams News Press, 1959. 44 pp., illus.
Fighting the Apaches, and the Graham-Tewksbury feud.

1904. WAY, W. J. *Ghosts and Ghost Towns: Southeastern Arizona.* Tombstone: The Author, 1966. 56 pp., illus., maps.
Brief histories, how to get there.

1905. ———. *"Postmarked" Arizona.* Tombstone: The Author, 1965. 39 pp., illus.
Subtitle: "A tour of the Grand Canyon state, its history, geography and people, as reflected by visits to the many post offices within its borders."

1906. ———. *The Tombstone Story.* Tombstone: The Author, 1965. 40 pp., illus., maps.

1907. WEADOCK, JACK. *Dust of the Desert: Plain Tales of the Desert and the Border.* Tucson: Arizona Silhouettes, 1963. 306 pp., illus.
Desert sketches, character sketches, Border Patrol. A facsimile of the original edition of 1936.

1908. WEBB, GEORGE. *A Pima Remembers.* Tucson: University of Arizona Press, 1959. 126 pp.
Customs and habits which are dying out.

1909. WEBBER, JOHN M. *Yuccas of the Southwest*. Washington: U. S. Department of Agriculture, 1953. (Agriculture Monograph no. 17) 97 pp., illus.

1910. WEBER, ROBERT H. AND H. WESLEY PEIRCE, EDS. *Guidebook of the Mogollon Rim Region, East-Central Arizona*. [Socorro, New Mexico?, 1962]. 175 pp., illus., tables, maps, diags.
Prepared by the New Mexico Geological Society with the cooperation of the Arizona Geological Society.

1911. *The Weekly Arizonan*. Volumes 1 to 4, 1859–1871.
Microfilm of the first territorial newspaper published in Tubac and Tucson and issued in this form by the Territorial Press, Tucson, 1964.

1912. WEIGHT, HAROLD O. *Lost Mines of Old Arizona*. Twentynine Palms, California: Calico Press, 1959. (Southwest Panorama 4) 76 pp., illus.
Mostly southwestern Arizona mines.

1913. ―――― AND OTHERS. *Wm. B. Rood; Death Valley 49er, Arizona Pioneer, Apache Fighter, River Ranchero*. Twentynine Palms, California: Calico Press, 1959. unpaged, illus.

1914. WEIST, W. G., JR. *Geohydrology of the Dateland-Hyder Area, Maricopa and Yuma Counties, Arizona*. Phoenix: Arizona State Land Department, 1965. (Water-Resources Report no. 23) 46 pp., maps, tables, diags.

1915. *Welfare Policies and Administration in Arizona*. A research compendium drawn from basic studies by College of Business and Public Administration, University of Arizona. Phoenix: Arizona Academy, 1963. 124 pp., tables.
Second Arizona Town Hall, April 1963.

1916. WELLES, PHILIP. *Meet the Southwest Deserts*. Globe, Arizona: Dale Stuart King, 1960. 82 pp., illus.
Intended as an introduction to the desert. Brief text and plentiful photographic illustrations by Marvin H. Frost, Sr. A second, slightly revised edition, Tucson, 1964.

1917. WELLS, JOHN D. *Stratigraphy and Structure of the House Rock Valley Area, Coconino County, Arizona*. Washington: U. S. Geological Survey, 1960. (Bulletin no. 1081-D) pp. 117–58, maps.

1918. WENDORF, FRED. *Archaeological Studies in the Petrified Forest National Monument*. Flagstaff: Northern Arizona Society of Science and Art, 1953. (Museum of Northern Arizona Bulletin no. 27) 203 pp., illus., tables, maps.

1919. ――――. *A Report on the Excavation of a Small Ruin near Point of Pines, East Central Arizona*. Tucson: University of Arizona, 1950. (Social Science Bulletin no. 19) 150 pp., illus.

1920. WENE, GEORGE P. AND OTHERS. *Winter Survival of the Pink Boll-worm in Arizona.* Tucson: University of Arizona Agricultural Experiment Station, 1965. (Technical Bulletin no. 170) 23 pp., illus., tables.

1921. WENGER, W. J. AND B. W. REID. *Properties of Petroleum from the Four Corners Area of Arizona, Colorado, New Mexico, and Utah.* [Washington]: U. S. Bureau of Mines, 1960. (Report of Investigations no. 5587) 25 pp., tables, diags.

1922. WENUM, JOHN D. *Spatial Growth and the Central City: Problems, Potential, and the Case of Phoenix, Arizona.* Ann Arbor: University Microfilms, 1969. 250 pp.
    A Northwestern University doctoral dissertation.

1923. WEPPNER, ROBERT S. *The Economic Absorption of Navajo Indian Emigrants in Denver, Colorado.* Ann Arbor: University Microfilms, 1969. 160 pp.
    A University of Colorado doctoral dissertation.

1924. WERHO, L. L. *Compilation of Flood Data for Maricopa County, Arizona, through September 1965.* Phoenix: Arizona State Land Department, 1967. (Water-Resources Report no. 31) 36 pp., tables, map.

1925. WERLING, JOAN. *History of Slavs in Arizona.* San Francisco: R & E Research Associates, 1968. 60 pp.

1926. WERNER, FLOYD G. AND OTHERS. *The Meloidae of Arizona.* Tucson: University of Arizona Agricultural Experiment Station, 1966. (Technical Bulletin no. 175) 96 pp., illus.
    Blister Beetles.

1927. WERNER, JANE AND OTHERS. *Walt Disney's Living Desert.* New York: Simon and Schuster, 1954. 124 pp,. illus.
    Based on the Disney film on the Southern Arizona desert; illustrated in color.

1928. WERNER, OSWALD. *A Typological Comparison of Four Trader Navaho Speakers.* Ann Arbor: University Microfilms, 1964. 169 pp.
    An Indiana University doctoral dissertation. "Trader Navaho is spoken by the white men . . . who trade with the Navaho Indians on and off the reservation in Arizona, New Mexico and Utah." Introduction.

1929. Westerners. Sedona Corral. *Those Early Days; Oldtimers' Memoirs: Oak Creek-Sedona and the Verde Valley Region of Northern Arizona.* Sedona, Arizona: Sedona Westerners, 1968. 240 pp.

1930. Westerners. Tucson Corral. *Brand Book 1 of the Tucson Corral of the Westerners: a Collection of Smoke Signals, Nos. 1–10, 1960–1964.* Edited by Otis H. Chidester. Tucson, 1967. various paging, illus., maps.

1931. WESTOVER, ADELE B. AND J. MORRIS RICHARDS. *A Brief History of Joseph City.* Winslow, Arizona: Winslow Mail, [1951]. 74 pp., illus.
> About half is devoted to family histories.

1932. ———— AND ————. *Unflinching Courage.* no publisher, no date. 704 pp., illus.
> Mormon genealogies and some Joseph City history.

1933. WESTOVER, WILLIAM H. *Yuma Footprints.* Tucson: Arizona Pioneers' Historical Society, 1966. 149 pp., illus.
> Stories of Yuma and the surrounding area and some outstanding Yuma personalities.

1934. WHARFIELD, H. B. *Alchesay, Scout with General Crook, Sierra Blanca Apache Chief, Friend of Fort Apache Whites, Counselor to Indian Agents.* El Cajon, California: The Author, 1969. 52 pp., illus.

1935. ————. *Apache Indian Scouts.* El Cajon, California: The Author, 1964. 113 pp., illus.

1936. ————. *Cooley: Army Scout, Arizona Pioneer, Wayside Host, Apache Friend.* El Cajon, California: The Author, 1966. 101 pp., illus.

1937. ————. *Fort Yuma on the Colorado River.* El Cajon, California: The Author, 1968. 183 pp., illus., maps.

1938. ————. *10th Cavalry & Border Fights.* El Cajon, California: The Author, 1965. 114 pp., illus.

1939. ————. *With Scouts and Cavalry at Fort Apache.* Edited by John Alexander Carroll. Tucson: Arizona Pioneers' Historical Society, 1965. 124 pp., illus.
> Activities in 1918.

1940. WHEAT, JOE B. *Crooked Ridge Village (Arizona W:10:15).* Tucson: University of Arizona, 1954. (Social Science Bulletin no. 24) 183 pp., illus., maps, diags.
> Excavations at Point of Pines. Part I of the author's doctoral dissertation.

1941. ————. *Mogollon Culture Prior to A.D. 1000.* Menasha, Wisconsin: American Anthropological Association, 1955. (Memoir no. 82) 242 pp., illus., diags.
> Part II of the author's doctoral dissertation. This material also appeared as Memoir no. 10 of the Society for American Archaeology.

1942. ————. *Prehistoric People of the Northern Southwest.* Grand Canyon, Arizona: Grand Canyon Natural Historical Association, 1955. (Bulletin no. 12) 38 pp., illus., maps.

1943. WHEAT, JOE B. *A Study of Mogollon Culture Prior to A.D. 1000.* Ann Arbor: University Microfilms, 1953. 644 pp.
A University of Arizona doctoral dissertation. Based on excavations at Point of Pines.

1944. WHEELER, ELDON H. AND JERE BOYER. *Costs of Operating Hay Conditioners in Arizona.* Tucson: University of Arizona Agricultural Experiment Station, 1958. (Report no. 179) 12 pp., tables, diags.

1945. WHEELWRIGHT, MARY C. *Eagle Catching Myth.* Told by Beyal Begay. *Bead Myth.* Told by Yohe Hatrale. Retold in shorter form by Mary C. Wheelwright. Revised edition. Santa Fe: Museum of Navajo Ceremonial Art, 1962. (Bulletin no. 3) 16 pp.
Originally issued in 1945.

1946. ———. *The Myth and Prayers of the Great Star Chant and the Myth of the Coyote Chant.* Edited by David P. McAllester. Santa Fe: Museum of Navajo Ceremonial Art, 1956. (Navajo Religion Series vol. 4) 190 pp., illus.

1947. ———. *Myth of Mountain Chant.* Told by Hasteen Klah. *Beauty Chant.* Told by Hasteen Gahni. Retold in shorter form by Mary C. Wheelwright. Santa Fe: Museum of Navajo Ceremonial Art, 1951. (Bulletin no. 5) 22 pp.

1948. ———. *Myth of Sóntso Hatrál (Big Star Chant).* By Yuinth-Nezi. *The Myth of Má-Ih Hatrál (Coyote Chant).* By Yoh Hatrali. Retold in shorter form by Mary C. Wheelwright. Revised edition. Santa Fe: Museum of Navajo Ceremonial Art, 1957. (Bulletin no. 2) 14 pp.
Originally issued in 1940.

1949. ———. *Myth of Willa-Chee-Ji Deginnh-Keygo Hatrál.* By Hasteen de Johly. *Myth of Natóhe Bakáji Hatrál.* By Estan Hatrali B'yash. Recorded and retold in shorter form by Mary C. Wheelwright. Santa Fe: Museum of Navajo Ceremonial Art, 1958. (Bulletin no. 7) 23 pp.
On cover: "Red Ant Myth (Willa Chee) and Shooting Chant."

1950. ———. *Navajo Creation Myth.* Told by Hasteen Klah. Re-written by Mary C. Wheelwright. Santa Fe: Museum of Navajo Ceremonial Art, 1953. (Bulletin no. 6) 25 pp.
Revised edition, 1960.

1951. WHIPPLE, AMIEL W. *The Whipple Report: Journal of an Expedition from San Diego, California to the Rio Colorado, from Sept. 11 to Dec. 11, 1849.* Introduction and bibliography by E. I. Edwards. Los Angeles: Westernlore Press, 1961. 100 pp., illus.
A reprint of Senate Executive Document 19, 31st Congress, 1st Session.

1952. WHITE, LARRY D. *Factors Affecting Susceptibility of Creosotebush* (Larrea tridentata) *(D.C. Cov.) to Burning.* Ann Arbor: University Microfilms, 1968. 108 pp.
A University of Arizona doctoral dissertation.

1953. WHITE, NATALIE D. *Analysis and Evaluation of Available Hydrologic Data for San Simon Basin, Cochise and Graham Counties, Arizona.* Washington: U. S. Geologic Survey, 1963. (Water-Supply Paper no. 1619-DD) 33 pp., tables, diags., maps.

1954. ————. *Ground-Water Conditions in the Rainbow Valley and Waterman Wash Areas, Maricopa and Pinal Counties, Arizona.* Washington: U. S. Geological Survey, 1963. (Water-Supply Paper 1669-F) 50 pp., tables, maps.

1955. ———— AND DALLAS CHILDERS. *Hydrologic Conditions in the Douglas Basin, Cochise County, Arizona.* Phoenix: Arizona State Land Department, 1967. (Water-Resources Report no. 30) 26 pp., maps, diags.

1956. ———— AND WILLIAM F. HARDT. *Electrical Analog Analysis of Hydrologic Data for San Simon Basin, Cochise and Graham Counties, Arizona.* Washington: U. S. Geological Survey, 1965. (Water-Supply Paper no. 1809-R) 80 pp., tables, diags.

1957. ———— AND CLARA R. SMITH. *Basic Hydrologic Data for San Simon Basin, Cochise and Graham Counties, Arizona, and Hidalgo County, New Mexico.* Phoenix: Arizona State Land Department, 1965. (Water-Resources Report no. 21) 42 pp., tables, maps.

1958. ———— AND OTHERS. *An Appraisal of the Ground-Water Resources of Avra and Altar Valleys, Pima County, Arizona.* Phoenix: Arizona State Land Department, 1966. (Water-Resources Report no. 25) 66 pp., maps., tables.

1959. ———— AND ————. *Effects of Ground-Water Withdrawal in Part of Central Arizona Projected to 1969.* Phoenix: Arizona State Land Department, 1964. (Water-Resources Report no. 16) 25 pp., maps.

1960. WHITEHOUSE, ARCH. *The Ace from Arizona: Frank Luke, the Hun Killer.* New York: Award Books, 1966. 223 pp.
Paperback biography of Arizona's World War I ace.

1961. *Who is Who in Arizona.* Phoenix: John H. Moore, 1958. 288 pp.

1962. *Wickenburg General Plan.* [Scottsdale, Arizona]: Van Cleve Associates, [1967?]. 1 sheet, illus., maps.

1963. [WICKENBURG] *The Comprehensive Planning Program, Wickenburg, Arizona.* [Phoenix]: Van Cleve Associates, 1964–66. 3 vols., illus., tables, maps.
Vol. 1, Data for planning.
Vol. 2, Planning studies.
Vol. 3, Plan implementation.

1964. *The Widening Gap: a Study of Alternate Taxable Wage Bases for Arizona's Unemployment Insurance Program.* Phoenix: Employment Security Commission of Arizona, 1962. 36 pp., tables, diags.

1965. WILDERMUTH, JOHN R. AND OTHERS. *Costs and Returns Data for Representative General Crop Farms in Arizona.* Tucson: University of Arizona Agricultural Experiment Station, 1969. (Report no. 253) 101 pp., tables.

1966. WILKEN, ROBERT L. *Anselm Weber, O. F. M., Missionary to the Navajo, 1898–1912.* Milwaukee: Bruce Publishing Company, 1955. 255 pp., illus.
The author's doctoral dissertation done at the University of New Mexico and also issued, 1955, by University Microfilms.

1967. WILKINSON, CATHERINE A. *The Effects of Veterans' and Widows' Exemptions on Arizona Tax Rates with Recommended Legislation.* Ann Arbor: University Microfilms, 1964. 148 pp.
An Arizona State University doctoral dissertation.

1968. WILLDEN, RONALD. *Geology of the Christmas Quadrangle, Gila and Pinal Counties, Arizona.* Washington: U. S. Geological Survey, 1964. (Bulletin no. 1161-E) 64 pp., illus., maps.

1969. WILLIAMS, AUBREY W., JR. *The Function of the Chapter House System in the Contemporary Navajo Political Structure.* Ann Arbor: University Microfilms, 1965. 260 pp.
A University of Arizona doctoral dissertation.

1970. WILLIAMS, FRANK E. *Urbanization and the Mineral Aggregate Industry, Tucson, Ariz., Area.* [Washington]: U. S. Bureau of Mines, [1967]. (Information Circular no. 8318) 23 pp., maps, tables, diags.

1971. WILLIAMS, JOHN A. AND TRUMAN C. ANDERSON, JR. *Soil Survey of Beaver Creek Area, Arizona.* [Washington]: U. S. Department of Agriculture, 1967. 75 pp., illus., tables, maps.

1972. WILLIAMS, THOMAS R. *Socialization in a Papago Indian Village.* Ann Arbor: University Microfilms, 1956. 269 pp.
A Syracuse University doctoral dissertation.

1973. WILLINK, ELIZABETH W. *A Comparison of Two Methods of Teaching English to Navajo Children.* Ann Arbor: University Microfilms, 1968. 232 pp.
A University of Arizona doctoral dissertation.

1974. WILLSON, ROSCOE G. *No Place for Angels.* Phoenix and Tucson: Arizona Republic and Arizona Silhouettes, 1958. 275 pp., illus.
Stories of old Arizona.

1975. ———. *Pioneer Cattlemen of Arizona.* Phoenix: McGrew Commercial Printery, 1951, 1956. 2 vols.
The second volume has the title: *Pioneer and Well Known Cattlemen of Arizona.* Pamphlets of 48 and 79 pp. respectively.

1976. WILMOT, CHARLES A. AND OTHERS. *Cotton Gin Fires in Arizona, California and New Mexico.* Tucson: University of Arizona Agricultural Experiment Station, 1960. (Technical Bulletin no. 144) 15 pp., tables, diags.

1977. ——— AND ———. *Cotton Gin Insurance in Arizona, California and New Mexico, 1956–57 to 1958–59.* Tucson: University of Arizona Agricultural Experiment Station, 1960. (Technical Bulletin no. 145) 23 pp., tables.

1978. WILSON, ANDREW W. *An Analysis of the Livelihood Problems of the Tucson Standard Metropolitan Area.* Ann Arbor: University Microfilms, 1956. 503 pp.
A Syracuse University doctoral dissertation.

1979. ———. *Selected Retail Trade Characteristics, the Tucson, Pima County, Arizona Area....* Tucson: University of Arizona Bureau of Business Research and the City-County Planning Department, 1953. 31 pp., diags.

1980. WILSON, EDWARD. *An Unwritten History: A Record from the Exciting Days of Early Arizona.* Santa Fe: Stagecoach Press, 1966. (Southwestern Series number 4) 62 pp.
Originally published in Phoenix in 1915. Briefly told reminiscences of Indian outbreaks, Wham robbery, Apache Kid, etc.

1981. WILSON, ELDRED D. *Geologic Factors Related to Block Caving at San Manuel Copper Mine, Pinal County, Arizona.* [Pittsburgh]: U. S. Bureau of Mines, 1957. (Report of Investigations no. 5336) 78 pp., maps.

1982. ———. *Geologic Factors Related to Block Caving at San Manuel Copper Mine, Pinal County, Arizona. 2. Progress Report. April, 1956–March 1958.* [Washington]: U. S. Bureau of Mines, [1960?]. (Report of Investigations, no. 5561) 43 pp., tables, diags.

1983. ———. *Guidebook 1 — Highways of Arizona: U. S. Highway 666.* Tucson: University of Arizona Press, 1965. (Arizona Bureau of Mines Bulletin 174) 67 pp., illus., diags., maps.
First of a series on the natural phenomena and man-made features along Arizona's highways.

1984. WILSON, ELDRED D. *Mineral Deposits of the Gila River Indian Reservation, Arizona.* Tucson: University of Arizona, 1969. (Arizona Bureau of Mines Bulletin no. 179) 34 pp.,tables, maps.

1985. ———. *A Resume of the Geology of Arizona.* Tucson: University of Arizona Press, 1962. (Arizona Bureau of Mines Bulletin no. 171) 140 pp., illus., tables, maps.

1986. ——— AND GEORGE R. FANSETT. *Arizona Gold Placers and Placering.* Fifth edition. Tucson: University of Arizona, 1952. (Arizona Bureau of Mines Bulletin no. 160) 124 pp., illus.

1987. ——— AND OTHERS. *Arizona Lode Gold Mines and Gold Mining.* Tucson: University of Arizona, 1967. (Arizona Bureau of Mines Bulletin no. 137) 254 pp., maps, diags.
Reprint of bulletin issued in 1934 with some omissions in Part III on mine laws.

1988. ——— AND ———. *Gold Placers and Placering in Arizona.* Tucson: University of Arizona Press, 1961. (Arizona Bureau of Mines Bulletin no. 168) 124 pp., illus.
Supersedes Bulletin 160 of which it is a modification with additional information.

1989. WILSON, JAMES A. *Cattle and Politics in Arizona, 1886–1941.* Ann Arbor: University Microfilms, 1967. 360 pp.
A University of Arizona doctoral dissertation. State government, federal control, and the cattle growers' gradual, reluctant involvement in politics.

1990. WILSON, RICHARD F. *The Stratigraphy and Sedimentology of the Kayenta and Moenave Formations, Vermilion Cliffs Region, Utah and Arizona.* Ann Arbor: University Microfilms, 1959. 401 pp.
A Stanford University doctoral dissertation.

1991. WILSON, ROBERT L. *Stratigraphy and Economic Geology of the Chinle Formation, Northeastern Arizona.* Ann Arbor: University Microfilms, 1956. 352 pp.
A University of Arizona doctoral dissertation.

1992. WINSHIP, GEORGE PARKER. *The Coronado Expedition, 1540–1542.* Chicago: Rio Grande Press, 1964. 403 pp., illus., maps.
A facsimile reprint of the Annual Report of the Bureau of American Ethnology for 1892/93. Includes the Castañeda narrative in Spanish and English, translations of letters from Mendoza and Coronado, and other contemporary reports.

1993. WINTERS, STEPHEN S. *Supai Formation (Permian) of Eastern Arizona.* Geological Society of America, 1963. (Memoir no. 89) 98 pp., illus., tables, maps.
Stratigraphy, paleogeography, and systematic paleontology.

1994. WILSON, TRELVA AND PHYLLIS HANCOCK. *Out of the Years.* [Culver City, California: Murray & Gee, 1953]. 36 pp., illus.
Mormon families in southeastern Arizona.

1995. WINTERS, WAYNE. *Campfires Along the Treasure Trail: True Treasure Tales.* Tucson: Tombstone Nugget Publishing Co., 1963. 88 pp., illus.
More lost mines and treasure in southern Arizona.

1996. WISHART, LUKE B. AND AARON G. NELSON. *Farm Adjustment Possibilities to Increase Income in the Wellton-Mohawk District, of Yuma County.* Tucson: University of Arizona Agricultural Experiment Station, 1963. (Report no. 218) 26 pp., tables.

1997. WITKIND, IRVING J. *Geology and Ore Deposits of the Monument Valley Area, Apache and Navajo Counties, Arizona.* Ann Arbor: University Microfilms, 1958. 224 pp.
A University of Colorado doctoral dissertation.

1998. ———. *Uranium Deposits at Base of the Shinarump Conglomerate, Monument Valley, Arizona.* Washington: U. S. Geological Survey, 1956. (Bulletin no. 1030-C) pp. 99–130, maps, diags.

1999. ———. *The Uranium-Vanadium Ore Deposit at the Monument No. 1 - Mitten No. 2 Mine, Monument Valley, Navajo County, Arizona.* Washington: U. S. Geological Survey, 1961. (Bulletin no. 1107-C) pp. 219–42, illus., maps.

2000. ——— AND ROBERT E. THADEN. *Geology and Uranium Vanadium Deposits of the Monument Valley Area, Apache and Navajo Counties, Arizona.* With sections on Serpentine at Garnet Ridge, by Harold E. Malde and Robert E. Thaden, and Mineralogy and Paragenesis of the Ore Deposit at the Monument No. 2 and Cato Sells Mines, by Donald H. Johnson. Washington: U. S. Geological Survey, 1963. (Bulletin no. 1103) 171 pp., illus., tables, maps, diags.

2001. ——— AND OTHERS. *Isopach Mapping by Photogeologic Methods As an Aid in the Location of Swales and Channels in the Monument Valley Area, Arizona.* Washington: U. S. Geological Survey, 1960. (Bulletin no. 1043-D) pp. 57–85, illus., maps.

2002. WOLCOTT, HENRY N. AND OTHERS. *Water Resources of Bill Williams River Valley near Alamo, Arizona.* Washington: U. S. Geological Survey, 1956. (Water-Supply Paper no. 1360-D) pp. 291–319, tables, diags., maps.

2003. WOOD, ELIZABETH L. *Arizona Hoof Trails.* Portland, Oregon: Binfords & Mort, 1956. 82 pp.
Reminiscences of Oracle in the Santa Catalina Mountains.

2004. WOOD, ELIZABETH L. *The Tragedy of the Powers Mine; An Arizona Story.* Portland, Oregon: Binsford & Mort, 1957. 63 pp., illus.

2005. WOOD, HARRY. *Lew Davis; Twenty-five Years of Painting in Arizona.* [Tempe?]: Arizona State University and Phoenix Art Museum, 1961. 72 pp., illus.

2006. WOOD, ROBERT C. AND DEAN SMITH. *Barry Goldwater.* New York: Avon Book Division, Hearst Corp., 1961. 175 pp., illus.
A paperbound biography.

2007. WOOD, WILLIAM H. *The Cambrian and Devonian Carbonate Rocks at Yampai Cliffs, Mohave County, Arizona.* Ann Arbor: University Microfilms, 1956. 321 pp.
A University of Arizona doctoral dissertation.

2008. WOODBURY, ANGUS M. *Preliminary Report on Biological Resources of the Glen Canyon Reservoir.* Salt Lake City: University of Utah Press, 1958. (University of Utah Department of Anthropology, Anthropological Papers no. 31) 219 pp.

2009. ———. *A Survey of Vegetation in the Glen Canyon Reservoir Basin.* Salt Lake City: University of Utah Press, 1959. (University of Utah Department of Anthropology, Anthropological Papers no. 36) 56 pp., illus., tables.

2010. WOODBURY, RICHARD B. *Prehistoric Agriculture at Point of Pines, Arizona.* Salt Lake City: Society for American Archaeology, 1961. (Memoirs, no. 17) 48 pp., illus., maps, diags.

2011. ———. *Prehistoric Stone Implements of Northeastern Arizona.* Cambridge, Massachusetts: Peabody Museum, 1954. (Peabody Papers, vol. 34) 240 pp., illus., tables.

2012. WOODIN, ANN. *Home is the Desert.* New York: Macmillan, 1964. 247 pp., illus.
Life on the desert near Tucson.

2013. WOODWARD, ARTHUR. *Feud on the Colorado.* Los Angeles: Westernlore Press, 1955. 165 pp., illus.
Establishes the claim of Alonzo Johnson as the first man to navigate the upper river by steamboat.

2014. WOZNICKI, ROBERT. *The History of Yuma and the Territorial Prison.* [Calexico, California: San Diego State College? 1968]. 116 pp.

2015. WRIGHT, ARTHUR A. *The Civil War in the Southwest.* Denver: Big Mountain Press, 1964. 214 pp., illus.

2016. WRIGHT, BARTON AND EVELYN ROAT. *This Is a Hopi Kachina.* Flagstaff: Northern Arizona Society of Science and Art, 1962. 28 pp., illus.
A well-illustrated introduction to the subject.

2017. WRIGHT, J. T. *Desert Wildlife*. Phoenix: Arizona Game and Fish Department, 1959. (Wildlife Bulletin no. 6) 78 pp., illus., map.
The land, the birds, and animals.

2018. WRIGHT, JEROME J. *Petrology of the Devonian Rocks in Eastern Pima and Cochise Counties, Arizona*. Ann Arbor: University Microfilms, 1965. 202 pp.
A University of Arizona doctoral dissertation.

2019. WRIGHT, L. NEAL. *Blue Panicgrass for Arizona and the Southwest*. Tucson: University of Arizona Agricultural Experiment Station, 1966. (Technical Bulletin no. 173) 27 pp., illus., tables, maps.

2020. WRIGHT, ROBERT A. *An Evaluation of the Homogeneity of Two Stands of Vegetation in the Sonoran Desert*. Ann Arbor: University Microfilms, 1965. 73 pp.
A University of Arizona doctoral dissertation. The area studied is the western slope of the Tucson Mountains and the adjoining Avra Valley.

2021. WRUCKE, CHESTER T. *Paleozoic and Cenozoic Rocks in the Alpine-Nutrioso Area, Apache County, Arizona*. Washington: U. S. Geological Survey, 1961. (Bulletin no. 1121-H) 26 pp., maps.

2022. WYLLYS, RUFUS K. *Arizona, the History of a Frontier State*. Phoenix: Hobson and Herr, 1950. 408 pp., illus., maps.
Comprehensive one-volume history, but rather dull. Minor inaccuracies.

2023. WYMAN, LELAND C. *Navaho Indian Painting; Symbolism, Artistry, and Psychology*. Boston: Boston University Press, 1959. 28 pp.

2024. ————. *Navaho Sandpainting: the Huckel Collection*. Colorado Springs: The Taylor Museum of the Colorado Springs Fine Arts Center, 1960. 88 pp., illus.
Introduction on sandpainting and a catalog of the collection.

2025. ————. *The Red Antway of the Navaho*. Santa Fe: Museum of Navajo Ceremonial Art, 1965. (Navajo Religion Series vol. 5) 276 pp., illus., tables.

2026. ————. *The Sandpaintings of the Kayenta Navaho; an Analysis of the Louisa Wade Wetherill Collection*. Albuquerque: University of New Mexico Press, 1952. (Publications in Anthropology no. 7) 120 pp., illus.

2027. ————. *The Windways of the Navaho*. Colorado Springs: Colorado Springs Fine Arts Center, 1962. 327 pp., illus.

2028. ————, ED. *Beautyway: A Navaho Ceremonial*. New York: Pantheon Books, 1957. (Bollingen Series no. 53) 218 pp., illus.
Myth recorded and translated by Father Berard Haile; variant myth recorded by Maud Oakes; sandpaintings recorded by Laura J. Armer, Franc J. Newcomb, and Maud Oakes.

2029. WYMAN, LELAND C. AND FLORA L. BAILEY. *Navaho Indian Ethnoentomology.* Albuquerque: University of New Mexico Press, 1964. (Publications in Anthropology no. 12) 158 pp., illus., tables.
The significance of insects in Navajo life and thought.

2030. ——— AND STUART K. HARRIS. *The Ethnobotany of the Kayenta Navaho.* Albuquerque: University of New Mexico Press, 1951. (Publications in Biology no. 5) 66 pp.
An analysis of the Wetherill ethnobotany collection.

2031. YAMADA, GEORGE, ED. *The Great Resistance; A Hopi Anthology.* New York: George Yamada, 1957. 75 pp., illus.
Hopi resistance to federal Indian legislation.

2032. YANG, TIEN WEI. *Vegetational, Edaphic and Faunal Correlations on the Western Slope of the Tucson Mountains and the Adjoining Avra Valley.* Ann Arbor: University Microfilms, 1957. 176 pp.
A University of Arizona doctoral dissertation.

2033. *Yavapai County, Arizona, Industrial and Commercial Summary.* [Phoenix?]: Yavapai County Chambers of Commerce and Arizona Development Board, [1963]. 32 pp., tables.

2034. *Yavapai County Junior College Survey.* [Flagstaff: Northern Arizona University], 1966. various paging, tables, maps, diags.

2035. [YAVAPAI COUNTY] *Atlas of Yavapai County.* [Phoenix]: Arizona Highway Department, [1967]. 45 sheets.
Detailed road and street maps in a spiral binding.

2036. YOST, BILLIE W. *Bread upon the Sands.* Caldwell, Idaho: Caxton Printers, 1958. 245 pp., illus.
Navajo trading post life 1914–1929.

2037. YOUNG, ALICE E. AND PATRICIA P. STEPHENSON. *Discovering Tucson in the Land of Sunshine.* Tucson: The Authors, 1954. unpaged, illus., maps.
A mishmash for the visitor.

2038. YOUNG, HERBERT V. *Ghosts of Cleopatra Hill: Men and Legends of Old Jerome.* Jerome, Arizona: Jerome Historical Society, 1964. 151 pp., illus.

2039. YOUNG, JOHN V. *The Grand Canyon.* Palmer Lake, Colorado: Filter Press, 1969. 44 pp., illus.
The Canyon, John Wesley Powell, and modern river running.

2040. YOUNG, JON NATHAN. *The Salado Culture in Southwestern Prehistory.* Ann Arbor: University Microfilms, 1967. 131 pp.
A University of Arizona doctoral dissertation.

2041. YOUNG, OTIS E, JR. *How They Dug the Gold: An Informal History of Frontier Prospecting, Placering, Lode-Mining, and Milling in Arizona and the Southwest.* Tucson: Arizona Pioneers' Historical Society, 1967. (Arizona History Series III) 162 pp., illus.

2042. YOUNG, RICHARD A. *Cenozoic Geology Along the Edge of the Colorado Plateau in Northwestern Arizona.* Ann Arbor: University Microfilms, 1966. 220 pp.
A Washington University doctoral dissertation.

2043. YOUNG, ROBERT W. *The Role of the Navajo in the Southwestern Drama.* Gallup, New Mexico: Gallup Independent, 1968. 94 pp.
History of the area and the tribe.

2044. ———— AND WILLIAM MORGAN. *Navajo Historical Selections.* [Washington?]: Bureau of Indian Affairs, 1954. (Navajo Historical Series, no. 3) 209 pp.
Selections from the Navajo language newspaper, selected, edited, and translated.

2045. ———— AND ————. *A Vocabulary of Colloquial Navaho.* [Washington?]: U. S. Indian Service, [1951]. 461 pp.

2046. *Your Heritage on the Public Domain in Arizona.* U. S. Bureau of Land Management, [1963?]. 27 pp., illus.

2047. *Yuma (Arizona) Drainage-Groundwater Problem.* Hearings, 84th Congress, 2nd Session. Senate Committee on Interior and Insular Affairs; Subcommittee on Irrigation and Reclamation. Washington, 1956. 69 pp.

2048. [YUMA] *Crane Elementary District: Report of Survey, June 1964.* Tempe: Arizona State University Bureau of Educational Research and Services, 1964. 92 pp.

2049. [YUMA] *Handbook of Yuma Environment.* Washington: Department of Army, Office of Quartermaster General, 1953. (Environmental Protection Branch Report no. 200) 59 pp., illus., maps, diags.

2050. [YUMA] *The Report of the Survey of the Yuma Union High School District, Yuma, Arizona, April 1950.* [Los Angeles? 1950]. 381 pp., tables, maps.
Irving R. Melbo, director of survey.

2051. [YUMA] *School Organization and Pupil Growth Survey, Crane Elementary District, Yuma County, Arizona.* [Tempe]: Arizona State University, Bureau of Educational Research and Services, 1965. 35 pp.

2052. [YUMA] *Soil Survey, City of Yuma, Arizona.* Portland, Oregon: U. S. Soil Conservation Service? 1969. 81 pp., tables, map.

2053. *Yuma County Soil Fertility & Agronomic Crops.* Tucson: University of Arizona Agricultural Experiment Station, 1962. 135 pp., tables, diags.
Called Report no. 1.

2054. [YUMA COUNTY] *Atlas of Yuma County.* [Phoenix]: Arizona State Highway Department, 1964. 26 sheets.
Detailed road and street maps in a spiral binding.

2055. [YUMA COUNTY] *Economic Survey of Yuma County.* Tempe: Arizona State College Bureau of Business Services, 1954. (Arizona Counties Economic Survey Series no. 2) 165 pp., tables, diags.

2056. [YUMA COUNTY] *Economy of Yuma County with Projections to 1985.* Los Angeles: Daniel, Mann, Johnson, & Mendenhall, 1969. 117 pp., tables.
Subtitle: "Report No. 2 of 1985 Comprehensive Plan, Yuma County, Arizona."

2057. [YUMA COUNTY] *1985 Comprehensive County Plan, Yuma County, Arizona.* [Phoenix: Jeffrey Holland, 1967]. 2 unnumbered parts, various paging, tables, diags., maps.
Population and housing; land use.

2058. ZIMMERMANN, ROBERT C. *Plant Ecology of an Arid Basin of Arizona.* Ann Arbor: University Microfilms, 1969. 199 pp.
A Johns Hopkins University doctoral dissertation. Middle San Pedro Valley.

2059. ———. *Plant Ecology of an Arid Basin, Tres Alamos-Redington Area, Southeastern Arizona.* Washington: U. S. Geological Survey, 1969. (Professional Paper 485-D) 51 pp., illus., tables, maps.
"A study of variations in the plant cover of an arid basin, primarily as related to differences in surface-flow regimen." The author's dissertation with minor changes.

2060. ZWOLINSKI, MALCOLM J. *Changes in Water Infiltration Capacities Following Burning of a Ponderosa Pine Forest Floor.* Ann Arbor: University Microfilms, 1966. 208 pp.
A University of Arizona doctoral dissertation. The area studied was on the Fort Apache Indian Reservation near McNary.

Index